C000141806

Cover illustration by Mario Hugo.

Inside front-cover artwork by Liniers.

The illustrations on the inside rear cover and pp. 9, 52, 69, 97 and 128 are by David Shrigley.

⌘

Download an exclusive Domino Records digital sampler for free with Issue 01, and discover new music from the label.

Visit www.loopsjournal.com for the full tracklisting and download information. When prompted, use the promo code: DT4G7KHT. This download expires 31 January 2010.

Editorial

LEE BRACKSTONE AND RICHARD KING

Words and music are a potent combination. In the hands of a once-in-a-generation singer-songwriter they can turn a moment of personal observation into a universal truth. The way the written word responds to music, however, has long been a subject of debate, if not irritation.

It is often, and often correctly, argued that the experience of music, whether communal, in a field or in a club, or in the solitude of the environment a certain record creates in the listener's mind, transcends the need for explanation or criticism. But few who have bathed in the glow of an LP at three in the morning or woken up with a bassline competing for room in their circulation would deny the impulse to communicate the feeling, explore the meaning and share the rush.

The way we listen to, buy, consume or discover, let alone read about, music keeps changing in the blink of an eye. In the meantime, here's the first issue of *Loops*. Whatever the word is for the relationship between the printed word and the head, the heart, a pair of speakers or a pair of headphones – we hope you'll find it here.

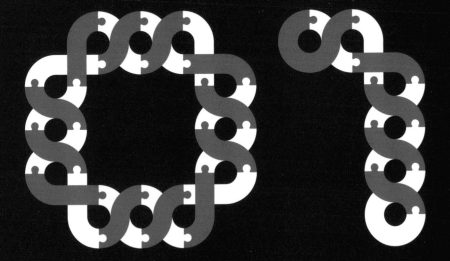

Bunny remembers the day he and Libby arrived home from the hospital with the baby. The tiny child's eyes, yet to find their colour, peered out of his scarlet, Claymation face as they laid him in the cot.

Bunny said to Libby, 'I don't know what to say to him.'

'It doesn't really matter, Bun. He is three days old.'

'Yeah, I guess.'

'Tell him he's beautiful,' said Libby.

'But he's not. He looks like somebody stepped on him.'

'Well, tell him that then,' she said. 'Only, in a nice voice.'

Bunny leaned into the crib. The child seemed to Bunny both terrifyingly present and a thousand light years away, all at the same time. There was something about him that he just couldn't handle, so full of his mother's love.

'You look like somebody put you through the mincer, little guy.'

Bunny Junior jerked his tiny bunched fingers in the air and changed the shape of his mouth.

'See? He likes it,' said Libby.

'You look like a bowl of Bolognese,' said Bunny. 'You look like a baboon's arse.'

Libby giggled and placed her raw and swollen fingers against the baby's head and the baby closed its eyes.

'Don't listen to him. He's jealous,' she said.

That was also the day that Sabrina Cantrell, Libby's workmate and 'oldest friend', came to pay her a visit. While Libby nursed the baby in the living room, in their tiny kitchenette Sabrina made the exhausted new mother a cup of tea. Bunny, who offered to help her, was suddenly and unexpectedly visited by a venereal compulsion that involved Sabrina Cantrell's arse and both his hands – something midway between a slap and a full-blown squeeze. It came out of nowhere, this compulsion, and even as he groped up great handfuls of her backside he wondered – What the fuck am I doing? Nothing came of it, of course, and it was the last time he ever saw Sabrina Cantrell, but a chain of events was set in motion that Bunny felt was beyond his control. There was a voice and a command, there was an action and there was indeed a consequence – shockwaves reverberated through the Munro household for weeks. Why had he done it? Who knows? Whatever. Fuck you.

Bunny rarely thought about that first marital miscalculation – what it was that guided his hands inexorably towards their forbidden resting place – but he did often think about the feel of Sabrina Cantrell's backside under the thin crêpe skirt, that wonderful contracting of the buttocks, the jump of outraged muscle, before the shit and the fan had their fateful assignation.

⌘

As he lies on his back, in his zebra-striped briefs at the Queensbury Hotel in Regency Square, working his way through a bottle of Scotch and watching with ancient eyes the tiny TV that blithers in the corner of the room, Bunny places a finger gently on the bridge of his nose and two thin rivulets of new dark blood emerge and run down his chin and drop soundlessly on to his chest. He curses to himself, rolls a Kleenex into plugs and inserts them up each nostril.

The room is a riot of psychedelic wallpaper and blood-coloured paisley carpet that appears to be designed around the ghosted, Technicolor nightmares of an Australian backstreet abortionist. The scarlet curtains hang like strips of uncooked meat and a paper lightshade that hangs from the ceiling writhes with fierce, whiskered Chinese dragons. The room reeks of bad plumbing and bleach and there is no room service and there is no mini-bar.

Bunny Junior lies on the other bed, in his pyjamas, engaged in an epic battle with his tormented eyelids – nodding off, then jerking awake, then nodding off again – a little yawn, a little scratch, a little folding of the hands to sleep.

'Daddy?' he mutters, rhetorically, sadly, to himself.

Bunny stops thinking about Sabrina Cantrell's backside and starts thinking about her pussy instead and quite soon he is thinking about Avril Lavigne's vagina. He is almost positive that Avril Lavigne possesses the fucking Valhalla of all vaginas, and in response to this late-night lucubration he carefully folds a copy of the *Daily Mail* over his semi-tumescent member. There is, after all, a child in the room.

Bunny lights a Lambert and Butler and focuses on the television. A woman on a 'confessional' talk show is admitting to being a sex addict. This holds no special interest to Bunny except that he finds it difficult to see how this woman, with her triplicate chins, flabby arms and lardy rear-end, could find enough guys willing to indulge her rank appetites. But apparently this was not a problem, and she gives a lurid and detailed account of her nympho-sploits. In time they bring on her husband, beaten-down and camera-shy, and she asks him to forgive her. The camera does a slow zoom on her tear-sodden face as she says, 'Oh, Frank, I have done bad things. Terrible, terrible things. Could you please find it in your heart to forgive me?'

Bunny pours himself another Scotch and lights up another Lambert and Butler.

'Kill the bitch,' he mutters.

Bunny Junior opens his eyes and, in a faraway voice that rises up from the soft curds of sleep, says, 'What did you say, Dad?'

'Kill the bitch,' answers Bunny, but the boy's eyes have closed again.

Then the sound seems to drop out of the television and the face of the host, a closet homosexual with a floppy yellow fringe and a salad-green suit, seems to morph into that of a braying cartoon horse or laughing hyena or something and Bunny, appalled, closes his eyes.

'zebra-striped briefs.'

He recalls, with a shudder, Libby standing in their kitchenette, red-eyed with confusion and disbelief, holding the baby and the telephone, and asking Bunny, point-blank, 'Is it true?'

She had been on the phone with Sabrina Cantrell, who had rung up to inform Libby that her husband had groped her in the kitchen and was, in all probability, a sexual pervert or something.

Bunny did not answer but hung his head and examined the monochromatic chequerboard linoleum on the floor of the kitchenette.

'Why?' she sobbed.

Bunny, in all honesty, had no fucking idea and he said this to her, shaking his head.

He remembered, quite distinctly, the baby, sitting like a little prince in his wife's arms, lift one well-sucked fist and uncurl his index finger and point it at Bunny. Bunny recalls looking at the child and having the overwhelming desire to go down to the Wick with Poodle. After half a dozen pints Poodle put a comforting arm around Bunny and bared his shark-like teeth and said, 'Don't worry, Bun, she'll get used to it.'

Bunny opens his eyes and sees the boy has raised himself up and is sitting on the edge of his bed, a look of concern on his face.

'Are you all right, Dad?' says the boy.

But before Bunny can think of what to answer, the TV comes alive with an urgent blast of music and a voice that cries, 'Wakey-wakey!' and the boy and his father look at the screen and see an advertisement for Butlins Holiday Camp in Bognor Regis. Various photographs framed in yellow cartoon stars cartwheel across the screen, showing the range of activities offered at Butlins – the Tiki Bar with its simulated electrical storms, the Empress Ballroom with its crimson curtains and tuxedoed band, the indoor and outdoor swimming pools, the world-famous monorail, the putting green, the adult quiz nights, the giant fibreglass rabbit that stands sentry by the pool, the Apache Fort, the Gaiety Building and amusement arcade. Smiling staff members in their trademark red coats show smiling patrons to their individual chalets and finally, in pink neon, blinking hypnotically across the screen, the Butlins Holiday Camp mission statement, 'Our true intent is all for your delight.'

Bunny's eyes grow wide, his mouth drops open and he says with genuine feeling, 'Fuck me. Butlins.' He sits straight up and jams another Lambert and Butler in his mouth. 'Are you watching this, Bunny Boy? Butlins!'

'What's Butlins, Dad?'

Bunny Zippos his cigarette and points at the TV, expels a noisy trumpet of smoke and says, 'Butlins, my boy, is the best fucking place in the world!'

'What is it, Dad?'

'It's a holiday camp,' says Bunny. 'My father took me there when I was a kid,' and with the mention of his father, Bunny feels a butcher's hook twisting in his bowels. He looks at his watch and screws up his face and says to himself, 'Christ, my old dad.'

'Why is it the best place in the world?' asks the boy.

'Has anyone ever mentioned you ask a lot of fucking questions?'

'Yes.'

Bunny reaches across to the bedside table and grabs the Scotch and, waving the bottle with an extravagant flourish, says, 'Well, let me just pour a little drink and I'll tell you.'

Bunny slops whisky into his glass, then lies back against the headboard and says, with emphasis, 'But you've got to listen.'

Bunny Junior's head suddenly wobbles dramatically on his neck and he falls back on the bed, arms splayed. He closes his eyes.

'OK, Dad,' he says.

⌘

'Don't bloody ask me why Dad took me to Butlins. He no doubt had some raunchy tête-á-tête or some liaison kangaroo with some slapper or something, I don't know, he was a squire of the dames, my old man, and he loved a bit of the fluff. Not bad-looking either, in his day,' says Bunny.

'When we arrived he changed his shirt, had a shave, put pomade in his hair, you know, then sent me down the pool, for a swim. He said he'd come by and get me later on.'

The boy's breath deepens and he brings his little square knees up to his chest and appears to sleep. Bunny pours the Scotch down his throat, then attempts to place the glass back on the bedside table but he misses and the glass rolls around the shrieking paisley carpet. He retreats deep into his memory and he sees the throbbing terraced lawns and the turquoise water churning with screaming children. He sees the fifteen-foot bucktoothed rabbit that stands by the swimming pool. His voice comes out tired and sad.

'So I went down to the pool, and I was doing this thing that I liked to do. I'd crouch down with just my eyes looking over the top of the water and glide around like a crocodile or a bloody alligator and watch all the kids jumping around and doing bombs and cavorting about. I used to feel like nobody could see me but, you know, I could see them.'

Bunny attempts to make some gesture with his hand to illustrate a point and for a brief moment he wonders how on earth he ever ended up this way.

'Anyway, on this particular occasion I started to get the feeling that someone was watching me and I turned around and there, sitting on the edge of the pool, was a girl . . . about my age . . . I was just a kid . . . '

Bunny sees, in his mind, the girl with her long wet hair and her nut-coloured limbs, and he finds that hot tears are running down his face, and once again he circles his hand in the air, his cigarette dead between his fingers.

'And she was smiling at me . . . watching me . . . and smiling at me and, Bunny Boy, I got to tell you, she had the most beautiful eyes I'd ever seen and she wore a tiny yellow polka-dot bikini and she was all caramel-coloured from the sun . . . with these violet eyes . . . and something came over me, I don't know what, but all the bloody emptiness I felt as a kid seemed to evaporate and I filled with something . . . a kind of power. I felt like a bloody machine.'

Bunny can see, in his mind's eye, the afternoon sun spinning in the sky and the glare of it as it touched the surface of the pool. He can see the water part as he floated slowly through it.

'So I kind of glided towards her and the closer I got the more she smiled . . . and I don't know what came over me, but I stood up and asked her what her name was . . . fucking twelve years old I was . . . '

The cigarette falls from Bunny's fingers and lands on the scarlet carpet.

'. . . and she said her name was Penny Charade . . . I kid you not. Penny Charade . . . I'll never forget it . . . and when I told her my name she laughed and I laughed and I knew that I had this power . . . this special thing that all the other bastards who were flopping around in the pool trying to impress the girls didn't have...I had this gift ...a talent...and it was in that moment that I knew what I was put on this stupid fucking planet to do...'

Bunny Junior, incredibly, opens one raw eye and says, 'What happened then, Dad?' and closes it again.

'Well, it was getting late and her mum and dad came and got her and I stayed at the pool, happier than I'd ever been, just floating around...all full of this gift until I was the last person in the pool...'

Bunny could see, deep in his memory, the night fall over Butlins and a spray of stars spritz across the sky, and he wiped the tears from his face with the back of his hand.

'Then it began to get dark and the stars came out and I started to get cold so I went back to our chalet.'

This time the boy keeps his eyes closed when he says, 'What happened to the girl, Dad?'

'Well, the next day my dad sent me down to the pool again and I looked for Penny Charade but she wasn't there, and I was moving through the water feeling sorry for myself when I noticed another girl who was smiling at me, then another one, and suddenly the whole pool was heaving with Penny Charades...on the side of the pool... swimming in the water, on the fucking diving board, waving and smiling and laying on their towels, playing with blow-up balls and there it was again...that feeling...that power...and me with the gift...'

Bunny gropes around on the bed until he finds the remote and, with a crack of static, it implodes into nothingness and he closes his eyes. A great wall of darkness moves towards him. He can see it coming, vast and imperious. It is unconsciousness and it is sleep. It moves like a great tidal wave but before it breaks over him and he is away, before he renders himself completely to that oblivious sleep, he thinks, with a sudden, terrible, bottomless dread, of Avril Lavigne's vagina.

HARI KUNZRU
Twice upon a Time (Listening to New York)
Reflections on Moondog

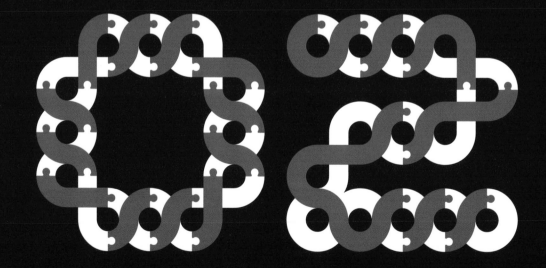

Machine were mice and men were lions
Once upon a time
But now that it's the opposite
It's twice upon a time

MOONDOG

Ear Cleaning: Any process that encourages
a person to listen more discriminately,
particularly to sounds of the environment.

BARRY TRUAX
Handbook for Acoustic Ecology, 1978

1 I♥NY

—

Lying in bed in my East Village apartment I can hear the ticking sound of a mechanical timer – perhaps the building's gas or electricity meter – turning round on the other side of the wall.

Strangeness of a new place:

> orange street light filtering through the thin blinds
> unfamiliar smell
> buzzing fridge, a few feet away from my head (studio)
> street noise outside the open window
> car goes past dopplering r'n'b
> laughter

A girl sits down on my gate post and makes a long phone call. Pleading, sobbing. '*Come on. I'll have the money for you on Tuesday. I swear. On my daughter's eyes. What do you mean? You don't know what I'm going through here.*'

And that metronomic clicking, relentless sound of time passing.

> *Time present and time past*
> *Are both perhaps present in time future,*

That doesn't sound like good news, Tom. I mean, in this economy? You want to keep your options open. You want to diversify. Try not to get tied into anything.

I have to go out.

I pull on some clothes. The heat is oppressive, even at 1 a.m. Tompkins Square is dark, filled with movement. A lot of people around tonight. Many reasons. Broken air con. Nowhere to sleep. Too wired. Too high. 104 degrees this afternoon, add another twenty in the underground. The sound of skate wheels on the basketball court, junkies conferencing on the benches of Crusty Row. Whole place smells of skunk. By the Avenue A gate some jazz musicians are conducting a discreet free-blowing session, begging the question – can a free-blowing session ever really be discreet? This feels that way, despite being basically very loud. Feels *clandestine*. They're watched by a small crowd, some of the street people who hang around outside Ray's Candy Store, others like me, forced out of their stifling apartments. The musicians honk and squeak. Everyone follows their own path, the tenor player and the drummer driving things along, half a dozen others dropping in and out, attacking everything from an upright bass to a set of bongos, meandering around with various degrees of competence, assuredness, purpose, strength of will.

Out of the pitch blackness of the basketball court steps a tall man in a wizard's cloak. He has a staff. Very metal. Seems to know the guy with the star tattooed on his cheek, the one leaning on his crutch, making his bottle of Olde English 800 perform a dance for the good people. For a moment I think it's Moondog...except this guy can see, is aged about 25 and looks totally wasted. I think he might be about to cast a spell.

> broken bottle smashes
> argument by the benches
>
> dog barking
>
> honk rattle

2 Be a hobo and go with me

—

I only got here a couple of weeks ago. Nothing but a stranger in this world. Every time I exit the underground I have to make a 360-degree turn to work out which way is downtown. I need a guide. Foodies have the Zagat, swingers have Adult Friend Finder. I choose ...

Moondog.

AKA Louis Hardin, born 1916, son of an Episcopalian minister who is also at various times, 'a merchant, rancher, real estate and insurance agent'.

Idyllic childhood in Wisconsin, then family moves to Wyoming, begins a slow process of disintegration that leaves the boy living alone with his father for long periods.

Hari Kunzru

On a visit to the Wind River Reservation, Louis receives a drumming lesson from an Arapaho Chief called Yellow Calf, learning 'the running beat, and alongside it the walking beat, which is also the universal heartbeat'.

He develops a lifelong taste for what he sees as a primal form of life, as opposed to the 'Coca-Cola culture' in which he has been brought up.

He will spend much of his life on Sixth Avenue in New York City.

3 We are all just prisoners here

—

Another humid August night, I'm drinking with a friend in a Bushwick bar. Important to keep hydrated. Equally important to be somewhere with air conditioning. This place is not what you would call fancy. It has a pool table and serves Pabst Blue Ribbon to guys who station themselves on their stools around five and try to maintain verticality until closing. The selection on the jukebox is so generic it ought to be shot into space as a memorial of white working-class American music taste (thirty-plus male demographic) in the year 2008. Pink Floyd, AC/DC, Bon Jovi, Springsteen. Someone puts on 'Stairway to Heaven', and I know what's coming next. It's inevitable. All other options have fallen away.

On a dark desert highway . . .

'Hotel California' is one of the few definitively globalised musical experiences. It walks the earth. It is abroad. I've heard it in every beach resort I've ever visited, and most other places besides – a bus station in Bolivia, floating towards my houseboat across the darkened water of Dal Lake in Kashmir. I've heard it in bars in Phnom Penh and Durban and Baku and Beijing. About the only place I don't remember hearing it is LA, though there's probably a California state law that says FM stations must clock up at least one play per day in order to qualify for a licence. It's a song whose lyrics take on a particularly sinister tone in tourist spots, with all that business about checking out but not being able to leave. Played on a crappy cassette recorder at 3 a.m. in a junkie beach shack in Goa, it's actively terrifying. In this bar its effect is comforting, a woozy affirmation that whatever we're all doing here has been sanctified by custom and tradition. We are guys, getting drunk. It has always been thus.

Later, walking towards the subway, I pass an auto-repair place. A group of men are playing cards on the sidewalk, listening to Reggaeton pumped out of a system somewhere in the back. Squat

Negro Modelo bottles are clustered on the crate they're using as a table. Down the street is a tortilla factory where women in white smocks and plastic caps are working a late shift. The door is open and I can see them, packing tortillas into bags. Machinery whirs and thuds. A radio plays Spanish language love songs.

amor / dolor
suerte / muerte

There's something devotional about the tableau, the repetitive gestures, the white uniforms, the plaintive declarations of love.

4 Blindness

Louis's parents divorce.

After a scandalous liason with a parishioner, Hardin senior is defrocked.

Father and son move from place to place.

In 1932, aged 16, Louis finds a detonator cap while wandering around near some railroad tracks and brings it home to tinker with. It explodes in his face, instantly blinding him.

He describes his time in hospital as like being 'smothered alive'.

He renounces his Christian faith. Later he will turn to the worship of Norse gods.

He attends the Iowa School for the Blind, where he startles people by his fierce independence. He studies music and begins to write poetry.

After a series of more or less platonic crushes on older women and a brief failed marriage, in 1943 he leaves for New York City to become a composer.

After this he never meets his father, mother, brother or sister again.

> My brother is blind. This is one of the major dynamics in my life. His blindness, my sight. I can only imagine how it would feel to negotiate this city as a blind person. The open delivery hatches in the sidewalk, the fierce commuters. With so much uncertainty, so much to go wrong, there's a need to make your own certainty, to find a system. The blind develop an appreciation for precision, repetition, knowability.

In New York Louis Hardin gives himself the name Moondog.

He makes money by:

life-modelling
selling broadsides and poems
playing music on the street

He composes canons, rounds and other highly formal pieces
He uses 'snaketime' rhythms, sevens, fives, nines
He invents a number of percussive instruments

the oo
the utsu
the uni
the trimbas

He gives up wearing factory-made clothes
He warns his readers of the evils of the Federal Reserve
He writes a hymn to the UN
He is taken up by the conductor of the New York Philharmonic, who lets him listen to orchestra rehearsals and introduces him to various famous musicians. Other musicians find their way to him. Steve Reich, Philip Glass. Charlie Parker. Stravinsky.

He makes his own costumes from squares of cloth
He cobbles his own shoes
He becomes preoccupied by the culture of Nordic Europe

ancient
prelapsarian
in harmony with nature
white race origin myth

In 1970, he compiles his 'Universal Reckoning', listing the key dates in five billion years of global history. Only five are in the last two millennia:

AD 0	Birth of Jesus
AD 9	Battle of the Teutoberger Wald. Three Roman legions annihilated in the Black Forest of Germania
AD 570	Birth of Mohammed
AD 1000	Discovery of America by Leif Eriksson
AD 1945	The coming of the atomic age

5 'Fifty-fourth and Sixth, a few yards from the north-east corner with the four-foot polished patio stone walls of the MGM building at his back.'

—

A twelve-block pilgrimage. I walk up from the New York Public Library, where I spend my days cocooned in an office overlooking Fifth Avenue. At weekends a breakdance troupe sets up, busking for money by Patience and Fortitude, the stone lions guarding the entrance to the library. For some reason, despite the huge variety of music recorded expressly for the execution of the boogaloo smurf, these b-boys always dance to 'Billie Jean'. Maybe they earn more money when they play a tune that doesn't make white midtown office workers feel threatened. There's only so much Michael Jackson you can listen to before you feel like throwing a baby off a balcony: sooner or later we usually get a guard to go down and move them on.

Midtown is a place of work. All other forms of human activity (most of which take place here, usually some distance above street level) are secondary. People walk fast. They hunt for gaps in the traffic, swerving past the charity muggers, the vendor pushing his pretzel cart across the intersection. The traffic on Sixth Avenue heads uptown, past the big hotels, the towers of media and money, status-conscious enough in this neighbourhood to need fussy little plazas, fountains, public art. The sounds: sirens, HVAC systems, 18-wheelers, car alarms, Mr Softee Ice Cream trucks, bass woofers, the subterranean rumble of the trains passing under the sidewalk . . . and shouting – not exclusive to midtown but an important topic for anyone researching the acoustic ecology of Manhattan. A whole book could be devoted to the reasons why New Yorkers shout in the street – to assert their control over their environment, to express joy or pain or rage or intoxication, to hail a cab, to abuse an acquaintance, to abuse a stranger, to abuse an authority figure, to abuse authority in the abstract, to apostrophise the buildings or the cars, to conduct one half of a conversation with an invisible interlocutor – or simply to express the intense feeling of vertigo generated by this particular world city:

FUUUUUUUUUUUUUUUCK

A cultural rule of thumb: Londoners conduct an internal monologue, New Yorkers just go ahead and say it.

internalise/vocalise

Hey! Ladies first! Goddamn jackass...

Looks like it's gonna rain. Radio said it's gonna rain. I believe it, look at that sky...

You are so beautiful, yes you are, don't let nobody tell you otherwise, hello puppy, yes hello puppy...

Moondog had a favourite corner. During his time in New York, roughly from the mid forties to the mid seventies, he spent most of his days in one spot. Despite his adoption by the Beats of Greenwich Village he didn't much like to improvise. All his music was carefully scored and copied.

Repetition, predictability, control.

Moondog's corner is just behind the new MOMA. I can't find the MGM building. Maybe it's gone. The Warwick hotel seems to occupy the whole corner.

> the hotel doorman's whistle summoning cabs da-*da*-da-da-da-
> da-*da*-da-da-da
> child's voice
> screech of tires
> thud of a cab door
> conversation in several languages
> rickshaw bell

The next day I take an MP3 player and I make the journey again, accompanied by Moondog's early music, recordings from the forties and fifties. The percussion rattles in snake-time cycles ('seven-four, eight-four, nine-four, and who for and what for I don't know...'), overlaid by delicate melodies. Sometimes you can hear trolley cars, traffic, a steam whistle, perhaps from a Hudson tug. Primitive tape overdubbing – the recordings were made in a studio. Sound leaks in and out of the iPod's earbuds, layering modern Sixth Avenue on to city noise of sixty years ago. Archaeology.

6 Ictus
—

The tone cuts silence (death) with its vibrant life.
   No matter how softly or loudly, it is saying one thing: 'I am alive'...
   Let us call the instant of sound-impact the 'ictus'. The accent of the ictus divides silence from articulation. It is like the dot in the painter's

vocabulary, or the period at the end of a sentence.

This dividing of silence from articulation should be one of the most exciting experiences possible. In medicine the 'ictus' refers to a stroke or sudden attack.

R. MURRAY SCHAFER, *Ear Cleaning, 1967*

I entertain the hope that if I look hard enough, I'll find Moondog's inheritor, standing on a street corner selling tracts. In this spirit, I give a few minutes to more or less everyone I come across on the subway, from the young woman dressed as a superhero doing unaccompanied Tina Turner numbers to the kora player whose new Air Jordans poke out imposingly from beneath traditional Senegalese robes. One night on the downtown 6 platform at Union Square I find an elderly black man in a velvet tuxedo. He sings 'Do Ya Think I'm Sexy?' and, just so we get the financial picture, 'Ain't Too Proud to Beg'. Another night a homeless-looking man bundled into a heavy down jacket improvises an incoherent and rather depressing song, with lyrics that seem to be a cut-up of 'Say You Say Me' and 'You Make Me Feel Like a Natural Woman'. There are slick acts, usually to be found in prime spots at Grand Central or Penn: Gypsy Kings copyists twirling in time, an inexplicably popular East Asian outfit who do schmaltzy covers of Kenny G and Lionel Ritchie. There's the same Andean pan-pipe ensemble I walked past in Paris, Milan, Sydney... I wonder if the Peruvian government regulates them, assigns them territories (*felicitationes amigos, you now have the exclusive Warsaw rights to* 'Flight of the Condor'...) or whether something even weirder is going on. Are they the *exact same musicians*? Are they following me? One day I discover the Kids from Fame have wheeled a rickety-looking upright piano into one of the interchange tunnels at Penn station. They're playing ragtime backing for a young woman who tapdances on a metal sheet laid out on the floor, like the chicken at the end of *Stroszek*. She's gonna live forever.

I like best the Mariachi bands who work the subway carriages. They shuffle in, carrying their instruments, always including an accordion and a little high-pitched vihuela guitar. They invariably look crushingly bored. Then they propel into a song, perfunctorily crunching into the silence of the carriage like a child biting into an apple.

Ictus.

It amazes me they can make such a joyful noise when they seem so dejected.

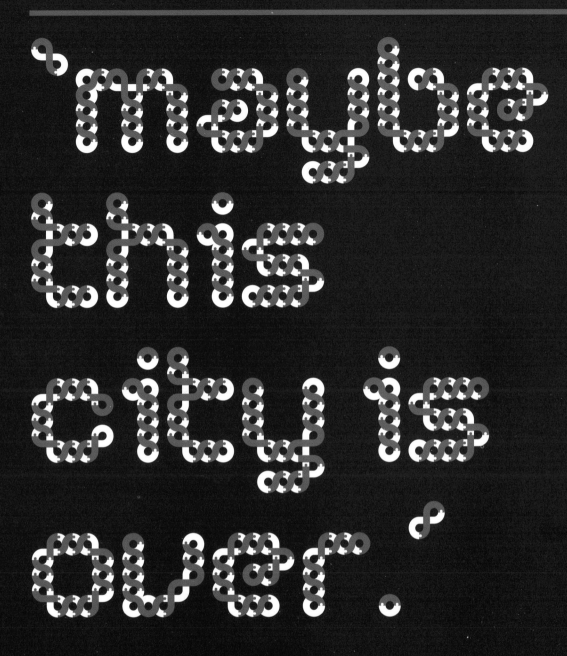

'maybe this city is over.'

7 Jobs all along

—

Curbing 'iPod oblivion' on city streets?
NY bill would ban the use of electronic devices in city crosswalks
CBS NEWS WEBSITE, 7 FEBRUARY 2007

So how many people on the platform have white wires snaking down into their collars? Rush-hour solipsism. Perhaps one in four. Privacy is just as valuable here as in any large city and of course there's a particular experience – of personal drama, control – that comes with navigating urban space to your own soundtrack. The ability to create an auditory environment and carry it around, to override the polluted city soundscape, is worth 300 bucks of most New Yorkers' money. In *Village Bells*, his study of church bells in rural France, the historian Alain Corbin explores the idea of an auditory territory. Until the nineteenth century, the range of the bells in the village clock tower defined the limit of a community, socially and administratively. The church bell tolled the end of the working day for those in the furthest fields, and the limit of hearing became the de facto basis for community boundaries. Now, auditory territory can extended infinitely, through amplification and broadcast technologies, while the iPod creates a community of precisely one. You could see it as a land grab, a radical privatisation of public space.

Certainly, between the mobile phone and the iPod, it's clear that people are only partially present in the physical space they occupy. When I'm on my bike, pedestrians often wander out into the road without looking. It happens far more frequently than in London, where people seem more used to cyclists. I get used to swerving, shouting insults, dealing with the aggrieved self-righteousness of iPhone owners who don't understand that natural selection press-ures are weeding their genes out of the communal pool. The future is for multitaskers, morons! You, my preoccupied friends, are going under a bus. Frankly I don't think a $100 fine would work on the Apple zombies. They're remote-controlled from Cupertino. When Steve Jobs throws the switch and starts beaming modem-like tones into their heads instead of Britney Spears, they'll stop what they're doing and march on the armouries and power stations, ready to fulfil their evil leader's plans for world domination. Don't you see? Bill Gates was just a diversion! It was Jobs all along! Jobs, I tell you! Jobs!

Hari Kunzru

—

'People usually ask why I'm dressed this way,' Moondog said, 'and I tell them it's my way of saying "no".'

NEW YORK TIMES, 15 MAY 1965

The first band I go to see in the city is a friend's intellectual rock outfit, who are playing the back room of a popular Williamsburg hangout. They're not a particularly serious act, knocking out songs for fun, though the singer seems to believe it; he clings to the mike-stand, lost in a skinny indie dream of hair and fuzzboxes. The bar is Ivy League Hipster central, a milieu of tattoos, irony, unacknowledged trust funds and sublet lofts. No figure (except perhaps the derivatives trader) is more reviled right now, particularly by other hipsters. Certainly no one will admit to actually being one. It's always someone else – posers, wannabes. Face-eating consumer of cool, ruiner of all that's new, the hipster is a sort of doomed wanderer, trudging about the blogosphere in search of the latest, greatest, most radical and transgressive cultural hit. He's hated (and hates himself) because he has no real allegiances, no real taste, no desires at all except to be safely at the centre of the edge, to be edgy just like all his friends, whereas in reality he's just at the edge of the centre, no more transgressive than the lamest suburbanite downloading the Jonas Brothers on iTunes. There's no 'niggaz 4 life /skinhead forever/born to lose' tribalism any more, at least not among the college-educated. You don't carve 'mods' into your arm with a box cutter (though on reflection perhaps that was an English thing) because no one's gauche enough to claim that what they like to wear or listen to will define them for longer than the next five minutes. The hipster is the cult of the absolutely new, the first true post-networked youth movement, its constant churn just a side-effect of the hard work of maintaining hip in a liquid world where information is easy to come by and everyone can acquire whatever cultural symbols they want with minimum effort. The tragedy of the hipster is his reverse Midas touch. He kills everything he loves. Once a thing is on his radar, blogged about, uploaded, it's immediately commercialised, branded and sanitised, then sold back to him. The transgressive danger he seeks is forever unattainable.

Hipster music can thus be everything and anything, but its essence is pastiche. Choose a style – '60s folk, African highlife, C86 English indie – and rock out. Every so often I trawl MySpace and the Pirate Bay, and listen to the new crop of bands. I try to be open-minded and occasionally find something that survives repeated listening, but for the most part I fall into the 'x sounds like y' game. Oh, this bunch like the Stooges. This lot like ESG…

Moondog makes music with Charlie Parker Steve Reich Tiny Tim Pete Seeger
    He lives for six months in Philip Glass's spare room
    Marlon Brando comes over to play bongos.
    He goes on the *Today Show*
    He makes an album of children's rhymes spoken by Julie Andrews
    Despite attempts to forge him a mainstream entertainment career he does not 'break out'
    During the '60s he develops a more elaborate Viking costume

     spear
     horned helmet

    Pursues larger scale musical projects
    Tries to distance himself from image as 'street musician'

One day I go to see LCD Soundsystem (favourites of mine), who are DJing with ex-DNA member Ikue Mori at an art gallery. They play Salsoul records to a packed crowd of bored and boring people, who spend most of their time looking around to see if anything cool is happening on the other side of the room. I'm desperate to dance, to lose it, but this party is inert, self-conscious. I'm getting texts from a girlfriend, who's on an E in the middle of a 10,000-strong outdoor rave in Serbia, having one of the peak experiences of her life. I leave, feeling angry, old and bland.

Maybe this city is over.

> *Oh, take me off your mailing list*
> *For kids who think it still exists*
> *Yes, for those who think it still exists*

Because it's all finished and they turned CBGB's into a boutique and we know we should have been downtown in 1979 because these days Laurie Anderson's at the Lincoln Center making booming noises by contact-miking her skull and Lou Reed looks like a grumpy wizened pixie and the Lower East Side is full of NYU students buying keffiyehs and in Tompkins Square there's a sort of rearguard action, a commemoration of a riot twenty years ago, with punk bands and fierce moshing and lots of ink and studs and army boots and cops standing at the back with a decibel meter, making the engineer turn the PA down when it tops 80 dB. Old guys with ponytails sell anarchist papers, one of the Ray's Candy Store drunks fist-bumps the singer of the Bullys (you can fuck my sister/but you might get a blister) who make way for Leftover Crack (a joke name: the joke being there's no such thing) and at some point we even get a Klezmer band. In the crowd is David Peel, local musical hero of the dope-smoking '60s, and it's all very defiant and withered and small and I understand why arty types say to one another at wistful parties that the one good thing about the coming recession is maybe it will go back to how it was in the good old days xeroxed flyers cheap speed muggings and free performance space for all and then at least pretty please perhaps those French bankers being so loud at the bar will just fucking disappear.

9 Not a game

—

According to Trainer Ron, they've had the same music at the gym since 2005.

Ron has arms like my legs. We talk about

> the financial crisis
> plasma TVs
> the honeys

then suddenly he's singing along

> *Made me learn a little bit faster*
> *made my skin a little bit thicker*
> *Makes me that much smarter*
> *thanks for making me a fighter*

I like that one, he says. Gimme twenty-five. Straight leg. Go.

10 Shout out to all my peoples

—

> *'WINS' UNFAIR*
> *This radio station*
> *Employs a Disc Jockey*
> *Who Plays My Record*

ROUGH TRADE

Rough Trade Multi Million pound Conglomerate
wish to announce that they are still trading
in the best records that can be found as well
as the hardest hard core sounds of the new wave.

Anyoneeinterested in acquiring these records
as a mail order customer or from the shops....

Please visit us at:

www.roughtrade.com

or

91, Brick Lane, London E1 6QL
phone 020 - 7392 - 7788
and
130, Talbot Road, London W11 1JA
phone 020 - 7229 - 8541

Remember: This is still the organisation
that doesn't give a shit about Joe Public

'Moondog Symphony'
and calls himself
'Moondog'
I AM MOONDOG

In 1954 Moondog sues the popular DJ Alan Freed for copyright infringement.

At first Freed, who has a huge audience (and is credited with the invention of the term 'rock'n'roll') does not take the case seriously. In court, Arturo Toscanini, Perez Prado, Benny Goodman depose for the plaintiff.

Moondog wins $5,000. Freed has to stop using the name.

With the damages Moondog buys land upstate, a refuge.

In almost six months of (intermittently) keeping this diary I've barely explored the radio spectrum. It seemed like it was the opposite of what I wanted to do – listening to sound in space, in the context of the city. Moondog not Freed. But radio is obviously a territory too, a profligate open sound-space, the counterpart to the iPod's solipsism. You phone in, request, talk to the presenter, make dedications. On a freezing Sunday night, just before Christmas, I sit down with a notebook and listen

> epic r'n'b ballad about singer vandalising her boyfriend's car:
> you'll probably think it's juvenile/but I think I deserve to smile

sarod and tabla players explaining sixteen beat structure of raag. Interviewer says to the two musicians: 'You come off as dudes. There's not like that whole back and forth.'

> Brooklyn we go hard
> We go hard
> Shout out to my dude XL I see you too, my moms, pops, my
>   whole family members
> See the future my boy Future we about to go big 2009
> Shout out to Mika
> All my peoples in Brooklyn

DJ mash-up of spacy electro and I kissed a girl. Katy Perry's perky lesbian titillation hollowed out, spooky, a suburban oxycontin high

> commercial rock
> in the first 30 seconds:
> road

bones
taste it
tonight
the greatest
sets me on fire

Hark the herald angels sing glory to the newborn king our next selection is going to be found on page 43 for those of you following along angels from the realms of glory yes angels

The worst part is I
Million reasons
do whatever it takes

La reina y el rey us against the world

Do it for the thugs
I'll do it for hip hop
a truck
a Benz

deals on electronics Mercedes slips and falls cases of cerebral palsy lead poisoning quadriplegic? We've recovered millions of dollars all expenses paid round trip by following the easy instructions on the website

Asesina, me domina
Cuando escucha el reggaeton en la bocina

dinner jazz walking winter wonderland simpering singer too bright piano

King Selassie I

Weird paedo Christmas song little altar boy I wonder could you pray for me what must I do to be holy like you little altar boy oh let me hear you pray oh it's the Carpenters

life is a highway knocked down back up again want to ride it all night long yeah

hard Latin bass DJ Cassanova takes calls ay baby gets the girls to simulate oral sex on the phone

All this in twenty minutes. Many simultaneous cities. NPR City, College Radio City, R'n'B City, above all the Latino City running in parallel to the Anglo one. Add to that the internet streams and you have a sort of infinite parallelism – Armenian City, Punjabi City, Ethiopian City, Mandarin City, New Age City, Ambient City, Faery City, Evangelical City, Adult Contemporary City, Singles City, Sports City, Pet City…

11 Two sounds, one high and one low
—

Each made it their work to return inwardly to the measure of grace in themselves, and not being only silent as to words but even abstaining from their own thoughts, imaginations and desires

ROBERT BARCLAY, QUAKER,
GOVERNOR OF THE COLONY OF EAST JERSEY, 1678

The jet-engine thrum of the air conditioning, that idiot on WNYC who plays show-tunes all weekend, the traffic jams and pointless horn-blaring whenever someone double-parks on Tenth Street. Machine were mice once upon a time. Now they're lions. Engines vibrate my windowpanes. Six months in and I still can't sleep, let alone return to the measure of grace inside myself. As the breakdancers outside the library work through yet another cycle of Michael Jackson, I Google 'quiet places in New York', which is how I end up in Tryon Park, crunching through the snow to the Cloisters, where the Metropolitan museum houses its medieval collection. It's like that Brueghel picture, *Hunters in the Snow*, except with kids sledding instead of peasants gathering wood. Sounds are muffled. The air is heavy, cold enough to sting. The Cloisters is a weird New World transplantation, bits of several French monasteries Rockefellered across the Atlantic and cobbled together to make a more or less Romanesque building, facing off against the housing projects on the neighbouring hill. It's a beautiful piece of fakery, but today it's full of people stamping snow off their boots and pointing objects out to one another, bubbly with pre-Christmas cheer. No silence here.

I crave the absoluteness John Cage describes in *Indeterminacy*:

> It was after I got to Boston that I went into the anechoic chamber at Harvard University. Anybody who knows me knows this story. I am constantly telling it. Anyway, in that silent room I heard two sounds: one high and one low. Afterward, I asked the engineer in

charge why, if the room was so silent, I had heard two sounds. He said, 'Describe them.' I did. He said, 'The high one was your nervous system in operation. The low one was your blood in circulation.'

When was New York last truly quiet? Some time before September 1609, when Henry Hudson sailed up the river to the isle of Mannahatta. There's a project to reconstruct the ecology of the island as it was then. A world without 'Billie Jean'. Imagine – it's easy if you try. Over the summer I spent a week alone in a house on Shelter Island. No distraction at all. The dark woods, the water lapping at the shore. The trouble, I think, was the early eighties décor of the place, which triggered memories of being terrified by slasher movies when I was young. In houses like that, teenagers drank and had sex and were punished by a chainsaw-wielding maniac in a hockey mask. I had to wedge a chair under the door handle. Not that kind of silence. I didn't like that kind at all.

Perhaps I'm better off in the city. Loneliness and silence are not the same. On Church Street in Tribeca, there's a compromise solution, the Dream House, set up by minimalist composer La Monte Young and light artist Marian Zazeela. A large apartment, empty but for grubby white carpet and a massive PA system, a few hippyish decorative touches, a small shrine to Pandit Pran Nath, coloured lights playing on the wall. From the speakers emanates a vast cosmic noise. A drone whose overtones are subtly, continually changing. The sound is huge, geological, pressing down on the ears. Lie on the floor, close your eyes. *In the life of the Tortoise the drone is the first sound. It lasts forever and cannot have begun but is taken up again from time to time until it lasts forever as continuous sound in Dream Houses where many musicians and students will live and execute a musical work. Dream Houses will allow music which, after a year, ten years, a hundred years or more of constant sound, would not only be a real living organism with a life and tradition all its own but one with a capacity to propel itself by its own momentum . . .*

In 1974 Moondog leaves US for Germany
Spends old age fêted
    tours interviews large perfomances
Dies in Germany aged 83, in 1999

There is, finally, only one true silence.

Hari Kunzru

12 Wake Me

I've been keeping this diary for six months now, listening to New York.

One day I think I've found Moondog's inheritor. A young, shirtless man, drumming on plastic tubs and bits of metal junk outside Penn station. Plastic tub-drumming seems to be a popular form of busking here, but this guy is extraordinary. His rhythm is locked down, metronomic and complex. Man lion sound for a machine city.

Descending into the subway at Astor Place. Beneath the street, ceramic tile, iron pillars. Industrial age archaeology. The downtown express shoots through without stopping, filling the space with metal on metal noise vast primitive ecstatic Gods of Manhattan howling

in the clatter of the carriage, the social world

close harmony singers

Why don't you wake me, shake me?
Don't let me sleep too late
Gotta get up in the morning
About a quarter to eight

boots on the stairs, mass migration, out into the street into yesterday's snowfall sloosh of slush and up into the marble quiet of the library and to my office where I put on my headphones free safe isolated and out of the drone in the silence at the centre of the city

June–December 2008

Most biographical information from *Moondog: The Viking of 6th Avenue* by Robert Scotto (Process, 2007) and Moondog's Corner www.moondogscorner.de

NICK KENT
Nick Drake
Songs of Waving, Drowning and a Sort of Sadness

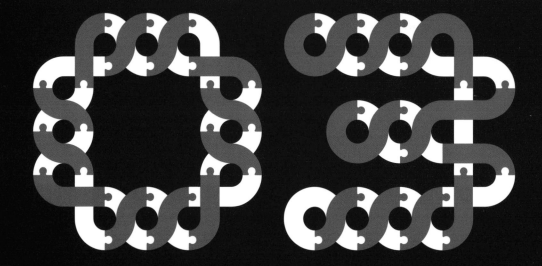

This piece is dedicated to Lucilla Vadja, a pearl of the rarest beauty, who first inadvertently turned me on to Nick Drake's music. Lucilla died from leukemia two years ago.

> You've been getting too deep;
> You've been living on solid air
> You've been missing your sleep
> And you've been moving through
> solid air.
>
> JOHN MARTYN 'SOLID AIR'
> *(written for and about Nick Drake)*

> If songs were lines
> In a conversation
> The situation
> Would be fine
>
> NICK DRAKE 'HAZY JANE II'

The noun 'enigma' can be defined as an 'unknown thing' or 'mystery'. In the desperate quasi-esperanto of contemporary rock literati, the term has been used with joyous abandon to describe the careers and lifestyles of all too many musicians and all-purpose rock personalities. In the vast majority of cases the term is ill conceived.

Nick Drake, however, was, and will forever more be, rightfully considered an enigma; a private, painfully shy individual who, between the years 1968 and 1972 created a volume of work so peerlessly self-contained, so slender on the one hand and yet so complete when judged in retrospect, that he carved out a musical niche so totally his own and one, moreover, that beyond its shimmering sensuousness and brooding mellifluousness is totally unfettered by the era of its creation. Drake's music is as timeless as it is irrepressibly beguiling in its distant seductiveness.

To refer to Drake as an enigmatic figure is most decidedly accurate, but the connotations of 'glamour' that have somehow become entangled within the word's true meaning find only cold comfort when trying to piece together the mystery of Nick Drake, his motivation (or lack of same), his existentialist melancholia – above all, the portrait one captures in sustained glimpses of a man lost within himself, an outcast and an outsider, all too painfully resigned to a confused and harsh destiny with no quarter left to belong in.

Even in his earliest compositions the overwhelming sense of resignation to a cruel mortality with no easy answers was overtly evident. The shimmering incandescence of Harry Robinson's arrangement to 'Riverman' from Drake's first album, at first obscures the essence of melancholia until the awesome intertwining strings and acoustic guitar blend together to reinforce the clinching stanza:

> Going to see the riverman
> Going to tell him all I can
> About the ban

On feeling free.
If he tells me all he knows
About the way his river flows
I don't suppose
It's meant for me.

Glimpses, glimpses. Sometimes sustained for a while, sometimes as fleeting and transitory as the unidentified pedestrian darting past Nick Drake, still as stone on the back cover of the aforementioned first album *Five Leaves Left*. But then there are facts and it's those facts that one should first document before darting into more uncharted terrain. Nicholas Drake was born on 19 June 1948 while his parents, Rodney and Molly, were stationed in Rangoon, Burma, where young Nick was to live along with his sister, Gabrielle, until the age of six. The Drakes then returned to England, choosing to live in the quiet village of Tamworth in Arden, not far from Stratford upon Avon.

The family was very much moulded in the upper-class social structure and Nick was immediately packed off to public school, where he excelled both academically and as a school athlete. Though plagued with shyness (a trait hardly uncommon among barely pubescent teenagers), the juvenile Drake quickly developed a passion for music. His mother had played the piano and actually written songs herself, and Drake started playing saxophone and clarinet in his early teens before, at the age of sixteen, starting to learn the guitar with the aid of a friend. Influences were not uncommon, with the likes of Dylan, John Renbourn and Bert Jansch to the forefront, but so speedy was his progress as a guitar player that, at 18, Nick had a fairly large repertoire of standard folk

songs as well as some of his own, which were steadily growing in number.

Indeed, while still living in Tamworth, Drake recorded a lengthy tape, apparently for his parents, of some twenty-five songs. Standards included Dylan's 'Don't Think Twice' and 'Tomorrow is a Long Time', Renbourn-styled 'Black Mountain', Jansch's 'Courting Blues' (a duet with sister Gabrielle), but the original material is what really mattered. 'Saturday Sun', 'Day is Done' and 'Way to Blue' were later to be found on that first album, while other self-penned works like 'Princess of the Sands', 'Joey' and 'Mayfair' have never been aired publicly (although Millie, of 'My Boy Lollipop' fame, recorded 'Mayfair' at arranger Robert Kirby's suggestion for an album since consigned to the bargain bins to be filed under obscurities).

Meanwhile, Drake's academic propensities scored him a place at Cambridge – Fitzwilliam College to be exact – where he went to read English Literature. Once in Cambridge, Drake became a part of both that cerebrally obsessive elitist capriciousness that the likes of Cambridge and Oxford seem fond of cultivating, and the activity on the outer periphery of the town itself. Cambridge was at that time (early 1968) starting to simmer with a certain well-honed, enthusiastic, self-enveloping energy: Pink Floyd had probably set the ball rolling the previous year, their appearance providing a spotlight for the area which carried on through to such cultural events as the staging of a 'Cambridge Free Festival', John and Yoko doing one of their dynamic displays of 'bagism' at Lady Margaret Hall – a four-hour avant-garde extravaganza which also featured John Tchicai (a saxophonist who had once worked with Archie Shepp), and the whole of Cadentia Nova Danica.

Drake had won his scholarship to study English Literature but, according to friends and fellow pupils, seldom attended lectures, preferring instead to get further into music – and his guitar-playing and song-writing in particular. (A previous article about Nick Drake has claimed that he went through an almost permanent depression while at Cambridge, which couldn't be further from the truth, according to Brian Wells, one of Drake's best friends at Cambridge and one of a number of 'frustrated' musicians resident there at that time.)

Cambridge, according to those who have resided there, has harboured a number of such figures in its time. Drake, however, easily shone forth from this company in almost every respect, a prolific songwriter, a dauntingly fine (to the point of innovative) guitarist and – a moot point, this – the possessor of a more than fair vocal style, a charming, almost breathy sound that fitted in somewhere between the incredibly diverse likes of Kevin Ayers and a male Astrud Gilberto. According to Wells, Drake was also always the first on his block to pick up on a new sound.

Randy Newman and Tim Buckley albums were to be found among Nick's collection before other music devotees had got the message; 'Astral Weeks' was another Drake Cambridge listening innovation. 'Blonde on Blonde' was never far from the stereo, neither was Donovan or Jim Webb's work from the 5th Dimension. Drake also loved Traffic as well as the little-known US songwriter Jackson Frank.

Friends are, in fact, only too eager to point out Drake's 'undying enthusiasm' for most things, principally music, during his two years at Cambridge, his own musical progress being most spirited. It was later brought to the attention of, amongst others, one Robert Kirby, a music student from another college in the University complex who became most eager to work on the arrangements for Drake's songs. One number for example, 'Way to Blue', Kirby saw in terms of endowing with a quasi-Handel string ambience.

Drake by this time had reached the stage where private performances in friends' lodgings (Wells mentions that certain facets of Nick's talents have never been brought to public attention, not the least being, for example, an adeptness at 12-bar blues improvisations) were turning into public performances in Cambridge itself. It was at one of these – he was supporting Country Joe McDonald at the time – that he was 'discovered' by Ashley 'Tiger' Hutchings, then bassist for Fairport Convention (later founder member of Steeleye Span and all-round die-hard ethnic English folk music pioneer), at that particular time very much the apple of Witchseason's eye. Witchseason was, of course, the company that managed numerous high-quality low-profile 'underground' acts motivated – and more or less run single-handed – by the incomparable Joe Boyd.

Boyd's credentials were, and still are for that matter, quite peerless. Absolutely *the* vital organising body for London's whole underground movement – the U.F.O. and Middle Earth – production credits on the Floyd's first single 'Arnold Layne', Incredible String Band svengali, the Fairports, of course...the list is endless and positively oozing with a kind of dead-eye sense of good taste and (a hackneyed word, sure, but most relevant here) *integrity*, easing up even to contemporary projects like the excellent Hendrix movie and production credits for Kate and Anna McGarrigle.

Boyd was informed of Drake's talents by Hutchings, went down to see for himself and at once became the third of the Drake–Kirby–Joe Boyd triumvirate which created *Five Leaves Left*. The title refers to the dilemma of roll-yer-own smokers when the cigarette papers are running out (Rizla placed a 'five leaves left' reminder before desisting from the tactic some years ago), and was of no particular relevance to anything much really, except that it sounded like it might be a good album title. It also fitted nicely with the autumnal feel of the music and package.

The cover said more: Drake the silent observer staring out of a window of a deserted house, dressed in an utterly non-descript, functional style, the corners of his mouth curling ever so slightly on a face that screams with a kind of low-profile sensitivity. On the back a stranger is caught by the camera, paralysed and in mid-sprint, while Drake leans against a wall quite motionless, his face betraying no semblance of an expression. The gatefold shot is unfortunate only in that it portrays Drake The Artist, head and shoulders cloaked in pitch-black darkness, prone, like some John Donne student of metaphysical introspection.

It's that word 'introspection' that constantly springs to mind when Drake's name is mentioned, which is a large part of 'the image', sure, but really Robert Kirby says it when he views Nick Drake the artist as remarkable for 'his ability to observe, mainly. I see his work above all as a series of extremely vivid, complete observations and not mere exercises in introspection as some might. They're almost like little epigrammatic proverbs. The music and the words are welded together in such a way as to make the atmosphere in all his songs the most important facet. I know that that was Nick's primary purpose – I don't think, for example, that he was hung up about his lyrics being "great poetry" or anything. They're to complement . . . to compound a mood that the melody dictates in the first place.'

The latter point seems to be one that meets with general agreement among acquaintances and admirers (though a brusque study of Drake as poet will be taken into account later in the article). Whatever, its omnipresence on all Drake's albums carves out a whole lustrous landscape that has seldom been touched and certainly never bettered by his singer-songwriter peers. *Five Leaves Left* is one of those albums that seem tied to exhorting and then playing on a particular mood in the listener – like *Astral Weeks* and *Forever Changes* – certainly and arguably stationed on that particular echelon of creativity.

The album's qualities are variable, of course, even if smoothed over by an utterly seductive continuity of mood (a *Time Out* review of *Pink Moon*, the third album, made mention of 'Nick Drake's exquisite 3 a.m. introspections').

'Riverman' is easily the album's finest track: an utterly hypnotic guitar coda played with a kind of deceptively ambling sensuousness, almost throwaway lyrics edged with an oblique mysticism that acts in exactly the way that Kirby states, and then Robinson's stunning string arrangement that suddenly

'let his music stand.'

swells up and levitates spiralling upwards and out, it is Drake at his most supremely, spine-tinglingly effective.

The rest of the album is charming, fragile, observant... the adjectives roll off as easily as the melodies.

Island Records (the company Drake was signed with through Boyd's Witchseason connection) loved it, critics drooled, everybody who made it their business to know exactly what was happening in music nodded in their arch, pseudo-sage-like pose and predicted great things and Drake immediately became the object of the 'But, my dear, have you heard?' conversations. The public largely ignored the album, of course, but it had sold 'encouragingly' if nothing else, and who could blame a highly elated Nick Drake, whose academic leanings had long become quite dormant anyway, for leaving Cambridge to pursue his musical bent?

More to the point, the company he was keeping in that sphere was perfect: Boyd produced and was a source of constant encouragement; illustrious folk like Richard Thompson were helping out; Chris Blackwell was a modest but admiring benefactor. And then there was John Martyn and his wife Beverley, another pair of Witchseason hopefuls, with whom Drake struck up a strong friendship and mutual appreciation society.

Drake was a great admirer of the Martyn acoustic guitar technique and this state of affairs was undeniably reversed to a point where John, according to friends, picked up much of the former's instrumental style, though Martyn himself denies this.

Robert Kirby, again: 'Nick was an absolutely phenomenal guitarist . . . that's a fact which is all too often merely glossed over. He very adept at highly complex double-pick rhythms with the thumb on the bass string and the other fingers working on as many as four tunes at a time. He was a master of counterpoint to that extent. I know for a fact that John Martyn was very influenced by Nick's work in that respect.' Martyn himself, though incredibly cagey talking about Drake, an intensely close friend (one mutual acquaintance of the pair claimed they were like Romulus and Remus . . . 'always arguing but as close as any two friends can get. It was closer to a brotherhood thing, really.'), allows himself to be quoted about Drake's guitar technique. Unlike Kirby's assessment Martyn claims that, like himself, Drake only used his thumb and one finger for picking, and that the secret behind his technique was in the tuning – mostly minor tunings that Drake kept very much to himself. Martyn also claims adamantly that he's never used Drake's tuning himself.

Drake's guitar-playing similarly revolved around several complex open tunings, principally certain mutations of the open-ended D and G chords. The instrumentals on *Bryter Layter* give one potent example of the personal technique which was to reach full fruition on *Pink Moon*. *Bryter Layter* is Nick's most outward-going and consequently commercial album. Very much a 'city' album, it is also the biggest seller, notching up something in the region of a humble 15,000 sales.

The personal positivism inherent in Drake's psyche at the time cannot be overstated (if only to act as a contrast for the depressing, bleak states that were to follow). Not that Nick was ever exactly one to be moved by a sense of 'drive' or ego – there is the story of the time Françoise Hardy, whose whole style and winsome breathy chantease must have obviously been drawn to Drake's similar superiority-wrought style, phoned Island Records, more or less ordering Drake over to France to write songs for her.

After much goading, Drake, ticket in hand, doggedly set off to the Hardy château and after a long journey arrived at the door which was answered by a maid. When asked who he was, Drake muttered, 'Um . . . I'm Nick . . . Nick,' prompting the maid to become suspicious. Upon questioning the guests present (Ms Hardy was unfortunately not there at that particular moment) as to whether they knew who 'zis Ne-ek is', and getting blank looks for replies, she more or less shut the door in his face. Drake, according to John Martyn, ever the romantic, consequently stood in the rain for two solid days waiting for Ms Hardy. She never arrived, leaving the bedraggled singer-songwriter to lurch back dejectedly to England.

It is said, however, that Drake and Hardy did eventually record together, though certain acquaintances deny this, citing concrete proof in the fact that nothing came of the sessions.

There is talk of some emotional attachment between the two, though little is known as to the exact nature of their relationship, or even it existed at all.

Back to city album *Bryter Layter* though. The cover wasn't as good this time. The front, for example, is a twee, unnecessary Nigel Waymouth photo of Drake the Homely Folkie sitting moon-faced and dozy-eyed poring over a Spanish guitar and fronted by a pair of 'bumper' styled brothel creepers.

The music though…well, for a start, there was more variety. The melodies were more fluid and easy. 'Hazy Jane II' was as close to rock as Drake was ever to get – with a freewheeling, swing-style that you could dance to plus horns, no less, and great Richard Thompson guitar work. The personnel were stronger and more varied than before, still using Fairport members plus Danny Thompson (with whom Drake talked about forming some sort of band along with Tristram Fry, without anything ever coming of it), encouraging excursions into a kind of atmospheric cool jazz like the wryly autobiographical 'Poor Boy', and 'At the Chime of the City Clock'. And then there was John Cale – at that point somewhere between his A & R gigs, first for Elektra and then Warner Bros, who was living with Joe Boyd at the time and played keyboards and viola on 'Fly' and 'Northern Sky', both, interestingly enough, very much precursors to Cale's own sound and style on *Paris 1919*.

The cover again – the back shot gets closer to the truth of the time. It's a follow-up to the running/standing still ambience number from the first album sleeve, except this time Drake's on a highway, watching a car speed by. He has his back to the camera.

Actually, Drake never really felt comfortable in front of a camera, though, strangely enough, photographs of him (principally those of Keith Morris, who was the only photographer to ever get anywhere near him) are all too depressing statements of his personal decline through intro-spection, depression and, above all – and this is the word that friends choose with great care – confusion.

From 1970, which marked the release date of *Bryter Layter*, Drake's final 'up' period of any length and consistency, up to and throughout 1973, Nick Drake's life reached a bleak, unhappy state of affairs that it is perhaps unwise to dwell on.

I earlier mentioned *Bryter Layter*'s commercial potential. It was released at the same time as Cat Stevens' *Mona Bone Jakon*. Both were artistes striving for public acclaim: Stevens received just that but Drake was pitifully ignored. The latter state of affairs was hardly aided by Drake's horrendous fear of performing before an audience. Here perhaps was the crux of the matter – Nick Drake, the intensely introverted artist thrust into a star-making machine that was the absolute antithesis of his fragile personality. He was in a very real and all too tragic sense a victim of following a vocation, the paradoxes of which would have torn him to shreds, had he at least not been with a more understanding record label.

Even so, the virtual lack of success meted out to *Bryter Layter* appeared not to have that much effect on a swiftly snowballing depression.

Drake was always the archetypal loner. He had his friends – Kirby, Wells, Keith Norris, John Wood, his engineer – but as often found himself in strange surroundings. He would occasionally consort with debutantes and the whole triple-barrelled moniker brigade, even though he found their chosen lifestyles utterly facile.

His confusion was something wrought via his destiny – though friends say there was no choice in the matter: no posing, no poetic gestures of the misunderstood troubador. It was all a matter of course.

Drake slowly became more introspective, less easy to communicate with, and everyone became concerned, worried and anxious for his well-being. He eked out a remarkably frugal existence, living in Hampstead on £20

a week and became so poor at one point he couldn't even afford a new pair of shoes. It never crossed his mind to ask a friend to give him a pair. It was just accepted as a fact of life.

It was Island records, indeed, that paid his way to Spain for a short stay just prior to the making of *Pink Moon*. This album was recorded in two sessions over at Sound Techniques with just Drake and John Wood in attendance. Joe Boyd was busy in the States at the time – but, strangely, even he wasn't missed.

Pink Moon is, I suppose, what you might call the Artist's Key Work. Brian Wells returned from abroad to find it already in the shops and marvelled at the fact that Nick, though quite lost in confusion and personal depression, could produce a work that captured him completely in the creative ascendant. His guitar playing, for example, is quite remarkable here – easily the best he ever allowed on to a record.

Pink Moon, though, is a strange, somewhat disturbing album. Wells likens it to a kind of Van Gogh statement (which is one way of looking at it); some of the songs do have obliquely sinister overtones to them: 'Know' is a kind of paean to schizophrenia that Syd Barrett would've loved to have written.

'Know that I love you/know that I don't care/know that I see you/know I'm not there' – while even supposedly placid songs like 'Harvest Breed' bear painful, oblique images of death in them: 'Falling fast you kiss the flowers that bend/And you're ready now for the harvest breed.'

Drake's lyrics occasionally ring with a certain positivism but mostly they are filled with a kind of dark sadness, and bitter, resignedly cold, observations. Photographs taken by Morris of Drake for the *Pink Moon* cover capture him staring into dull air, his face bearing that horribly doomed dough-like pallor of the terminal depressant – the one that ends up on the gatefold sleeve is inverted into a kind of mysterioso, doomed negative; while a shot of him shuffling away from the camera with a dog running by his legs was used in advertisements for the album.

After *Pink Moon* Drake spent some time in various mental hospitals. He had left London in despair and returned to his parents' house in Tamworth, and it was there that he sought help. Mostly, though, it wasn't followed up. Nick would check himself in and leave the same day. Everything, from the taking of all manner of pills to electric shock treatment, was advised, but the advice was seldom heeded. Friends became resigned to the imminent news that Nick Drake had taken his own life. It seemed all too inevitable.

And then something happened. The first thing anyone knew about it was the news that Joe Boyd had driven to Island Records' Hammersmith offices and promptly entered to inform said company that Nick Drake was ready to record again. Drake stayed in the back of the car.

Sessions were laid on at Sound Techniques and in a couple during the summer of 1974, Nick Drake, with Joe Boyd and John Wood, got to lay down four new tracks. To all intents and purposes Nick Drake was back on something approaching the right track.

Certain associates of Drake's claim that this renewed interest in recording – compared with the point just after *Pink Moon* when Joe Boyd, attempting to drag Nick out of the quagmire of his depression, gave him a pep talk, only to be told blankly 'I don't

have any more music in me' – is only half the story.

What had occurred, they claim, was something approaching a total psychic rebirth for Drake; he looked and sounded happier than he had in years, literally. He was writing songs again and one source claimed that he even had a steady girlfriend.

His parents, who had been living with that daunting imminence of suddenly finding their son dead, were not unnaturally elated. Everyone was. Up until the night of 25 November 1974, that is.

Drake, always a perfectionist as regards his music (even when verging on the point of catatonia in previous recording sessions, he would still make sure that only the best was to be laid down), had scrapped four tracks – 'Voice from the Mountain', 'Rider on the Wheel', 'Black Eyed Dog' and 'Hanging on a Star' (though both Boyd and Wood considered them quite beautiful, an opinion shared by yours truly, and, I can only imagine, anyone else besotted with the man's music) – and appeared determined to return to the studio again and record them better.

Also, anticipating Boyd's return from the States, he had gone over to Paris to live communally on a barge. Again sources say that he returned 'more contented than ever'.

Which all leads up – with a brutal finality – to the 25 November date, when, in his bedroom, supposedly practising guitar and working out riffs and germs of songs, recording said morsels on his cassette player, he ingested a quantity of Tryptasol, a highly potent anti-depressant that he'd been prescribed. One of the newer drugs on the market, this medium-sized orange capsule relieves depression but its potency is such that only a small overdose could prove fatal.

At about 6 a.m. the next morning, Nick Drake, aged 26, died in his bedroom from just such an overdose.

The coroner's verdict was suicide; in an attempt to write a biography of Drake (I had in fact started the project before his death but his unavailability, coupled with Boyd stuck in America, had scotched the work temporarily) I encountered a number of Drake's old cronies, including principally Brian Wells, himself a student doctor, who was adamant the coroner's verdict was wrong. Thus convinced, I zealously contested the verdict in an article published early in 1975.

⌘

Over three years have passed now and my feelings concerning the circumstances of Drake's death have become blurred. At the time I made great play of the fact that no suicide note, no grand flourish, had accompanied the act – yet this in all honesty is probably exactly the way Drake would have wanted to end it all. With absolutely no fuss.

John Martyn, who not only had to bear the loss of Nick Drake but that of his good friend Paul Kossoff, while noting that both died and lived in radically different circumstances, stated that the lowest common denominator of their twin problem was simply 'oversensitivity'.

Finally, it is worth checking out an obscure critique on Drake's work to be found in *The London Magazine* of October 1978 entitled 'Some Get By'. Its author, Neil Powell, believes that Drake committed suicide, not because of any particular factual

evidence but more from studying intensely his work, his lyrics in particular. Powell notes certain motifs in Drake's work – colours, for example – blue being a symbol of ease, freedom and fulfilment ('Way To Blue') while pink is cryptic, leading to the song of death ('Harvest Breed'). Powell notes a recurring theme in Drake's work of the quest that often shades off into a land of fairytale, with oblique characters appearing and disappearing (Betty in 'Riverman', Jeremy/Jacomo in 'Three Hours', even Hazy Jane, who could be Drake addressing a female alter-ego), ending always with the feeling that there are in any case no answers, or at least none for Drake. And yet there is that gorgeous music that totally transcends rock-jazz-folk-fusion music – you name it. Stolidly English, a little old-fashioned (a trait Drake always seems high self-conscious about and not a little embarrassed of) – Powell hits the nail squarely on the head when he likens Drake's music at its best to the pastoral works of Delius.

The beautiful thing is that it's still alive, imbued with a spirit that is timeless. John Martyn, when asked for his final thoughts, chose these succinct but heartfelt words: 'I loved him. Let his music stand.'

My own feelings coincide perfectly with Neil Powell, however, when, in his final sentence, he states perhaps the most perfect critique of Nick Drake's work yet made:

That is where Drake's strength lies and why it is not melodramatic to speak of his death as an artistic inevitability: he delineates more tellingly than any other contemporary songwriter the hinterland between despair and fragile happiness which is the territory of a peculiarly

English melancholia. He has nothing to say about the glossy and superficial world of the popular performer. But when the pretensions of the showbiz kids are forgotten, the listener of the future will be able to discover from Nick Drake what it was like in our time to be honest, English and a bit screwed up.

Author's note

In 1978 Island Records asked me to contribute a text for the booklet in *Fruit Tree*, Nick Drake's first boxed set. This is the result. Unfortunately it went unpublished; the reasons why are lost in the mists of time. This is the first time it has ever appeared in any kind of public forum.

RICHARD MILWARD
Drugby Union

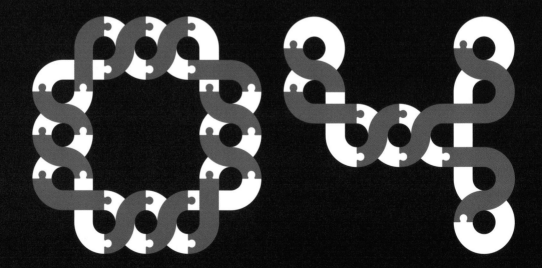

Drugs and music make a wonderful couple. Without wanting to sound like a soggy-eyed grandmother-in-law, it's like they really were made for each other. The best drugs make the best sounds sound even better, like replacing your old worn-out ears with new, state-of-the-art surround-sound speakers for a few sacred hours.

Along with drinking cups of tea and daydreaming, taking drugs and listening to music is one of my all-time favourite pastimes. Acid transforms Donovan into the most gorgeous, hilarious twee psychedelia, putting me in stitches just by the way he rolls his Rs. Ecstasy and the Beatles makes me fall hopelessly in love, Cupid-like, with whoever happens to be nearby, especially if they like the Beatles too. But it's Spacemen 3, with their Timothy Leary-like guidance and delightful hypnagogic drones, who turn taking drugs into a riotous, near-religious experience.

A very long time ago, the hole in the middle of Karl Marx's beard said, 'Religion is the opiate of the masses.' A bit more recently – between the years of our Lord 1982 and 1990, to be precise – Spacemen 3 were the opiate for a modest number of drone-drenched disciples. Nowadays, more people get their kicks from drugs and music than from the stuffy shackles of religion – although, essentially, the experience is quite similar; going out every weekend in your best clobber, singing along to enlightening, happy-clappy music, receiving wine, getting scolded and told what to do by men in smart black suits. Likewise, both getting lashed and going to church have that cruel ability to make you wake up feeling a bit guilty now and then.

With all the references to 'God' and 'the Lord' in their lyrics, Spacemen 3 seemed a bit like sonic shamans themselves, blending heavenly, hypnotic guitar and synth with mantra-like melodies whispered lovingly in your inner ear. Often, people would sit on the floor at their gigs, as if in prayer, the altar-like amplifiers churning out layer upon layer of enlightening white lightning.

Spacemen 3 enjoyed sitting down at their gigs, too. Not ones for onstage amateur dramatics or daft cock-rock showmanship, the band delivered their sermons sitting on stools – a bit like your local dusty, folky church band, except with more intentional feedback, more stroboscopic brain-sizzling lightshows, and more songs about smack. They are a wonderful companion to any trip – be it drug-fuelled or otherwise – transporting you softly to a strange world where you can walk and talk with Jesus, fall in love, and come down easy.

⌘

There are lots of marvellous, magical things about Spacemen 3. Born on the very same day (19 November 1965), by some cosmic law of attraction Pete 'Sonic Boom' Kember and Jason Pierce met and formed Spacemen 3 in 1982 at art college in Rugby, Warwickshire – the home of cement, radio masts, odd-shaped balls, and plentiful odd-shaped pills and potions. Affectionately known as 'Drugby', in the Eighties the town was awash with cheapo narcotics. Wearing their musical influences on their sleeves (as well as the odd cheeky track-mark underneath), the lads started out making music combining the primal raw power of the Stooges with the rolling greased lightning of Krautrock. Their early demos (captured on *For All the Fucked-Up Children Of This World We Give You Spacemen 3* and *Taking Drugs to Make Music to Take Drugs to*) seemed like the work of a hippyish Velvet Underground, Natty's Neanderthal drumming summoning up the spirit of Mo Tucker, all the while Pete and Jason injecting their amps with sloppy melodic distortion in a similar vein to their moody sunglassed heroes, Reed and Cale.

At times, during the early days, Spacemen 3 might have been seen as a sort of cosmic covers band – reworking and remodelling the musical threads of their idols (the MC5, the Red Krayola, the 13th Floor Elevators, etc.) into new, woolly sonic tapestries. It's perhaps due to these – then obscure – '60s influences that, in 1982, the band sounded like nothing else around. Set against their contemporaries (for instance, it took the

Jesus and Mary Chain until 1985 to treat us to their delicious *PsychoCandy*, and it was not until 1986 that alleged Spacemen 3 'rip-offs' Loop formed in London), Spacemen 3 were more like artists reinterpreting the work of their favourite Old Masters, rather than trying in vain to reinvent the colour-wheel.

⌘

On a chilly Friday evening in autumn, me and a pal took some LSD out from its hiding place in the back of *To Kill a Mockingbird*. The acid had blue suns on it. A few hours later, after the obligatory giggling along to Donovan, I decided to dash home before the effects wore off, to surrender my surround-sound speaker-ears completely to Spacemen 3. It seemed like the decent thing to do, since I was limbering up to write an essay about them and all.

Laid out perfectly horizontally on my bed, I figured the best place to start was to stick on both versions of 'Suicide' (the band's notorious one-chord metallic noise-orgy) off the remastered *Playing with Fire* album, on headphones. Since intense tear-jerking laughter had been the theme of the night's trip, as soon as the song kicked in, both me and the guitars were cackling uncontrollably. Instant pleasure! At times it was like being serenaded by a lynch mob of randy robots squealing 'DANGER DANGER DANGER DANGER DANGER', the music wahwah-wahwahwahwahwahwahing away, rising rising rising to the point of a supersonic starburst. Oh yes!

You see, it's the tones – not specifically the notes – that ooze pleasure in Spacemen 3's music. Applying a strict, puritan ethic of 'less is more' (the band's legendary manifesto was

'Three chords good, two chords better, one chord best', so says Chris Barrus, in the *Live in Europe 1989* liner notes), the Spacemen eschewed fancy fretwork for jaw-dropping simplicity. In their infancy, the band were more or less shunned for their particular brand of repetitive psychedelia (whereby songs could go on for twenty-odd minutes, the lads seemingly stuck in a one-note groove, like statuettes in a broken music-box), but went on to inspire legions of fans and bands who enjoy getting high on the crest of a steadfast soundwave.

⌘

My Friday night of 'Suicide' was truly heavenly, though perhaps the only daft thing about doing acid is its ability to turn you into a freakish insomniac. By five or six in the morning, I was still wide awake, gazing zombie-like at the photos in the middle of Erik Morse's newish Spacemen 3 biography. The blue suns had already begun to wear off and set in the dusky lower sanctums of my brain, leaving me with sore limbs, sticky trip-fingers, and heavy bushbaby eyeballs. As is always the case with LSD, once you get to that stage, you're just sat there wishing the visions would come back. Music – and life in general – seems so much blander and sad.

Head stinging, I found myself staring listlessly at this photo of a young Pete and Jason, sat together on some Rugby railing or other. Yawn yawn! I was just about to slip into the shallow waters of sleep when – I kid you not – I saw Pete hop off the railing! Admittedly, the acid was too weak now to make him do anything else exciting (like hop downstairs and make me a nice cup of tea), but the fact that he'd made himself known to

me in such a dire druggy malady made me chuckle again.

Then, finally, I dropped off to peeps.

⌘

I became acquainted with Pete Kember again a couple of months later, this time by a similarly mystical process: the internet. Still buzzing off the randy robot chorus of 'Suicide' (itself more a homage to the art-rock duo of the same name, than the art of topping yourself), I asked Pete if he finds certain drugs especially helpful – and others particularly detrimental – to the creative process. After all, it was Pete who came up with the title *Taking Drugs to Make Music to Take Drugs to*, which begs the question: which drugs does Pete like to take to make music to take drugs to?

'Different strokes for different folks,' he replied. 'I dunno, it's very personal, I guess. DMT I find awe-inspiring and very stimulating creatively. I think smack can be, in its own way. Coke – sure. LSD/mushrooms – definitely. Speed – of course. In the same way though, any of these can be destructive to creativity. It's a fine balance – and I firmly believe a reasonable route to the sublime – BUT only with adherences to a certain respect for these things.'

It's important to stress here that Spacemen 3 were far from being wastrels. The lads may have been explicit about what drugs they've been on in their interviews, but only because journalists enjoyed hounding them about it, coaxing them into being controversial. Honesty is far more of a virtue than drug-taking is a sin, after all – from the very outset, all the Spacemen tried to do was tell the truth.

'NICK CAVE WILL OBVIOUSLY LIVE FOREVER, JUST BECAUSE THE DEVIL's SCARED OF HIM.' *Rolling Stone*

'Put Cormac McCarthy, Franz Kafka and Benny Hill together in a Brighton seaside guesthouse and they might just come up with **THE DEATH OF** *Bunny Munro.* A compulsive read possessing all Nick Cave's trademark horror and humanity.'

IRVINE WELSH

The first novel in twenty years from the legendary

NICK CAVE

Coming in

SEPTEMBER 2009

CANON||GATE
www.meetatthegate.com

Published in hardback at £16.99 and in audiobook format read by the author and with musical score by Nick Cave and Warren Ellis at £18.99

'I don't subscribe to the "all drugs are bad and dangerous" thing,' stresses Pete. 'I take each on their own merits and downsides, and fully realise that they have both.'

Taking Drugs... aside, the band was far less chatty about narcotics in their music. In fact, the lyrics retain an intentional ambiguity – when they sing about 'getting high' or 'losing touch' with their minds, anyone who has ever been in love or felt utterly alone can relate as much to the lyrics as your average pot-headed hippy.

Even the most heartless of humans are interested in emotions – and drugs are interested in heightening them for us. In turn, Spacemen 3 were interested in condensing these feelings for us into song, like rock-and-roll research scientists. Ultimately, it is the timelessness of these songs – and the emotions wrapped up in them – which has ensured the band's longevity.

Admittedly, 'Walkin' with Jesus' (the band's wondrous first single, released in November 1986) originally contained the lyric 'So listen sweet Lord please forgive me my sins, cos I can't stand this life without sweet heroin'; however, after a bit of deliberation, the band substituted 'sweet heroin' for the more universal 'all of these things', exemplifying their wish never to alienate the listener. In other words, they didn't care about forcing drugs down the listener's throat; only their own, in private, for their own ends.

Incidentally, the reference to 'sweet heroin' in 'Walkin' with Jesus' stemmed from some obligatory writings Pete penned in a clinic for addiction outside Rugby. 'It was analogising life with drugs to drinking water, or drinking orange squash!' explains Pete, who has been on and off the drug for much of his life. '[But] it soon became apparent that if I wanted to get out of the clinic and avoid sectioning, that proselytising about drugs was not going to work. I met some interesting characters in there: drug burnouts, alcoholics, bored housewives. It was a good intro to the music biz...'

⌘

By the latter stages of 1986, Spacemen 3's lift-off into the music biz was well underway. Their first full-length album, *Sound of Confusion*, was released in July of that year; a record apparently 'written about taking speed'. From *Raw Power* to *Metal Machine Music*, some of the most wonderful, ear-splitting records have been influenced by that white-coloured powder, and *Sound of Confusion* is no less masterful. Chockfull of churning, gurning distortion, the album seems like a distant nephew of the Velvet Underground's *White Light/White Heat*, the primitive guitars smothering the delicate, sentimental melodies with the softest of fuzzy pillows. However, unlike the VU – who notoriously didn't like each other very much when they were recording *White Light/White Heat* – *Sound of Confusion* captures four young friends (Pete, Jason, Pete 'Bassman' Bain and drummer Nicholas 'Natty' Brooker) guiding each other blindly on their maiden sonic voyage, with only a few meagre chords packed in their suitcases.

In the early days, perhaps the 'Three chords good, two chords better, one chord best' manifesto was just a convenient cover-up for a lack of competence. However, listening to *Sound of Confusion*, the strict repetition seems less a crutch, more the crux of an extraordinary idealism. As opposed to the idle bash-bash-bashing of calamitous cavemen, Spacemen 3 made music with a specific, sophisticated aim: to transcend the trappings of consciousness through trance-like mantra and fuzzy distortion, like how a snake-charmer lifts his snake from the basket through mere music alone.

'We were very much [making music] for ourselves,' Pete explains, 'but anyone who says they don't care what people think about them are lying, or a little desperate, I guess. We hoped there would be other folk like us out there who would appreciate out adjunct to their lives in the same way we did. This music was obscure and unpopular – sometimes even within the band. We had high hopes – but low estimations – for it.'

⌘

Despite the initial low estimations, by the end of the '80s there were a lot of folk who found themselves hopelessly snake-charmed by the band's psychotropic sentiments.

Spacemen 3 were on the telly once, with Alan McGee, standing about all sullen in their denim jackets. At one point, Alan asks the band, 'If you were to describe your group, what drug would it be?' After a long hesitation, Pete Kember replies, 'A cocktail. Definitely a cocktail of different drugs.'

While their one and only concept album, *The Perfect Prescription* (released September 1987) was supposed to map the highs and lows of the drug experience in song (from the clashing come-up of 'Take Me to the Other Side', to Pete's overdose opus 'Call the Doctor'), in fact the band's entire chronological history seems to follow the rocky peaks and troughs of a twirly-whirly psychedelic trip. Starting out with youthful

wonder and abandon, by the time Pete and Jason divorced the band in 1990, they were a wreck of p-p-paranoia and detachment. Like a doomed space-shuttle; what went up, came back down, horrendously.

But let's not jump the gun. As the story goes, Pete and Jason were on fine, friendly form during the recording of *Perfect Prescription*, getting stoned together and tinkering about with their new Fender Jaguars and Farfisa organs in VHF Studios, in Rugby. The pair came up with the gorgeous 'Feel so Good' after injecting palfium (a morphine-like opioid), Pete singing over Jason's strum-strum-strumming while the goo slid softly through their veins. The songs all point towards some sort of joyous surrender: getting drunk on love, getting high on life. As Jason croons on 'Come Down Easy': 'In 1987, all I wanna do is get stoned, and all I want for you to do is take my body home.'

More wistful and dreamlike than the leathery, amphetamine-dusted *Sound of Confusion*, *The Perfect Prescription* is notable for the Spacemen's most extreme, delectable foray into minimalism: their instrumental magnum opus, 'Ecstasy Symphony'. Taping down one of the A keys on a Vox organ, the lads fed the note through a series of wacky oscillators and tremolos and autopans and phasers, creating this orgasmic ambient soundscape, which pushed their minimalist manifesto to its furthest, purest limits. And, with MDMA slowly beginning to rear its acid-smiley head in Britain, it could be argued Spacemen 3 unwittingly pre-empted the birth of the lovey-dovey 'Ecstasy Generation'.

Back on telly, in 1989, Alan McGee probes the band: 'Would you describe your sound as the Ecstasy sound?' Pete Kember smiles. 'I think, yeah,' he answers. 'Amongst other things; you could, yeah. Definitely some of our tracks...are aimed at that type of listener.'

Today, Kember admits wryly, 'Alan was on a big E kick back then.' By the time dance floors across the UK became swamped with dummy-sucking, whistle-blowing divvies spouting 'Es are good, Es are good' at each other, it became clear Spacemen 3 were not ones to jump on the 'unpsychedelic' band-wagon of Acid House. After all, Ecstasy did not create Spacemen 3. Supplementing their cornucopia of trusty chemicals, by the close of the '80s the Spacemen had tapped further into another, equally well-trodden route to the sublime: love.

As Kember explained to *Melody Maker* in 1988, 'Most of the feelings we try to sum up are attained through cannabis or ampheta-mines or whatever. Or that really intense feeling of being close to someone you're totally in love with and who's totally in love with you. That intense oneness is very druglike. I mean – all those drugs are in our bodies anyway. There are ways of releasing them other than with chemicals.'

⌘

Ultimately, Spacemen 3's music is about romance. While, in 1989, the lads were more or less at each others' throats (Pete's strict 'no girls on the tour bus' policy was shunned by Jason and his then-girlfriend Kate Radley; meanwhile, everyone had to suffer the brunt of each others' grumpy hangovers and junk withdrawal), conversely the music was more loved-up than ever. Spacemen 3's third studio album, *Playing with Fire*, is the musical equivalent of going to church with

Martin Rev, Brian Wilson and a packed-lunch of magic mushrooms. And it's beautiful. As is sometimes the way with bands, the less you get on with each other, the more you feel the need to prove your own worth; a bit like lovers trying to make each other feel jealous when they're aware they're on the cusp of splitting up.

Playing with Fire fluctuates between sparse, glistening pop (Jason's '[So Hot] Wash Away All of My Tears' is a sun-ripened peach of a song) to raucous electric freakout (indie #1 single 'Revolution' rattles away with fuzzy vehemence). The distance and venom found in the music owes itself in no small part to the increasing detachment between Pete and Jason – they were no longer collaborating on each other's songs; in fact, Pete argued that Jason was purpose-fully not writing him any guitar parts to play.

After they cut the album, every single writing credit was contested, and the band appeared to be going down the shitter, but somehow *Playing with Fire* still sparkles with unassuming beauty. It's the first Spacemen 3 album I ever heard, and still my very favourite. The beauty seems to come, in part, from the new blood in the group – Pete 'Bassman' Bain made way for Will Carruthers, while Jonny Mattock took over from Stewart 'Rosco' Roswell (grafted in for *The Perfect Prescription*) on drums. In contrast to Bassman's plodding, pounding tribal bass lines, Will's so-called 'bass vibrations' elevated the Spacemen's music to new, more melodic heights. At times, he seemed to treat his bass more like a lead guitar, holding the tracks together like the lead in a lovely stained glass window; not to mention holding the band together, what with his wanderings back and forth from Pete's studio sessions to

Jason's and so on and so on.

All hail *Playing with Fire*! After I first plucked the album from the dusty racks of HMV, I thought Spacemen 3 came across a bit like an incendiary religious campfire band, the way they sung so softly and sincerely about the Lord and Jesus and sainthood and sinning, occasionally with the accompaniment of sweet church organ sounds. While the lads themselves didn't seem like your typical clean-living Christians, they clearly held a belief in some kind of all-encompassing enlightening presence, whether it lives in the heavens, or in your wacky-backy tin. When Pete dropped ET acid in Amsterdam, apparently he saw Jesus in the wallpaper. But has he ever been interested in going to see him on his home turf; church?

'It's a metaphor for something unattainable,' Pete explains. 'The use of phrases like "Jesus" or "Oh Lord", etc., are more a part of human vocabulary in an unliteralised way.'

Again, it harks back to the timelessness of the lyrics. Like the cloaked, ambiguous drug references, so too the religious aspect is muddied, made universal. It's almost like a secret language – if you want to find drug references in the music, they're there for the taking. Otherwise – say, if the Spacemen landed on a planet where drugs or religion didn't exist – I'm sure the extra-terrestrials would understand their worldly wise sensibilities, and perhaps even shake their hips a bit.

Pete validates these universalised words – such as 'higher' or 'sweet Lord' or 'babe' or whatever – referring to the liner notes of Otis Redding's album *Dictionary of Soul*, 'where . . . it gives definitions for phrases such as "ooooeee", "baby", etc.. . . .[These] vocalised rather than verbalised words [were] a sort of generation-proof language that you could nudge and wink about, but your folks couldn't bitch about.'

In other words, whether you're young, old, a tea-drinker, a daydreamer, or an acid-sucker, there's something in Spacemen 3's music for everybody.

⌘

However, by the time the curtain fell on the '80s, it appeared it was the Spacemen themselves, not anyone's folks, who were bitching. While *The Perfect Prescription* may have been the band's one and only 'official' concept album, their last record, *Recurring*, is a kind of concept album in the art of breaking up. Taking the animosity first unearthed during the *Playing with Fire* sessions (and which continued to harass them on tour round Europe in 1989, like a horrid hitchhiker) to new depths, Pete and Jason were like a pair of lovers splitting up, fighting over each others' belongings before finally agreeing to disagree and go their separate ways.

As before, the two of them recorded the album separately, grafting in Will and Jonny as well as guitarist Mark Refoy (later to found Slipstream) to help hammer in the final nails of the spaceship-shaped coffin. While Kember maintains he had guitar parts worked out for Jason to overdub, the favour was apparently not reciprocated. After a host of heated arguments, Pete threatened to release *Recurring* with his songs on side one, and Jason's on the other. Perhaps out of spite, or exasperation, Jason called his bluff, and agreed.

And so *Recurring* was born. The album feels more like two solo mini-albums loosely Sellotaped together than one cohesive mass: Pete's sugary-sweet dream-pop numbers are both transcendent and foot-tappingly gorgeous. On the flipside, Jason's tracks are more like avant-garde church hymns or slow-motion gospel, all seven of them submerged in the same sumptuous reverb. Despite the lack of cohesion, both efforts make breaking up sound absolutely blissful.

A truly beautiful, swoony swansong, *Recurring* is charged with equal parts melancholy and hopefulness, like a dead swan absolutely certain it's going to be reincarnated into something very pleasant. Essentially, the separate sides of *Recurring* paved the way for Pete and Jason's successive musical incarnations: Spectrum and Spiritualized. Pete's love of r-r-r-repetition, analogue machinery and lullabies seems not to have faltered over the years (for extreme tribalism, see his Experimental Audio Research side-project), while Jason's delicious brand of soft, plaintive gospel sees him touring with choirs and orchestras large enough to fill a small church.

Ultimately, *Recurring* seems to heed the advice intoned by Pete on *Playing with Fire*'s 'Let Me Down Gently'. Over a sublime, wishy-washy backdrop of synth and beating-heart bass line, Pete speaks on the track: 'Darling, if you find your love ever starting to fade, let me down gently honey, ever so gently, and then maybe, just maybe, and it's only a maybe, well maybe I won't feel a thing.' It may only be a 'maybe', but – while the animosity seemed inconsolable between the band leaders – there appears to be no malice in the lyrics of *Recurring*. Pete's tracks sing of joy, adoration and longing ('I Love You', 'Just to See You Smile'), while Jason

presents a sort of manic-depressive palette of introspection ('Feelin' Just Fine', 'Feel So Sad'), held together by those lovely, rich lashings of reverb.

Looking back on the Spacemen experience, Pete does not seem downhearted, or spiteful. 'It was a lot of fun,' he says. 'A whole slew of trippy nights.'

⌘

It's thanks to those trippy nights that Spacemen 3 have got into the veins of many recent noise-enthusiasts and purveyors of so-called 'space rock'. The Brian Jonestown Massacre, for one, have adopted the ethos of the Spacemen, preaching to another wonderful bunch of 'honeys' and 'Lords' over a backdrop of charged, Stones-esque guitar jangle. At times the BJM feel like a sexed-up Spacemen 3, expressing more of those primal, seedy desires usually kept behind closed doors. Ex-Spaceman Will Carruthers even pops up on stage with them now and then, amongst all the guitars, sitars, tambourines, and testosterone.

The Spacemen 3 influence lives on elsewhere; not only in the physical manifestations of Spectrum, Spiritualized, E.A.R., and the Brian Jonestown Massacre, etc., but also in a whole host of bands harking back to the head-spinning days of '80s hallucinogens, hypnagogia and repetitititititititititition. When Rocket Girl released *A Tribute to Spacemen 3* in 1998, its contributors – from Mogwai to Bardo Pond to Low – were more or less unknowns. Now, these bands command a heady sort of respect with their own brands of quiet/loud sonic splendour. Just as the obscure '60s references in the Spacemen's music were given new life by the Rugby-ites, so too the Spacemen have found themselves resuscitated by the lungs – and guitars – of their fans.

In fact, it was through the 1998 *Tribute to Spacemen 3* that I first became acquainted with the band. Embarrassingly, the band itself was already two years old by the time I'd popped out of the womb. I often wish I was around to see them play live, to be one of those disciples sitting cross-legged before the lightshows and the dry ice, rather than being sick on myself in a buggy. Unlike some of their noisy '80s counterparts, like My Bloody Valentine or the Jesus and Mary Chain, it seems doubtful Spacemen 3 will ever make a comeback. Too much bad blood, I think; and too many good side-projects.

While the sum of the Spacemen's parts can still be found nesting in the music biz to this day (Stewart/Sterling 'Rosco' Roswell DJs regularly in and around Camden, Pete 'Bassman' Bain has his own recording studio in Rugby), there is nothing quite like the trippy treats of the original band. But at least we have the records forever. And at least we can still get our hands on acid now and then, and put headphones on, and commit 'Suicide' to our memories forever; not to mention all their other lovely songs.

With thanks to Vinita Joshi and Pete Kember

SATURDAY MORNING

WASP

HEAD
OF
NEIGHBOUR

TABLE

MUG
OF
TEA

Richard Milward

The *England's Dreaming Tapes* Outtakes

These three interviews were conducted in 1988 and 1989, during the research for *England's Dreaming*. Comparatively little of them were used in the finished book. When last year I came to edit the interviews together into 'The England's Dreaming Tapes', they didn't fit either, so I'm pleased to present them here.

One of the things I wanted to do in *England's Dreaming* was reflect a fact that had not been recognised up until that point: that punk began as a movement of outcasts, that it offered a brief moment when the isolated, the marginal, saw that they could get together and, suddenly, realise their own strength.

Class was a very important element in this, as were various types of radical politics, but so was gender and sexuality. As Siouxsie Sioux told me with a decade's hindsight, punk was 'a club for misfits, almost. Anyone that didn't conform. There was male gays, female gays, bisexuals, non-sexuals, everything.'

There were many gay, bisexual and severely non-conformist young men and women involved in early punk, and they helped to create its look, its patchwork of deviant influences, and its curious, early distance. That all got flattened out as soon as punk did what it was always intended to do, broaden out into the wider culture.

The gender polemics implicit in *England's Dreaming* still remain relevant, after a decade and a half of the New Lad counter-revolution. Current histories of punk ramp up the boys groups, forgetting the strong women and the hopeless, introverted men who made some of the period's best music.

The first two interviews address this topic. Jane Suck and Jayne Casey redrew the possibilities of what women could do in popular culture. A fierce believer in her home town, Casey also gives a partial history of the Liverpool punk scene – as well as outlining the difficulties faced by severe stylists like herself in the late '70s.

There was this intense urge in 1976 and 1977 to be new, and regional autonomy was part of this. The final interview, with the Pop Group's Gareth Sager, tells a story often obscured by London, Liverpool and Manchester – that of the Bristol scene that helped to pave the way for Massive Attack and Tricky.

*Jane Jackman, aka *Jane Suck*, was my friend and colleague at Sounds and, I thought, the most naturally talented writer of all the Punk generation. After leaving the music press under the circumstances that she relates below, she got a BA at the University of East Anglia and resumed writing under the name Jane Solanas. Her current whereabouts are unknown.*

I was born in Middlesex and brought up in Chertsey, Surrey, until I was 14, when I was dragged off to Weston-super-Mare. I was 18 when I came back to London.

Was that move traumatic?
Very. I felt it was like going from New York to the deep south in the States. I went as a skinhead, and everyone there was still a hippy. I didn't talk to anyone at my new school for six months.

Were you very interested in pop music?
Yeah, when I was nine I discovered the Beach Boys, and I wouldn't buy any other records but the Beach Boys, until I discovered Bob Dylan. I became a Skin girl when I was 12. There was one greaser in my class, she was universally scorned. You didn't have much choice, it was such a local thing.

Unfortunately I had more money than all my friends, so I had the best clothes, the only time in my life when I was leading any kind of fashion scene, just because I had more money. I had a real Crombie, while they all had theirs off the market. I had about three pairs of Sta-Prest. It wasn't DMs at that point, you went to Ravels and got loafers with tassels, and Ben Shermans.

What were the records?
Filthy ska records, like 'Spunky Spunky Night' [Big Five], that we didn't understand a word of. 'Wet Dream', by Max Romeo.

Did you ever do any gang things?
Oh no, you just went to the youth club and went home. I was always a bit of an oddball, I was into amateur dramatics, I joined an acting group. So just before we moved, I was moving out of the rough element. All the girls were getting laid by Skin boys, the virginity level had gone down quite drastically by 14, and I wasn't interested in all that, so I got into the intellectual side.

That's when I became a record collector. I never had close friends, but I started going to Bristol, the Virgin Records shop had just opened. I got into West Coast music, the Doors, and then Iggy Pop, Velvet Underground. Jefferson Airplane were my favourite group at one point. I liked the harmonies. I was a complete American freak.

I wrote from when I was 12, compulsively, but I never wanted to be a journalist, I did the usual, writing poetry. Journalism happened by accident.

I left Weston under a cloud, when I was eighteen, March or April 1977. I had my first piece published in *Sounds* in February, and there was a terrible drama at home and they virtually pushed me on to the train, to get me out of Weston. I'd hit a girl at school, I was madly in love with her. I was doing a secretarial course in Weston, after I'd gone punk. I was in this room full of would-be secretaries with pictures of Patti Smith all over my typewriter.

How did you hear about punk?
Through reading the music press. I'd read them all, cover to cover, and I read a John Ingham piece in *Sounds*, and it was the first time something lifted me out of my chair and I wanted to be a part of it. I heard 'Horses' in a record booth in Weston and, to use the old cliché, it blew my mind. Patti Smith was very influential.

What was the first punk gig you went to?
Patti Smith at Hammersmith – my background was provincial, so I missed a lot of it. I only ever saw the Sex Pistols once, at the second Screen on the Green. The first one was seeing Generation X at the Roxy. I went up on the train, hung around for hours waiting for the Roxy to open. I got off with this bloke, one of John Rotten's friends, John Gray, 'cos I needed a place to stay. He was sweet, turned out to be just as naive as me.

I wrote the thing for *Sounds*, and when they printed it, I thought, hey, I'm in print, get up there! I wrote this piece about going to the Roxy. I was always pissed off that I didn't win the *NME* Young Hoodlum competition, or whatever it was, that Tony and Julie won. So I thought, I'll write to *Sounds*, they could probably do with someone. I would read *Sounds* and think, this is crap, I could do better than this.

Then Alan Lewis published my piece and wanted something from me every week, so that made moving to London feasible. I went and lived with my grandmother in Ruislip when I first got here, and commuted every day until I found an awful flat in Finchley.

When did you start with *Sounds* properly?
The first piece went in in March 1977. I was writing regularly by about April. I was only with them for fourteen months, not very long at all. I would go to seven gigs in seven nights.

What music did you particularly like?
Oh, hardly anything. I really didn't like punk music very much. I loved the Sex Pistols, liked the Damned, hated the Clash, and liked the odd American thing.

What did you think of the Pistols when you saw them at Screen on the Green?
I enjoyed it, but we'd all taken speed and got there really early and sat there for hours and hours, and there was no bar, hours and hours coming down off speed, so by the time the Pistols came on we were all a bit frazzled. It was Sid's first gig, and it was quite exciting, but I wasn't in quite the right state of mind for it. No one likes to wait for anything, do they?

Who did you go with?
Gaye and Tim from the Adverts. I interviewed them very early on, and they became friends. People are slowly coming to recognise the worth of the Adverts, but they were really shat upon, there was so much snobbishness, I got a lot of flak for liking the Adverts and writing about them. It was to do with them coming from Devon. It was difficult if you hadn't been going down the Kings Road since the year dot.

What was the situation like at *Sounds* at that time?
It was a joke. Everyone was so ageist then, you didn't dare confess you were over 22. I

hadn't really been around 'adults' before, and they seemed very straight. The only one who was warm and open was Vivien Goldman, and Dave Fudger. They went out on a limb. In *Sounds*' defence, though, I must say they put up with a lot of very bad behaviour from me. I was taking a lot of speed . . .

Sulphate or blues?
Sulphate. Within a couple of months I started injecting it, so I wasn't interested in anything other than what could be put in a syringe. I was a needles freak.

Were many people doing that?
Not as many as you'd think. It was the stupid ones, the Iggy Pop fans, basically. I'd show my scars and scabs to anyone. I wanted people to know I had a habit. It's trite, but it was a sexual thing as well. I was a virgin throughout punk, and once I started injecting speed I didn't have to worry about my sexuality, it wasn't an issue. I became asexual. I think many people were, it was an incredibly unsexual movement.

Do you think there was much puritanism against gays at that time?
No. But that surprised me, because what was coming across with punk to me was something bisexual, so when I became part of it I was surprised that I never met many gays or bisexuals. Everyone had done the camp David Bowie thing, and I thought they would have experimented.

Did you have any plans about what you wanted to do?
I wanted to be in a band, I didn't want to write for *Sounds*, that was a stop-gap. I put up notices in Rough Trade and tried to form a band, but drugs took over everything. I

wanted to be Iggy Pop. I interviewed him, and he was everything one could ask for, really. He did a complete number on me. He becomes whatever you want him to be when you walk into the room. He'd asked Julie Burchill about me, and Julie said, oh she's a lesbian with drug problems.

I was put in this room with him; he was stark naked and I thought, 'Oh my god, Iggy Pop is going to rape me,' and he sat down and leaned over to me, and said, 'Hi, I hear you're a lesbian with drug problems,' then he put his clothes on. The interview was conducted with me on his lap, and ended up with me asking for a kiss from Iggy. We had a great time, got really drunk.

When did you change your name to Jane Suck?
Before I started writing. I wanted a punk name for a group, and it was a woman at secretarial college who came up with Jane Suck. It was Jane Suck and the Vacuum Cleaners . . . !

What sort of reactions did you get to that name?
Oh, wonderful. Miss Suck. The worst was when my mother rang the office and Vivien Goldman didn't know whether to answer, yes, Mrs Suck.

When did you think punk had run its course?
By the summer of 1977 I thought it was all over, 'cos you got all the idiots that were buying rather than making the clothes, more or less the time bondage trousers came out, I thought that was the death knell. More or less the time that Sid joined and Johnny dyed his hair black. The stench of something

rotting. It was burned out in about six months, because the whole world wanted it, and it couldn't exist like that.

The other thing that killed it off was the Americans coming in with their heroin. That was the significant point, when the Heartbreakers came along with their very jaundiced, sophisticated New York attitude, and smack. I didn't know anyone that was using the stuff before they came along. It didn't get into my circle, but we know the ones who did.

The Americans were treated like royalty when they came over, 'cos we'd all been listening to our New York Dolls albums. But they were scum. I was in the Roxy dressing room when they were parading up and down. I got on with Leee Black Childers, I would go to parties at the various squats.

What do you remember about *Sounds'* 'New Musick' issue?
I remember writing my little bit for it, and arguing with *Sounds* because I wanted them to do an all-black cover, so that people would get covered in newsprint when they bought it, and they compromised and put Siouxsie on the cover . . .

What made you think that electronics were the music of the future?
Kraftwerk were a brilliant band, and because I'd never really liked punk music, this was something new, that was satisfying me. Everything else I liked had been and gone, like Iggy or the Velvets. I didn't really want punk in my record collection, whereas Kraftwerk . . . I was a bit slow discovering them. I liked *Magic Fly*.

I was too late to follow the Pistols around, they weren't playing. There were the Banshees. With Siouxsie it was lust at first sight, and she had that wonderful self-possession, she had a bit of class, and I also liked the music, which was very black, but witty. It was different to what other people were doing.

When do you think the Banshees were at their best?
When they started, up until they did their first album. When Kenny and John left, the chemistry had gone.

You have to remember that this is where my memory becomes really quite blurred. I was in a pitiful state, I was just about for the chop at that point. It all came to a head with *Sounds* in the spring of 1978 – I upset EMI on two occasions which followed in the same fortnight.

I upset Suzi Quatro and then upset the press officer of Capitol, when I was taken to Paris for the launch of *The Man-Machine* by Kraftwerk. I behaved atrociously. I'd been up all night, on a massive speed comedown, didn't want to go to Paris, but Vivien gave me no choice in the matter.

I was very very rude, reduced the press officer, Deborah Bennett, to tears on the coach, left the launch party very early and demanded to be flown back earlier than everybody else. I did apologise for my behaviour before I left and everything was fine until I wrote about her and named her in print, and she went running upstairs to one of the directors of EMI, sobbing, who happened to be a friend of Jack Hutton, the managing director of Spotlight, and that was it.

I couldn't really argue my way out of the Suzi Quatro incident: I turned up with a bottle of vodka, out of my mind, and proceeded to insult her. She didn't mind, she was from Detroit, she'd probably seen it a lot, but her road manager complained. They couldn't sack me, 'cos I was freelance. I was already banned from the building, because I had gone berserk, smashed windows and ripped a phone out.

I was drunk and unhappy, a drug-addled little girl.

Do you think *Sounds* could have helped you?
If I'd been a man, because Nick Kent had done all this and survived it, and was considered a living legend for it, *NME* played upon it. But because I was a woman behaving badly, I had to be got rid of. I was beyond help, I think. [Assistant Editor] Dave Fudger had tried to help, Vivien had tried to help, to the extent that she had me staying in her flat, but anyone taking that amount of speed anyone is going to be a depressive, and a psychotic, a risk.

Don't you think that the way the music press operates is very exploitative?
Yes, and if you're a woman you mean nothing in the music press. You are the lowest of the low, and no one will support you. And if you're a lesbian, and I think I was the only out lesbian in the music press, then you are really out on a limb. The managing director, Jack Hutton, even called me up, sat me down and said look, I knew Brian Jones. Drugs, that's it, you're on the slippery slope. We are dispensing with your services.

Then I was effectively blacklisted, and I still hear rumours about what I'm supposed to have done. I threw an ashtray through *Sounds'* office window, which has been variously reported as a typewriter and a person. Then there were all these Jane Suck stories, my name was trouble. So I gave up, I didn't write, I didn't even listen to music. I wouldn't even turn the radio on.

Was there something self-destructive about punk at that time?
I can't be objective about it. I think I would have been destructive whether I'd found punk or not. I threw out all my punk clothes, I deliberately wore the most disgusting clothes that I could, I grew my hair and I looked like shit. I practically had flares at one stage.

What did you think when the Pistols split?
About time. I thought Sid was a very bad thing. The Pistols became a joke. They were a mess.

Were you aware of Mrs Thatcher getting in?
No, I was ignorant of anything that didn't affect me. I would trade having gone through the punk experience for having discovered the gay community in London instead. That made a real difference to the way my life is. Those years were wasted, in a way. I didn't go into a gay club until 1985. I hadn't seen other lesbians until then. I had affairs with either bisexuals or heterosexuals. I'd missed Louise's. I arrived too late and stayed too long.

2

Jayne Casey, *style queen and frontperson of Big In Japan. With her outrageous outfits and confrontational courage, Casey was one of the handful of people who created the Liverpool punk scene, but, as she tells me, this was how she had been for years. Casey has remained at the heart of the creative industries in Liverpool: she has worked for Cream, the Moores Foundation, and most recently has been Artistic Director for the city's year as European Capital of Culture.*

I was born in Moreton, and I was in children's homes, so I travelled all over, and I ran away to New Brighton when I was 15. It was the nearest place with lights. It was quite a dramatic childhood. I had a bedsit that was £3.99 a week. I used to babysit for prostitutes who worked on the boats. I used to listen to music, and love it, and whenever I was taken to a new place to live, I'd look for a record player. If there was a record player, I could handle it. I liked Motown, and soul, '60s music.

Then the headmistress of the school I'd gone to found me, and asked me to come back to school and get some O levels, 'cos she thought I was quite clever although I was very naughty. So I went back and lived with some foster parents, then left again and got a job as a receptionist in a hairdressers in Liverpool. That would have been about 1972, '73. It was really boring, so I used to get my hair done all the time.

I started as a bleach blonde Marilyn look-alike, and it got shorter and shorter. I was totally into clothes. Then one day I got my hair shaved off. A receptionist in a hairdressers with a bald head used to cause hell. I started attracting weirdos to the shop, and every weirdo in town, of whatever age, came to the shop to get their hair done. Then we started getting people like Pete Burns coming to work for us, and Lynne, who was later his wife.

Before Punk was there any place in Liverpool for weirdos to go?
No, you went to gay clubs like the Bear's Paw, and the Masquerade later on. A lot of the boys were very young, and at that time were just discovering their sexuality, you weren't gay, but you were obviously different from other people. None of the straight clubs would let us in. The music was disco, and David Bowie, of course, 'Walk on the Wild Side' and all that '70s stuff. Bowie was quite influential.

It gave people a licence to look weird. Liverpool was going through a very straight time, you couldn't believe this was the city all these things had happened in during the '60s, there wasn't a trace of it. People were very aggressive to you if you looked different. People had moved out to the suburbs.

Around that time I opened a second-hand clothes shop in a building in Matthew Street called Aunt Twacky's [old Scouse malapropism for antique]. It was started by this guy called Peter O'Halligan, who took over this warehouse and declared it the Liverpool School of Language, Music, Dream and Pun. He was into Jung and Dada, he put the plaque on the building, about Liverpool being the Pool of Life.

Different people came into the scene at that point: Ken Campbell put on *Illuminatus* at Aunt Twacky's. I was selling second-hand American stuff, mainly, '50s stuff. I used to go around the rag yards. Roxy Music were still going and all the girls from Kirkby used to come in and buy '50s ball gowns. Swimsuits and things.

While we were at the hairdressers we discovered 'SEX' and wearing 'SEX' clothes. We used to go down to get them. Earlier than that we had gone to Biba, and then we discovered 'SEX' [this was a boutique run by Vivienne Westwood and Malcolm MacLaren on the King's Road]. I think we'd seen an article in a magazine, *Honey* or something like that. There were plastic trousers, and T-shirts with nipple zips. Then we started buying from sex shops in the north: rubber stockings, things like that.

When did the music start happening?
During the Roxy Music era we'd also started to go and see Deaf School, a local band, and they used to rehearse at Aunt Twacky's so I became friends with Clive Langer, and Bette [Bright]. Eric's was opening, and this giant guy came into my stall and said, here's some free tickets for this club I'm opening next week. Tell your friends.

On the night it opened I went down with Clive and Kevin Ward who used to do Deaf School's artwork. It was either the Runaways or the Stranglers. It started off as a punk club. Punk had broken. People used to think we were all different things. We had perverts following us round, thinking we were into heavy sex.

Then punk happened and taxi drivers started calling us punk, and we hated it,

hated it so much! We'd looked this way for so long, and we hated being called punk. Now, looking back, you can say, yeah, we were punks, but at the time we hated it. The process of definition. Suddenly people had a handle for you.

Tell me about seeing the Sex Pistols.
Eric's was like a door opening. It took off instantly. It was great when the Sex Pistols played. It's just a blur, really. It wasn't so much that they were the greatest thing you'd ever seen, as much as everything that surrounded it. It was the feeling that something was happening, and that was the most exciting thing you'd ever experienced. The bands were just a part of that. People were coming together. We went and talked to them afterwards.

We met them again, a year or eighteen months later, when Big In Japan were playing in Manchester, and they were doing a promo somewhere, and they were horrible and obnoxious. They were vile.

Did people start forming bands quite quickly?
Yeah. Big In Japan was the first band to form out of that scene. It was Clive and Bill Drummond and Kevin who used to do the artwork, wrote some tunes and decided to get a band together, and they supported Deaf School somewhere, one gig, as Big In Japan. Then they came to me and they kept asking me to be the singer, and I wasn't into the idea at all. Then Clive was going to America and he left all this equipment and said, I really want this band to get it together by the time I come back. So I started singing.

We rehearsed in Eric's. At that point, Aunt Twacky's closed. The guy who ran it had a

FOYLES FOR MUSIC

BOOKS, SHEET MUSIC, CDS, DVDS

Foyles Bookshop
113-119 Charing Cross Road
London WC2H 0EB

Also at:
Royal Festival Hall
St Pancras International
Westfield London

www.foyles.co.uk

breakdown and locked us all out, threw flour bombs at us from the top windows. Somebody ran to get his brother, who put a ladder up to the window, and Peter leaned out and pushed the ladder. He was dressed in a gold ballroom dress and high-heeled shoes, and a beard and everything. His brother broke loads of bones, lying there in Matthew Street.

By that time we'd discovered loads of shops in Liverpool where they still had stuff from the '60s, so me and Paul Rutherford used to buy these up and go sell them, at Beaufort Market on the King's Road.

We'd all come from these repressive backgrounds and we'd all discovered the Velvets, and Andy Warhol, and William Burroughs, and *Leaving the 20th Century*. It was an instant bonding, and it was very deep, because we'd all arrived at the same place, individually. It's amazing when that happens.

The best interview Big In Japan ever did was with Paul Morley. We were all in Eric's, and by this time Holly Johnson had joined, and this was out first interview with the *NME* and we were thrilled. He walked into Eric's, and we were expecting some trendy, and he had red trousers on, and a sort of feather cut, and one of those quilted Chinese jackets with big red roses all over it. We were flabbergasted.

We used to go to Manchester quite a lot. The Fall had happened, and we were massively into the Fall. We used to play with them sometimes. I lived in Manchester for a couple of years, in Aunt Twacky's days, and got the train every day. I used to get on the train and get my electric razor out and shave my head, and then get out the vanity case and do my make up and paint my head with everybody watching.

One time I had this little ground floor flat just off Croxteth Road, and I was so paranoid with all these perverts following me around that I used to sit in the bathroom all the time, cos it was the only room without a window, and I ran the kettle in there and I'd sit in there reading, if anyone came round I'd take them to the bathroom.

One day I was sitting there reading in the bathroom, and I noticed that the keyhole of the bathroom was in line with the keyhole to the front door, and I got up and stuffed clothes in the keyhole! I was stared at so much, it was getting too much.

When Biba's closed they sold off all the make-up and stuff on market stalls, and Pete Burns called me up one day and said, they're selling Biba's make up at Birkenhead Market. Fantastic! It was a Saturday, and on Saturdays we'd get dressed up extra special, and so we got the train over there.

We were walking around the market looking for this stall, and I noticed that the crowd appeared to be just around us and nowhere else, there were all these people following us, it was really heavy, so we walked out to the entrance real casual, and just legged it for the bus stop.

There was a queue and they wouldn't let us jump the queue and all these people chased after us, and they were battering us, really badly, and the bus driver saw what was happening, and got off the bus, dragged us inside, shut the door and detoured the bus to the train station. Before the bus pulled away there were all these people shaking the bus. They really wanted to get at us.

It was horrendous. We got to the station and hid until the next train came. The next day in the papers there was this little thing about a riot in Birkenhead, and people trying to turn a bus over.

Why such a strong reaction?
It was to do with sex. It was always to do with sex, and we never really thought about it.

What do you think are the differences between Manchester and Liverpool?
You'd walk down the street in Manchester, and the crowds would part for you, as if you were diseased or something, but they wouldn't comment; and you'd get on the train to Liverpool and as soon as you got off, you'd get some scallies having a go, and you experienced the difference every day.

Liverpool is a far more violent city than Manchester is. I preferred Manchester music, and that's why me and Holly were always different from what was going on around, 'cos we liked Manchester music, and my idea of the North that I love is Manchester.

Punk started spreading out, you had the weekend punks coming in. The Spitfire Boys started and they were a sort of acceptable Eric's band. There was the Naughty Lumps, Iggy Pop's Jacket. Then there was the Accelerators, who weren't acceptable to the Eric's crowd. Then the Swinging Apple opened, and that crowd hated Eric's. It was a punk club that was quite National Front. The NF and punk got quite big in Liverpool at one point.

Roger Eagle wouldn't allow any of that element into Eric's. He was a great expert on black music, they played lots of reggae in Eric's, and there was a big split between the right-wing kids who wore the swastikas and stuff, and the Eric's kids. It was very heavy. Those kids were just kids who were carrying on the politics of their parents.

I think I only set foot inside the Swinging Apple once. We had this friend called Leila, who was a transsexual, and she got stabbed in the Swinging Apple so badly she nearly died. But in Eric's we listened to a lot of dub, there was a big rasta connection. The fascist thing took a long time to die down. Some of them got jail sentences for racial attacks, and that cooled the scene down.

Did you see any of the other punk groups when they came up to Liverpool?
We saw them all. I became good friends with Billy Idol, and with Dave Vanian from The Damned. Everybody who was there was really into seeing different bands...the Adverts, the Human League. The one I particularly liked was the Fall, 'cos they introduced repetition.

Punk became very boyish. The Clash were massive, and I felt isolated 'cos there weren't many girls in Eric's, not in our scene. The way all the boys loved the Clash made me not like the Clash, even though I like the tunes. We became pissed off with it quite quickly. But then I remember Roger getting 'Warm Leatherette' (the first single by the Normal), and things like that were having more influence by that time. Suicide, electronic things, Sylvester and the gay clubs, distracted us for ten minutes. Shortly after that we got back to the gay clubs, while people were still heavily into punk.

Big In Japan split up fairly quickly. Ian Broudie joined, and it was getting a bit professional, learning to play their instruments and things. We were really into Patti Smith and everything, and we felt that the boys had taken over, so we got bored.

You never had any record company interest?
No, well, when we split up, Virgin called up and said, oh we wanted to sign you. Bill would have signed a record deal, but we wanted to do other things, and we were

irritating to the others, 'cos we weren't serious enough. Pete Burns was on the sidelines then, and he used to sometimes sing 'Paint it Black', with Big In Japan, while Holly and I stood at the side of the stage, glaring at him!

The Teardrops did their first gig at Eric's with the Bunnymen supporting. I never really liked the Teardrops, but the Bunnymen just did a song called 'Monkeys' for fifteen minutes and it was fab. We knew that they were going to be special. They had a coolness that had been lacking in Liverpool bands. They were the first real band that had happened, all the others had been silly, and art school, very fashionable and crazy.

Bill had learned quite a lot from his Big In Japan experience, and he took the Bunnymen. Bill had been a set designer for Ken Campbell's theatre company when they moved into Aunt Twacky's, and Ian Broudie was playing guitar, and Budgie was at the art college and lent his drum kit. Budgie was a sweet, sensitive person really, and that wasn't the thing to be around people like us, 'cos we were horrible and vicious.

Did record labels and clothes shops start appearing?

Roger released some records, the Big In Japan single and some others. Bill started Zoo. Pete Burns had a punk clothes shop inside Probe, and I had a clothes shop and a cafe called Blood and Lipstick, just off Matthew Street. I had a shop in the back of 69a, Leila's shop, for a while. Everyone used to hang around there.

Was there a time when you thought punk, or whatever it had been, was over?

Definitely. By the time Eric's closed, it was full of different people. There was the march to save Eric's and we didn't go on it, 'cos we felt it was time for it to close.

Why did it close?

There was some confusion about that. It got raided for drugs. They'd been approached for protection money and had refused to pay, and then the police raided because they'd heard that they paid the bands in drugs, so they ripped the place apart looking for drugs. But it was running into financial trouble, so we knew it was going to close. Most people think it was police trouble that closed it, but it wasn't, really.

The bands were getting more expensive, so Roger Eagle could only get bands very early on in their careers, 'cos of the size of the venue. The second time round they'd go to the Empire. Roger tried to buy the Royal Court, but it didn't come off. It's a frustrating business, having a small venue, 'cos you get bands just before they break. Also that end of the market had died off. Disco was coming back.

Did the police see punk as a problem?

They definitely wanted to get rid of Eric's. I think they knew that drugs were coming in. There weren't any drugs in Eric's at first, but by the end there would have been. Punk had spread to the boy's gangs, it had gone mainstream.

3

Gareth Sager *Teenage guitarist for the Pop Group, bright new hopes when they arrived in London during 1978, with their passionate fusion of funk, jazz, punk and radical politics. Later formed Rip Rig and Panic with Neneh Cherry. In 2003 he released an excellent album,* The Last Second of Normal Time *and has since collaborated with Jock Scot on the 2006 album,* Caledonian Blues. *Had a difficult reputation, but I've always found him engaging and witty.*

We moved down from Edinburgh to Bristol at age 10. My father works in theatre and is also a dentist. Went to a school with Bruce Smith, Mark Springer. I bought *Funhouse* and my first Dolls album at age 12. I was also into James Brown and the club scene of the time.

Bristol is a very pleasant place, aesthetically, to grow up, but also one of the nastiest, most aggressive places, 'cos there was nothing to do, and everyone seemed to have a bit of money, so they were all out in the pubs when they were 15 years old. Lots of drugs, speed early on. Lots of hippies.

There was this hybrid club called the Dug Out. That was where we all went. It was basically a black club, a meat market but with the weirdest mix of people. Hippies, dreads and straight blacks, townies. Then, the kids that wore the right gear were called 'kitten wicked', and they were the people who became all the second generation punks, in all the fights and everything. People might call them soul boys, but that was a really old-fashioned word.

I'm not a good person to talk about the West Country. I only lived there for a brief time, it was just during an incredible creative flow that we all got going, that step away from London that allowed us to get into our own ideas. There might have been a better crossover of ages, you had old people and young people in the same pub.

When did punk first come down to Bristol?
We all saw early Pistols shows, 100 Club. You should get that big picture from the *Observer* of Mark and Simon Underwood at the Caerphilly show. Mark's got big black shades on.

We all dug Patti Smith, so it's very difficult to know the line between . . . me, Jeremy Valentine and Mark went to the Ramones at the Roundhouse, and we couldn't believe there were no other punks there, apart from Sid and Viv Albertine, who we basically tried to get into a fight with, because that's what we thought we were meant to do. They were petrified, 'cos there was five of us. We were really horrible.

How did you form the group?
Me, Mark and Bruce just wanted to be part of what the scene was. We were coming up for the first night of the Roxy, and we thought, fuck, we can do this. I was always disappointed when I heard what the bands sounded like, I expected them to be much more wild. I liked Subway Sect. I loved the Pistols' attitude, but I was disappointed at how they sounded. I wanted 'Little Johnny Jewel', with those lyrics . . . those were the two that I liked, the rest were piffly. The first Buzzcocks single was good.

What did you like about 'Little Johnny Jewel'?

It sounded completely new. I'd listened to John Lee Hooker and John Coltrane and this came in from a completely different angle. It had something to do with Iggy Pop, but it felt free. In a way it was more like when you first read Rimbaud.

When did you form?

January 1977, I think. We didn't do anything until about May. There was a review of our first ever gig, a very good one, which shows the period of time it was.

There was no punk scene in Bristol per se, was there?

Not really. The Cortinas was the band that went and played the Roxy. Everybody thought they were a bit of a joke, but I think they had an influence on the Undertones, and all that. Lots of people started wearing the gear, and if the Clash came to town they'd all turn out. There was a Subway Sect gig in Swindon, and the place they were going to play burned down, so they had to get a place really quickly, and that's when the kitten wicked kids started wearing safety pins and everything.

Did you call yourselves the Pop Group from the start?

Yeah. I think we picked the name the day we started the group. It was ironic. We knew that whatever we did, we wouldn't be what a pop group is meant to be. It caused a lot of problems when the police stopped us.

What did you start playing?

We had one called 'Let Me Talk To The Driver', which was like our version of Artaud!

Had you read all this stuff?

Mark had an elder brother, Paul, who was fantastic, he was a big Burroughs fan, only about three years older than us. He had his nose down to the ground. He might have been at art school in London when it was all happening. Burroughs was the man. You heard Iggy Pop and David Bowie, so you read William Burroughs, and then you found out that Burroughs had read Artaud and Céline. I didn't know what the fuck was going on, but I loved it. It was different. I didn't read what you were meant to read, I went straight to Wilhelm Reich and that stuff.

How did you get that look, the baggy trousers and double-breasted jackets?

Bristol was a very style-conscious place. I just wanted anything that would annoy the people in London who thought they were super-hip. Ended up wearing dresses. It was anti things like Siouxsie and the Banshees, who looked crap to us. We were influenced by cinematic things. We were against the scene already, so we just wanted to look good.

When did you start picking up speed as the Pop Group?

Winter of 1977–8. I remember playing the Marquee the night of Elvis's death, and lots of people couldn't work out what the fuck was going on, 'cos we were all wearing arm-bands, and we did a version of Heartbreak Hotel.

Had you started with a bit of funk in there?

That was our heritage, basically. Every club we had ever been to had played black music. We liked *Funhouse*, but we liked James

Brown and George Clinton and all those things. So that was the music we wanted to play. A lot of bands then sounded to me like Hawkwind, and I hated that stuff. We really did hate hippies.

What were the first songs you wrote?

I think 'Trap' was very early. There was 'Hypnotised by the Radio', real catchy things, but then we got into the other stuff pretty quick. We knew where we wanted to go straight away. Mark would do the lyrics. There were two guitars, both like Subway Sect. Lead guitar was an alien concept to me, still is. Someone takes a break, someone doesn't.

You never did serious interviews with anyone, did you?

Well we read Dylan's interviews, and we were very much that way. You had serious journalists coming along asking us about the unemployment problem, that was ridiculous to us. It's much better to do something that stimulates your imagination than to give some boring, dogmatic doggerel.

It was much more exciting to read a good quote by Patti Smith that's got nothing to do with the employment figures. You wouldn't be reading the pop press if you'd rather be reading the *Financial Times*. You have to put the right thing in the right place.

Were you courted by record companies?

Not really. I think Virgin turned up at a gig where John Waddington, the other guitarist, had a complete freakout and smashed up all his equipment – not in a Pete Townshend way, he just freaked out. You remember we just had that blue and white light, and the strobes? He probably had an epileptic fit, and

we didn't realise. We never knew or cared.

I remember doing gigs at the Roundhouse when there was seventy fucking Hell's Angels from Amsterdam backstage, and people going, you did a song lasting ten minutes, that's not the punk ethic, and we didn't give a shit about the punk ethic. We were all teenage Rimbauds, dedicated to creating hell on stage.

The big one was the Electric Ballroom, with us, Linton Kwesi Johnson, Nico, Cabaret Voltaire. Johnny Thunders was playing across town, the old school, and if you were really hip, you came to us, and if you wanted rock'n'roll punk roots, you went to Thunders.

People made us suffer for that, 'cos everybody had a lot more power than us. I was playing guitar with a hammer, then. A Vox Teardrop. I remember the Heartbreakers playing the Roxy and suddenly everyone was taking heavier drugs than speed. It was old school, I had no interest in that.

When did you get signed to Radar?

It must have been mid-1978. It might have been before. 'Beyond Good and Evil' must have been recorded in September. I have no recollection of signing a record deal whatsoever.

When did you pick up Dick O'Dell as your manager?

1977. He'd been a tour manager for Alex Harvey and things like that. He did lighting for David Bowie, got into the business very young.

Did you go to the States?

Yeah, we played New York and Philadelphia, did some outrageous things, had to do another concert to get our flight back. They wanted the Clash, so they hated it. A few people loved it.

Did you like the 'No New York' record?
I loved DNA, I was there when it was happening with the Slits. I saw some great things, but it was very drug-induced.

Did Radar drop you?
No, we wanted to leave, we went through massive dilemmas, Mark especially, he thought it was contrary to everything we were about, that we were on Warner Brothers. It was easy to get off, 'cos we sold about five thousand records and they didn't want to spend any more money on us. 'Good and Evil' was a critical hit, but the sales were minute.

Then we did 'We Are All Prostitutes', which spawned the famous T-shirt that we never made a penny out of. That was a classic single. Then there was the album, which should have been great 'cos we were getting more obviously funky, but the lyrical content was getting clearer to the punters, which I didn't enjoy half as much.

What happened with Mark?
I shouldn't really talk about it, but I think he got hyper-paranoid. He'd got on to the front of every pop paper by the time he was eighteen, and his conscience got very tapped, and we met a few people, one particularly who got him into lots of conspiracy theory stuff. I suppose I was tougher about it all, I took what I enjoyed, and Mark took it all to heart, wanted to go and fight in Cambodia, sort out Pol Pot . . .

Is that why the group split up in the end?
Yeah, well, we didn't really split up, it was very amicable. Mark wanted to get into that, and I wasn't into it.

How did you feel about the state of the country by that time?
The first riot was in Bristol, in St Pauls. We knew it was going to happen, we sang about it on 'How Much Longer?' It wasn't hard to predict, if you were still on the street and not touring America.

SELF - CONFIDENT

SAM DAVIES
Not Bad Meaning Bad . . . but Bad Meaning Good
Hip Hop and Susan Sontag's 'Notes on Camp'

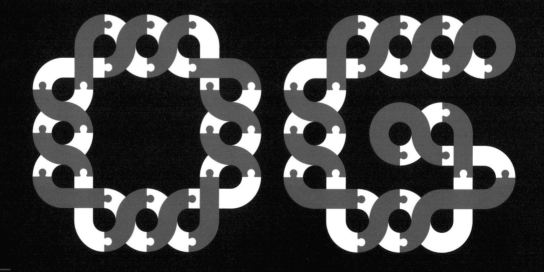

That, I would venture, is how most people would define the idea of Camp taste if pressed. They might not phrase it quite that way – I'm quoting from 'Peter Piper', by Run DMC. 'So bad it's good,' is the more usual version. Someone like Graham Norton would probably also figure as shorthand for Camp: gay, waspish, effeminate, never serious. So goes the popular conception. It's a misconception; it sells Camp short.

Camp is more complex, more serious, and more important than simply a craving for the trashy and end-of-pier innuendo. And one of the ways to complicate it is to insist that it describes an enormous swathe of modern music: not just factory pop, glam rock, snowball disco, or the kind of art-school punk that lies in the gutter, gazing at the stars. But all of them, and hip hop too. I think hip hop – rappers, rap music, the whole culture – is Camp. Camper than a row of pink velvet tents.

It was a brief sketch of an idea that first made me think about hip hop and its relationship (or otherwise) with Camp. Writing about disco on *The Wire* magazine's blog in 2008, Derek Walmsley asked, 'What's become of Camp in urban music today?' He continued:

R'n'B and rap videos these days look airbrushed, as if hidden behind a plastic wall, a distancing effect exacerbated by the constant use of slow motion and fast cross-cutting. The big names of urban music are synthetic products of the studio system as much as (arguably more than) Hollywood stars. The overall impression is a fear of people finding out what they're like. This look-but-don't-touch sexual politics is, for me, deeply un-sexy, and it's music's loss.

But that sounded pretty Camp to me; like a reasonable working description of the average Kylie video. It also reminded me of something else I'd once read, and after some trawling online, eventually I found a post by Mark Fisher, of the esteemed blog k-punk, from a few years previous:

Dare it be admitted, but isn't hip hop the problem these days? . . . There's nothing unsettling about it any more. On the contrary: hip hop is quotidian, everyday . . . Isn't hip hop now a kind of anti-glam? It is an ultra-masculinist refusal of glam and its feminizing threat.

This seemed somehow right and wrong, and also a reason to go back to the main source and reread Susan Sontag's 'Notes on Camp', the aesthetic's urtext from 1964.

Approaching the essay with rap culture in mind, the results were bizarre. Time and again, Sontag seemed to be anatomising not only mid-century Camp, but pre- and post-millennium hip hop. In fact, when I first planned this piece, I considered simply taking Sontag's essay, excising all occurrences of the word 'camp', and replacing it with 'hip hop', 'rap' or 'bling' as appropriate. To do so would have had a certain formal affinity with both subjects. 'Camp sees everything in quotation marks', according to Sontag, and hip hop is pretty keen on them too: whether musical (the sampler) or lyrical (the tradition of crafting choruses and refrains from scratched snippets of older raps). All the same I decided not to risk copyright infringement.

Sontag used the fragmentary form of notes to avoid having to join all the dots of her argument; I've taken this as licence to do the same.

Notes on ~~Boot~~ Camp ~~Clik~~

Sontag: 'Camp taste transcends the nausea of the replica.' I think it is safe to say that hip hop long ago transcended the nausea of the replica. It never suffered from this nausea. Hip hop doesn't just like, it loves, adores and fetishises the replica, from Run DMC in their Kangols and Adidas shelltoes, to the mid-'90s vogue for Tommy Hilfiger sportswear, to Busta Rhymes allegedly accepting payment for the product placement of 'Pass the Courvoisier' (from guess who?). By 2005 McDonald's were openly offering to sponsor rappers per radio play of any song mentioning their food. Not only that, the more entrepreneurial modern artists feel no nausea about replicating themselves, as commodities, brands, and soon no doubt, franchises, leveraging their fame to diversify into clothing, fragrance, sneakers and more.

Sontag: 'To perceive Camp in objects and persons is to understand Being-as-Playing-a-Role. It is the farthest extension, in sensibility, of the metaphor of life as theater.' The relevance of this to hip hop and its narratives may not be immediately obvious given the music's obsession with 'realness'. Reality – meaning street reality – is one of hip hop's governing tropes. As the pattern for the ideal big-name rapper developed and hardened in the '90s, it became essential to have had a rough childhood, ideally in a known ghetto; and failing that, to be able to construct or imply one. Which is exactly what many of hip hop's biggest stars did. Sean Coombs, P. Diddy, attended the private Mount Saint Michel Academy, and dropped out of the solidly middle class university, Howard, to pursue his ambitions as a music mogul. Tupac Shakur switched high schools in Baltimore to attend the local stage school where he took ballet classes and acted in productions of Shakespeare. Christopher Wallace, the Notorious B.I.G., lied about where he grew up in Brooklyn to look tougher, and attended a private Catholic school.

Elsewhere in hip hop, the reality principle is less important, but life is no less a theatre, and being is no less of a role. Take Keith Thornton, more commonly known as Kool Keith, whose personas have included Dr Octagon, Black Elvis, Dr Dooom and Keith Korg. Or Russell Jones – initially known with the Wu-Tang Clan as Ol' Dirty Bastard

Sam Davies

or ODB, and later as Dirt McGirt, Dirt Dog, Osirus, Big Baby Jesus, Sweet Baby Jesus and more. The Wu-Tang Clan went through a period in which every solo album the individual group members produced had to have a corresponding film, which was sliced up to provide atmosphere and background, a kind of audio mise-en-scène. The GZA's *Liquid Swords* had Robert Houston's *Shogun Assassin*, Raekwon's *Only Built for Cuban Linx* had John Woo's *The Killer*. Ghostface's *Ironman* weaves in clips from *The Education of Sonny Carson*, *The Usual Suspects* and *Carlito's Way*. The metaphor here being updated from life-as-theatre to life-as-cinema.

Sontag: 'Clothes, furniture, all the elements of visual décor, for instance, make up a large part of Camp. For Camp art is often decorative art, emphasising texture, sensuous surface, and style at the expense of content.' Hip hop's obsession with clothes is inescapable: Clipse and their Cavalli furs, Ghostface and Raekwon on the cover of *Ironman*, surrounded by Clarks Wallabees of every hue, as though raiding the den of some shoemaking elves, the clothing ranges developed by P. Diddy, Jay-Z, and more. Alternatively, just take in a random sample of hit rap videos on YouTube and try to keep a mental tally of the designer goods, vehicles, yachts and jewellery. (Is hip hop the only genre of popular music to have made the career of a jeweller – as in Jakob the Jeweller?) And think of MTV's *Cribs* – for which it wasn't uncommon for those featured to rent houses that were then passed off as their own in order to make themselves appear more successful. In 2004, Ja Rule was sued for illegally using a home to film a *Cribs* episode which his corporate sponsors had merely rented for him during a Memorial Day weekend in Miami.

Sontag: 'The relation of Camp taste to the past is extremely sentimental.' Where to start? With an album like Nas's *God's Son* and its obsessive tributes to his mother? With Ghostface's 'All I Got Is You', a misery memoir of his childhood which succeeds in sampling the Jackson Five's 'Maybe Tomorrow' and making it even more schmaltzy? With the high-water mark of hip hop sentimentality, Puff Daddy's elegy for Notorious B.I.G., 'Missin' You'? With the obsessive glorification of the old school, of rap's early glory days? Even Missy Elliott, sonically speaking one of hip hop's arch-futurists, decided in 2002 to telescope back to the mood and feel of early-'80s block parties, and her albums since have largely stuck with this retro schtick.

Sontag: 'Camp is art that proposes itself seriously, but cannot be altogether taken seriously because it is "too much".' Shakespeare's *Titus Andronicus*, continues Sontag, could be claimed and performed as Camp. *Titus Andronicus* is Shakespeare's proto-Peckinpah, proto-Tarantino moment: it takes physical violence so far that it becomes practically an absurdist comic spectacle, with a character being fed family members cooked in a pie, and another clutching a bowl in the severed stumps of her arms to catch the blood from the murder of her rapists. Hip hop adores this kind of Grand Guignol. Gravediggaz spawned a subgenre of their own, horrorcore. Method Man in a skit from *Enter The Wu-Tang (36 Chambers)* brainstorms torture techniques to delirious background giggles: he'll 'sew ya asshole closed, and keep feeding you, and feeding you and feeding you . . .' Big L's taste in violence is pure cinema: in 'Casualties of a Dice Game' the protagonist, shot by police, dies in a park, watching clouds of his own discarded cash settle on the grass, where kids collect it. *Scarface*, surely hip hop's favourite film, features a man's arms being removed by chainsaw early on, and concludes with its anti-heroes mowed down, weltering in orgiastic gore. Violence comes in quantity in hip hop; sharing the sensibility of *Scarface*, it has never felt that less is more.

Sontag: 'Camp is the glorification of "character". What the Camp eye appreciates is the unity, the force of the person. In every move the aging Martha Graham makes she's being Martha Graham.' It's easy to think here of hip hop and its relationship to acting: not only the hip hop persona as a theatrical construct, but what happens when rappers cross over into film roles. Time and again, they play themselves: Eminem in *Eight Mile*, 50 Cent in *Get Rich or Die Tryin'*. These are not examples of acting, but of a pre-existing persona around which not so much a film, but a 90-minute promotional video is constructed using the biopic form. You could point also to the films adored by hip hop – especially Hong Kong action flicks. Bruce Lee plays Bruce Lee, regardless of his character's name, in every single Bruce Lee film.

Sontag: 'Camp is esoteric – something of a private code, a badge of identity, even of small urban cliques.' Sontag's regret is like that of a snitch, a rat: 'To write about Camp is to betray it.' Her essay, she fears, could have a kind of quantum effect: to have exposed Camp to observation will compromise it, alter it.

Now, hip hop is no secret society. 'Esoteric' doesn't quite ring true as a tag for the music that dominated the American pop charts to such an extent that it had to be fenced off into the Hot 100. But again, there's a connection to be made. Hip hop slang after all originates as the private idioms of small urban cliques, is popularised by record sales, and then assimilated into wider society. New verbal codes are then needed: the old slang is no longer private. So while hip hop may not be a small or private concern anymore, at its heart is a kind of linguistic engine, turning over new codes, new slang. (A sidenote: even that word, 'clique', with its effete connotations of gossipy gangs, has entered hip hop usage – though it's pronounced with a short 'i' as in 'click' – like the hammer of a gun, not the long 'i' of 'eek'. As in Boot Camp Clik, the supergroup featuring Smif-N-Wessun, Black Moon's Buckshot and others.)

But hip hop does hate a snitch. New York rapper Cam'ron even insisted once to a CBS interviewer that he was so anti-snitch, he wouldn't even tell the police if his neighbour was a serial killer. Cam'ron has to come up in any discussion of Camp in relation to hip hop sooner or later – a rapper who wore his favourite pastel tone so much he ended up calling himself 'The Pink Panther', yet whose (irony-free) slogan is a reflex yelp of 'No homo!' whenever he does anything that could possibly be construed as indicating homosexuality. In an interview on New York's Hot 97 FM, after being questioned about the necessity of this verbal tic, Cam'ron was invited to 'rock the mike' and accepted – but only after a muttered 'No homo'. *Hamlet*, Act 3, Scene 2, line . . . ? Cam'ron's feelings towards 'snitches' do make you wonder what kind of confessional burden he carries round on his shoulders.

Sontag: 'Allied to the Camp taste for the androgynous is something that seems quite different but isn't: a relish for the exaggeration of sexual characteristics and personality mannerism . . . The corny flamboyant female-ness of Jayne Mansfield, . . . the exaggerated he-man-ness of Steve Reeves, Victor Mature.' Hip hop doesn't value the alpha male so much as the alpha-plus male. Pick out the back cover of Gang Starr's *Mass Appeal*, where Lil' Dap stares out with his chest out – or the video for 50 Cent's 'In Da Club'. In a secret underground facility, an ultra-pumped, ultra-sculpted 50 Cent is doing sit-ups, hanging by his legs from a chin-up bar, supervised by Dr Dre and Eminem, like some hip hop Universal Soldier, a super-rapper, which they have designed and are preparing to unleash on the world.

In the 'Notes', Sontag provides a capsule history of Camp as an aesthetic, tracing its roots to mid-eighteenth century England and the figure of Horace Walpole, perpetually renovating his villa Strawberry Hill in Twickenham. (Sacha Baron Cohen take note: one of hip hop's main sources, located a mere stone's throw from Staines.) Walpole, Sontag writes, is the godfather of the Camp inversion of traditional values in which one is 'frivolous about the serious, serious about the frivolous'. This injunction echoes down the centuries, honoured in the observance by Oscar Wilde, the Bright Young Things – and every rapper who ever obsessed over 20-inch rims, before dispatching a one-liner about the murder of a rival.

Some notes on bling from 'Notes on Camp': 'The hallmark of Camp is the spirit of extravagance. Camp is a woman walking around in a dress made of three million feathers . . . One should either be a work of art, or wear a work of art . . . The old-style dandy hated vulgarity. The new-style dandy, the lover of Camp, appreciates vulgarity . . . Camp is the attempt to do something extraordinary. But extraordinary in the sense, often, of being special, glamorous. . . . Not merely in the sense of effort.'

99 Problems

Camp doesn't map perfectly on to hip hop from the music's earliest roots to the present. It declares itself early: Big Daddy Kane's '80s album covers alone tick the boxes of alpha male idolatry, materialist excess, an epicene view of women. But it comes into play most powerfully by the mid-'90s, when the music practically becomes the pop mainstream (introducing its stars to an altogether different scale of wealth), and thereafter becomes practically the genre's hallmark.

I would identify the shift as taking place at some point in the years 1993 and 1994. These are the years in which hip hop undergoes massive labour pangs as it effectively gives birth to a new commercial order. 1992 had been a year of convulsive controversy: the open-armed, almost ecumenical ethos of De La Soul, A Tribe Called Quest and The Jungle Brothers was sidelined by the cultural firestorms of the Rodney King race riots in LA, Ice Cube's *Predator* (practically a concept album meditating on the riots), the vein-bulging intensity of Onyx, and Ice T's censor-baiting 'Cop Killer'. The negative energies, the dark charisma of hardcore or gangsta rap, decisively sidelined other currents in the music which prioritised the party, or more introspective, interpersonal directions. Ice T's 1993 album, *Home Invasion*, while

www.dominorecordco.com
www.dominorecordco.com/mart
digital.dominorecordco.com

*Domino was founded to release and represent artists
who had no choice but to reproduce the sounds in their head*

You can hear it in the ecstactic yells of Animal Collective

Or in the graceful ire of Robert Wyatt

It's loud and clear in the phase patterns of Four Tet

And in the snare of Franz Ferdinand

In the burr of James Yorkston's voice

And the white heat of Arctic Monkeys

It's in the high notes of Bonnie 'Prince' Billy

And the inner workings of Juana Molina

*All unique, alive and uncompromising
though they all have one thing in common,*

The sound of people doing whatever they want

overlong and mediocre, spelled out what was happening in those years through its cover, in which a white teenager is depicted in his bedroom, cross-legged with headphones on, while from murky background clouds Ice T plays puppet-master, beaming messages into his brain. But these fulminations – predatory, invasive, inked in distilled testosterone – were still in thrall to Public Enemy's cracked walls of noise.

When the dust settled and gangsta/hardcore stood alone, it was Dr Dre's *The Chronic* that had quietly established a new sonic paradigm. It modulated the sound and fury of hardcore or gangsta rap into a kind of lackadaisical aggression, a laid-back, almost limp-wristed (pimp-wristed?) thug aesthetic. Its sound was so luxuriant that *New Yorker* music critic Sasha Frere-Jones argues it made hip hop 'music for driving' with its heavy bass 'literally massaging the passengers' through their car seats. The ideal to strive for was no longer paramilitary: the stick-up kid, the urban guerilla in the mist or at the window with a gun like Malcolm X, disappeared, to be replaced by 'the playa'. The playa was no less dangerous, but they waved guns around less. Shoot you? They had people to do that for them.

There are other elements in Sontag's analysis of Camp which, while acutely relevant to hip hop, nonetheless connect less to recognisable features of the music, more to unstable areas, to faultlines at the culture's core. For instance, Sontag claims that it can be taken as read that 'the Camp sensibility is disengaged, depoliticised – or at least apolitical'. It's true that mainstream hip hop rarely engages explicitly with politics. Since Public Enemy's demise, political radicalism has been the preserve of one-hit-wonders like Dead Prez, or stalwart commercial sideshows like Common or Talib Kweli. At this stage of hip hop history, what Sontag would recognise as 'a daring and witty hedonism' seems determined to leave politics out of the equation.

But to try to do so is still to make an inescapably political gesture. Written out of the political framework, hip hop attempts to rewrite the terms of its discourse, to hold a conversation of its own in which establishment politics in turn has no place at all. Hip hop opts for bling consumerism, the pragmatic self-reliance of the hustler, out of frustration with its disenfranchisement. As Nas raps in 1993 on 'The World is Yours', to an answering chorus of disbelief:

> I'm out for presidents to represent me.
> [Say what?]
> I'm out for presidents to represent me.
> [*Say what?*]
> I'm out for dead presidents to
> represent me.

The idea that he could hold out any hope for a politician to make a difference is presented as ludicrous. It's only cold cash (dead presidents) that will empower him in any meaningful way. The irony of this political aspect to bling is that it only reinforces the structures that keep the American black underclass down: it follows the Darwinian logic of capitalist market economics, replicating its view of individuals as mere units of consumption.

Sontag: 'Camp taste is by its nature possible only in affluent societies, in societies or circles capable of experiencing the psychopathology of affluence.' This is a trickier assertion to apply to hip hop; given its roots in a low-income social group, you could argue that hip hop exhibits different symptoms altogether – those of the psycho-pathology of poverty. It remains to be seen what happens to materialist hedonism, this gourmandising escapism, on the downslope of an economic depression, with a box-fresh President who *is* out to represent Nas now in power.

Sontag: 'Camp is the triumph of the epicene style. (The convertibility of "man" and "woman", "person" and "thing"). But all style, that is, artifice, is ultimately epicene.'

This is also a statement with plenty of pitfalls as applied to hip hop and its culture. In one sense it chimes perfectly with the sexual politics, implicit and often XXX-plicit, in much of the music. The videos alone make it clear that most rappers believe in the 'convertibility' of 'woman' and 'thing' (or at least in the commercial value of treating them as such). But it's somewhat harder to argue for the interchangeability of man and woman in hip hop, even if Snoop Dogg did used to have a perma-curled hairstyle which he dubbed his 'Shirley Temple'.

This brings us to the sheer *straightness* of hip hop. Camp is now considered by common convention to be an essentially gay sensibility, hence the reflex instinct to object instantly if it's proposed that hip hop, awash with an unashamedly toxic homophobia, is Camp. But Sontag is absolutely clear throughout 'Notes on Camp' that it should not be regarded in any crude way as synonymous with homosexuality. 'Camp', she writes, 'is much more than homosexual taste . . . one feels if homosexuals hadn't more or less invented Camp, someone else would.' Gay metropolitan cliques are simply

Camp's standard bearers, its avant-garde, its reconnaissance units. Hip hop in this case could be seen as the heavy artillery bringing up the rear. (No nudge, no wink, etc.)

So, how else to conceive of hip hop and Camp. Isn't hip hop intrinsically un-Camp due to a sense of humour failure? Doesn't the unceasing frivolity of the dandy founder too often on po-faced masculinity? Isn't Camp without the jokes a contradiction in terms? Not necessarily. 'The pure examples of Camp are unintentional', writes Sontag; 'they are dead serious.'

Then perhaps, as much as hip hop can be viewed anew through the lens of Camp, Camp has been rewritten by hip hop – or rather, sampled? The quoters quoted; the biters bit. Maybe the two cankers at hip hop's heart, its misogyny and homophobia, do not invalidate it as Camp, but are simply what mark it out from classic Camp. So hip hop Camp is like a mutant Camp, Camp gone wrong – a new kind of Camp which bears the same relationship to the original as the Y chromosome does to the X: a malformed variant of the original.

I guess that's the commonsensical verdict. But I prefer not to draw the lines between gay and Camp and hip hop too sharply in this context. Not least because to do so would deny us one way of reconsidering homo-sexuality as hip hop's great unspeakable. Better instead to imagine a Venn diagram, with three interlocked circles, so that all three can overlap in every combination. If hip hop is reconsidered as a chapter of Camp sensibility, the insubstantial spectre of homosexuality in rap begins to become incarnate; it's no longer a question of cherchez la ghost. The elephant in the room is a purloined letter, hidden in plain sight. If you dwell on these connections, Sontag offers us the possibility that this taboo that can never be discussed is actually, subtly, omnipresent, sublimated into fevered creative energies of the whole culture. And Cam'ron's bleat of 'No homo' can begin to mean something very different; or rather, nothing at all. There's no need to whisper rumours on internet forums, start YouTube beefs, or pre-empt innuendo because, in terms of much of their mental furniture (décor again!), *everyone* in hip hop is gay – at least a little bit.

Sontag's definition of Camp it should be remembered was far broader – either more severe or more forgiving, depending on whether you are irritated or delighted by Camp's inversion of values – than that in circulation today. She names *The Maltese Falcon* and *All About Eve* as classic examples of cinematic Camp. The first is regarded now as the inception of hardboiled noir as a genre; the latter as melodrama without kitsch. In music, jazz is not Camp – but French *yé yé* and 'concoctions of Tin Pan Alley and Liverpool' are. So Camp includes early Beatles. Not to forget the kind of chatty film criticism that lists 'The 10 Best Bad Movies I Have Seen'; and *The Wings of the Dove* by Henry James. Given this comprehensive reach, I don't think Sontag would have had trouble finding room for hip hop, nor should hip hop take offence at the tag. 'Not only is Camp not necessarily bad art, but some art which can be approached as Camp . . . merits the most serious admiration and study', writes Sontag.

There's another reason to anoint hip hop as high Camp: it offers a way of expanding on Sontag's argument, a way of going beyond it. Perhaps the essay's boldest claim is made almost in passing, when she argues that 'the modern sensibility' has been formed essentially by two social forces: 'high-minded Jewish liberalism and urban homosexual aesthetics.' The instant I read that it rang, if not false, then not quite sufficient. I'd say Sontag identified only two out of the three formative cultures of the twentieth century; she was writing in 1964 of course, so two out of three is roughly par.

Maybe the Jewish intelligentsia and an urban gay subculture defined the modern sensibility in 1964, but surely in 2009, with practically every popular music traceable to roots in various black music subcultures, the modern sensibility is actually tripartite, with black music and voices completing the holy trinity. These voices and this music are there from early in the century. They can be found in T. S. Eliot and Ezra Pound, writing letters to each other in the dialect of Joel Chandler Harris's *Uncle Remus*. Or in Picasso's *Les Demoiselles D'Avignon*, the paradigmatic modernist painting, in which the fracturing faces are borrowed from African masks. If the twentieth century is the century of the edit, of the cut-up, of the collage, the aesthetic quote mark, then hip hop's sampler-wielding producers are its arch-editors. As the RZA, the musical architect of Wu-Tang Clan, once observed with glorious hubris: the sampler means that hip hop can absorb any music, any sound, but never be fully comprehended within the reach of any other form. And in this meta space, it can remain the sower of shark-toothed quotation marks – and, perhaps, the final arbiter of whether something is bad meaning bad, or bad meaning good.

AMANDA PETRUSICH
Blues in My Condition

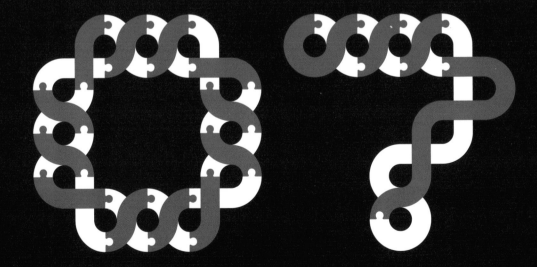

Desire and nostalgia, saving and loss, the urge to erect a permanent and complete system against the destructiveness of time . . . [Modern collectors exist] at the margin of the human adventure, that pivotal point where man finds himself rivaling God and teeters between mastery and madness.

JOHN ELSNER AND ROGER CARDINAL
The Cultures of Collecting, 1994

John Heneghan's East Village apartment is crammed tight with dusty American artifacts: antique wooden furniture, pulpy paperback books, a *Beverly Hills, 90210* pencil case (with matching ruler and eraser), an unopened can of Bahamas Goombay Punch, a yellowing *Planet of the Apes* cereal bowl. All available surfaces are littered with collectibles; all accessible closets are bursting with vintage clothes, discerningly acquired by Heneghan's striking live-in girlfriend, Eden Brower. Two exceptionally skittish house cats, both rescues, nip in and out of cardboard boxes, eyes wary and wide. Alongside the far living-room wall, sixteen squat wooden cubes – each filled with about a hundred 78 rpm records, most recorded before 1935 – loom, parsed into genres like Hillbilly, Blues, Hawaiian, or Comedy and organised alphabetically by artist. Each section is marked off with a neatly labelled cardboard divider; each 78 is housed in an unmarked brown-paper sleeve. It is an impeccable display. I ask Heneghan if he ever sits in his living room and gazes at his record collection, mesmerised by each perfect row. 'All the time,' he answers.

'I have a recurring dream about finding Skip James's "Devil Got My Woman",' Heneghan says, leaning in, voice low and solemn. 'It's so vivid, so clear – the first time it happened I woke up in the middle of the night certain that I had the record. I was like, *"This is amazing"*. So I got up to check, and it wasn't there, and I was like, *"Fuck"*. So then I have the dream again, and it's so vivid the second time, and I think maybe the part about *not* having it was the dream. So I get up to check. Then I have the dream the third time, and the fourth time . . .'

At 40, John Heneghan is one of America's youngest collectors of 78 rpm records. Although he's careful to establish a clear distinction between collectors of 78s and folks who shamelessly stockpile LPs or 45s (for Heneghan, the distinction is acute, comparable to collecting pebbles vs collecting diamonds), his own collection began with an LP – a reissue of a Charley Patton record, which he acquired when he was 16 years old. Heneghan can still describe, in remarkable detail, the subsequent moment of catharsis: picking up the record, feeling its weight in his hands, squinting at the photograph on the cover, flipping it over to read the date printed on the back, placing it on his turntable and dropping the needle into the groove, feeling transported, feeling changed.

'I'm not even sure that I liked it at first,' he admits. 'I liked the idea of it. It was really hard to listen to. But I was a guitar player – I had played the guitar since I was a kid – and I thought "What is this? What is he doing?" It was only a matter of time before I started seeking out the original records, the 78s. I resisted it for a long time because I knew it would be nearly impossible, and I knew it would be a financial burden beyond what any rational mind would consider a wise decision.' He sighs.

78s range in price from 50 cents (or less) to \$30,000 (or more), depending on the cachet of the artist, the condition of the record, and the rarity of the pressing (as Heneghan puts it, a record commands \$10 when one person wants it, and \$5,000 when two people want it – the 'Fuck you, I'll pay more' effect). Still, beyond their fetishistic and material worth, 78s have significant archival value, a fact often employed by collectors – justifiably, in many cases – to rationalise or validate massive collections. Because they were produced in such limited quantities to begin with (although a CD player is a fairly common accessory in most American homes now, gramophones were hardly standard in the early 1920s) and because so few people are interested in salvaging them, a good portion of the country's remaining 78s – it's impossible to say how many are even left – are also singular representations. Meaning that if they break, or are crammed in a flood-prone basement, or tossed in the trash with a sack of old clothes and some crappy paperback books, that song is gone, forever.

John Heneghan is glib (and, at times, aggressively self-deprecating) about his fanaticism, but his collection is, independent of its personal worth, an extraordinary cultural document: collectors of 78s, maybe more than any other curator of music or music memorabilia, are doing essential preservationist work, chasing – often desperately and with unchecked vehemence – after tiny bits of art that would otherwise be lost. Even though their pursuits are inherently selfish, fuelled by the same (at times uncontrollable) obsession that drives all collectors, without Heneghan and his peers, a good slice of American popular song would be absent from the contemporary canon. And while academics, anthropologists, reissue labels, university- or government-sponsored archivists and field recorders all assume essential roles in the preservation and diffusion of early American songbooks, the bulk of the material being released or reissued is still being sourced from the original 78s – which are found, almost exclusively, in the cramped basements and bedrooms of collectors of 78s.

Still, the historical responsibility imposed by his efforts doesn't mean Heneghan is free from the neuroses that characterise so many collectors; his collection is historically significant, but it is also deeply personal, even pathological. 'On a good day, you look at yourself like, "I'm preserving American history. I'm an archaeologist." But the bottom line is that there's seriously something wrong,' he says. 'The first time I bought a record, I remember thinking, "I have to see if this band has any other records." And then when I got the other records, I thought, "I need to figure out which one came first so I can put them in order." I remember going to friends' houses and they just had their records anywhere, and it was like, "How can you *do* that? They have to be in order!" I just spent so much time thinking about the perfect way to put everything in order.'

Heneghan leans back in his chair, scratching a craggy blonde goatee. He re-adjusts the black bowler hat he frequently sports. He is a formidable physical presence, and his narrow, slate-grey eyes belie an intolerance for certain strains of bullshit; he is exceedingly pleasant but uninterested in pleasantries, and it occurs to me that I wouldn't ever want to be standing between Heneghan and a copy of 'Devil Got My Woman'. He asks me what I'd like to listen to, and we huddle around his turntable, taking turns to pull heavy 78s from his shelves. My hands shake. Unlike vinyl records, which are forgivingly pliable, 78s are thick, brittle, and about as easy to crack as a dinner plate (and infinitely less replaceable).

Heneghan spins Mississippi John Hurt's 'Big Leg Blues', The Cannon Jug Stompers' 'Walk Right In' and a 1920s test pressing of Frankie Franko and his Louisianans' 'Somebody Stole My Gal'. A diamond-tipped needle digs deep into the disc's thick, ink-black grooves. The room fills with crackle. We pause, relishing the indescribable richness of original analogue sound, the spits and sputters that reduce audiophiles to shivering, swooning heaps. As a seasoned consumer of contemporary music, I don't necessarily buy into the oft-repeated clichés of hot vinyl supremacy, nor do I think that CDs are intrinsically stupid or cold or soulless, or that MP3s are innately disposable, a wicked plague upon sound. But for a quick second, I crumple, submitting to a sudden communion with every other human being who has ever listened to this song, this way: each strum and pop feels precious, beloved,

timeless. I hiccup, conjuring up dozens of ingenious ways to obliterate every pair of cheap earbuds I have ever purchased and stuffed, stupidly, into my ears. If I squint, I think I can see smoke curling up from the surface of the turntable. It might even be on fire.

Heneghan's collector pals – including the famed illustrator Robert Crumb – are the type of folks who went door-to-door in the 1960s, asking people if they had records in their attics and snatching up 78s for a quarter a piece. When I ask Heneghan where he buys the bulk of his records now, he looks at me as though I've commanded him to disrobe. 'You don't expect me to answer that question, do you? I'm not sure I should answer *any* of these questions,' Heneghan guffaws, incredulous. 'Do you realise how limited . . . These aren't LPs! All it takes is a dozen more people interested and . . .' He trails off again. 'It amazes me. It's American musical history and it's forgotten about, and there are only a handful of people out there preserving it.'

I understand why Heneghan might be protective of his sources. 78s are a finite reserve, first introduced around the turn of the twentieth century, about thirty years after Thomas Edison, camped out in Menlo Park, NJ, developed his long, shiny phonograph machine and revolutionised the ways in which human beings thought about sound. Initially, Edison's phonograph played cylinders – little tubes, smaller than cans of soup, which were crafted from metal (later wax, and then hard plastic), stored in cardboard canisters and coated with a strip of tin foil. Sound transcriptions were pressed into the foil with a cutting stylus, and the phonograph then translated the textures back into sound. The catch was that after a dozen or so plays at 160 revolutions per minute, the cylinders wore down and became unlistenable, and they could only hold about 120 seconds' worth of music until 1912, when Edison conceived and introduced the Blue Amberol cylinder, which contained up to four minutes. In 1887, the German-born inventor Emile Berliner, now an American citizen, unveiled the gramophone, which worked similarly to Edison's phonograph but played flat, grooved discs instead of stumpy cylinders. At first, the technology was employed mostly by toy companies, but in 1895, Berliner established the Berliner Gramophone Company, and, later, the Victor Talking Machine Company, and began expanding his business.

Berliner's disc records – which were flat, 5 to 7 inches wide, made of various materials (often rubber), and whirled, on hand-cranked players, at around 70 revolutions per minute – were easier to produce and store than cylinders, and, unsurprisingly, Edison's little tubes became obsolete by 1929. Around the same time, the production of disc records standardised: most were 10 inches wide (which yielded about three minutes of sound), crafted from a precarious jumble of shellac, a cotton compound, powdered slate, and wax lubricant (shellac was the prevailing substance, although precise percentages varied), and spun at 78 rpm – the pace of the first electric turntable motor. 78s, as they later came to be known, were in relatively wide use until 1960, when they were ultimately replaced by 7-inch, two-song 45s and 12-inch, long-playing 33⅓ records (themselves replaced by cassettes, which were eventually supplanted by compact discs, which are already being exchanged for MP3 players). As Mark Coleman writes in *Playback*, his history of recording formats, 'By the 1920s, Thomas Edison was a sideshow.'

Since there is so little popular interest in the format, even hunting down a turntable capable of playing 78s properly is a challenge. Modern LPs contain microgrooves, which measure about 0.0006" to 0.0007"; the grooves in a 78 are four to five times larger, at 0.0028" to 0.0030", so a different kind of stylus is required in addition to a motor that rotates at 78 rpm, rather than the standard 33⅓ or 45. Instead of obtaining all the equipment necessary to get a 78 to play, most people just tossed the records away without much thought – which makes them even harder to find now, almost a decade into the twenty-first century.

After some mild cajoling, Heneghan reluctantly confesses to acquiring most of his records through eBay, private auctions, antique dealers or from trading with other collectors who are also good friends; rarely do worthwhile 78s pop up in Salvation Army stores or at flea markets, although most hunters never entirely give up the fantasy. 'You hear these crazy stories still, about guys who go into a junk store in Philadelphia – there was a guy a few years ago who found a Son House record that had never been discovered. He got it in a junk store for a dollar. That's a record that's worth thousands and thousands of dollars. I haven't had anything like that happen yet,' Heneghan grins. 'But the amazing thing about 78s is that so much of the music is 100 per cent undiscovered. There are still so many records out there that are so rare there are only one or two copies, or no copies – you've never heard it. I'm still often discovering things. You find some weird band name, you don't know what it is, and you take a chance on it, put it on, and it's some incredible masterpiece. Or it's someone that you know, but you've never heard this one song.'

The bulk of Heneghan's collection consists of early blues and hillbilly records, and they range in quality and tone. Until about 1920, recordings were made acoustically, meaning the musicians would have to bellow and pluck directly into the phonograph's diaphragm cone, where the resulting sound vibrations would nudge the cutting stylus and create a transcription, which could then be played back. There are considerable drawbacks to the technology: drums and bass were rarely recorded because the depth of their vibrations would knock the cutting stylus from its intended groove, while sounds from cellos or violins and even the human voice weren't always resonant enough to render themselves fully. By 1930, engineers had worked out how to use a microphone (another Edison gadget, from 1876) to collect sound, which could then be amplified with vacuum tubes and used to power an electromagnetic recording head, meaning a far wider range of frequencies could be picked up and reproduced, thus yielding a richer, more authentic sound. Still, if you are not prone to romance and nostalgia, it all seems rather silly now that error-free digital recording – in which analogue sound is converted into perfect streams of binary code – is the standard, and things like styluses and diaphragm cones are about as relevant as the iron lung.

Unsurprisingly, for traditional record collectors – ones who, like Heneghan, came of age in the late 1970s – digital sound, and MP3s in particular, remain mostly irrelevant.

Although he owns an iPod (he bought it for Eden, who rarely uses it) and a few shelves of CDs (mostly releases from the famed reissue label Yazoo, founded in the late 1960s and run, in part, by his friend and fellow collector Richard Nevins – who worked, almost exclusively, from original 78s) he is not particularly romanced by digital files, which, being intangible streams of noughts and ones, are about as far from clunky shellac discs as possible. I can see how Heneghan might find the transition from music-as-precious-object to music-as-insubstantial-stream a bit unsettling. Even CDs, with their little shiny faces and lack of texture, are inherently unappealing. 'If I find a great record, and a friend of mine says, "How about I keep that record and just make you a CD of it?" it's like, "Are you *insane*?"' Heneghan snorts.

The record ends. The room feels emptier, colder. I ask Heneghan if he thinks that, given technological advancements in the way music is disseminated and stored, record collecting is a dying art. 'I think it's funny that you even call it an art,' he says. 'I think it's more of a disease. There has to be something really wrong with you to want to possess these objects in the first place. You have to have them, and it's never enough, and you get that strange, tingly feeling when you get one. Anyone who collects anything is obsessive–compulsive and neurotic. The need to put things in order, to file by number, to alphabetise and label, to be constantly reassessing how you've ordered things – that's neurotic behavior. I've always thought I was really crazy, that there was something really wrong with me. Especially when I started collecting 78s, because I didn't know anyone else who collected them, and I felt really isolated and weird,' Heneghan says. 'But then when I met guys like Crumb and Nevins, everyone was like, "Yeah, we're all crazy." I never met [another 78 collector] who wasn't like, "This is sick, we're all sick," ' he says. 'When I finally gave in and started buying 78s, it was a conscious decision to embrace my sickness and do what I always wanted to do. It's probably like when someone dabbles in drugs their whole life and finally decides to shoot heroin. There has to be something in your mind that says "I give up". If I really wanted a big house in the suburbs, I wouldn't be able to buy records as often, if ever. But the thing is, I don't really want a house in the suburbs. I'm happy, which is a little bit of a problem.'

⌘

On a gleaming afternoon in early May – the kind of late spring day when New Yorkers abruptly rediscover things like light and air, inching out of their apartment buildings in bare legs, eyes large and slightly suspicious – I plod down Second Avenue towards Heneghan's apartment, toting a warm six-pack of Brooklyn Lager. Outside Mars Bar, on the corner of Second Street, three very young men are seated in the crosswalk; the one in the middle is too drunk to stand, his neck limp and wilted, head drooping. The one on the left is eyeing my beer, and I preemptively cross the street. Today, John Heneghan is hosting a listening party with a few of his collector pals, and I understand that I will, in all likelihood, be made privy to artists and recordings that I would never otherwise be able to hear. Beer seems like a modest trade; I don't want to lose it en route.

I'm the first to arrive. As always, Hene-

ghan's apartment – despite being packed with stuff – is exceptionally neat and clean. As he hands me back a lager, Heneghan points out a new acquisition: a small, weathered banjo, signed in fading pencil by the '20s folksinger Chubby Parker. The banjo is hung above Heneghan's computer, alongside a framed headshot of Parker. A tiny silver star – inlaid deep in the instrument's head – shines. I smile; it reminds me of a Christmas tree.

Heneghan explains that he also recently scored an extremely rare 78 of Parker's 'Davey Crockett', which he purchased on eBay for $110 (he would have paid as much as $1,200). Parker was one of the first performers to be featured regularly on Chicago's *National Barn Dance*, itself a precursor to the *Grand Ole Opry*, but his legacy is middling, at best, and he is mostly known, when he is known at all, for chirping goofy folksongs like 'Nickety Nackety Now Now Now'. As is often the case, Heneghan was the only serious bidder. 'When I first saw it on eBay, I had a weird panicky feeling,' he says. 'This was it, this was the day I'd been waiting for. But you just don't know. All it takes is one other person. I have my arch-enemies on eBay – I don't know who they are, but their monikers haunt me. When I saw "Davey Crockett", I didn't sleep that well for a week. I knew this was it – I was never gonna see it again. All my crazy friends saw it and knew that I wanted to get it and valiantly stayed away, and then they congratulated me when I got it.' He smiles.

Until he manages to locate a copy of 'Devil Got My Woman', Heneghan placates himself with small victories, which may be all he ever gets: there are only three or four original known copies of 'Devil Got My

Woman' remaining, two of which are so damaged as to be inconsequential. While a good-quality copy could easily command $30,000, the song exists, in infinite quantities, in a re-mastered digital format, and can be purchased instantly on iTunes for 99 cents (thanks, mostly, to Yazoo Records co-director Richard Nevins, who possesses an original copy). As Nevins later explains in an email, almost any time anyone listens to 'Devil Got My Woman', regardless of the individual source, the chances are that it actually originated from his 78: ' "Devil Got My Woman" was first reissued on LP in the '60s, and, like for almost all old 78s of back-country music, no masters have survived,' he writes. 'I'd say that all reissues of this came from my copy, which is close to new and which previously belonged to [late Yazoo founder] Nick Perls. Many of the European labels that reissued this just dubbed it off the Yazoo release [1994's *The Complete Early Recordings of Skip James*].'

The track itself – James's signature song – is meandering and almost structureless, comprised of little more than a three-bar vocal phrase and two guitar chords, embellished and augmented by various vocal and instrumental flourishes. It's the kind of song – mysterious, unpredictable, pained in a way that's also intensely (if uncomfortably) intriguing – that you'll want to hear again immediately after it ends. Consequently, it's not hard to catch yourself playing and re-playing it, over and over and over again, face twisted, trying to decipher James's cries and strums: when Bob Dylan featured the track on his *Theme Time Radio Hour*, he introduced it by declaring, 'Skip had a style that was celestially divine, sounded like it was coming from beyond the rail, magic in the grooves

. . . rare and unusual, mysterious and vague, you won't believe it when you hear.' Dylan, unsurprisingly, is right; 'Devil Got My Woman' is so strange and volatile, so other-worldly that I can understand why James's biographer Stephen Calt called it 'one of the most extraordinary feats of vocalizing found in blues song'. I can also see why Heneghan has been so wholly consumed by it.

For now, Heneghan's most valuable 78 is a copy of Charley Patton's 'High Water Everywhere', which he acquired in a trade with another collector (he gave up an Ishman Bracey record, which he claims not to miss). Given the sliding price-scale of records, Heneghan is hesitant to assign the disc a precise market value, although Nevins eventually tells me that a good quality 78 of 'High Water Everywhere' could probably fetch $10,000. Patton, who died in 1934 on the Heathman-Dedham plantation in Mississippi, has long been considered the originator of Delta blues (insomuch as one exists) and is as elusive as he is esteemed: in his book *Deep Blues*, the scholar Robert Palmer claims Patton 'personally inspired just about every Delta bluesman of consequence . . . he is among the most important musicians twentieth-century America has produced. Yet we know very little about his formative years, and practically nothing about how he learned his art.'

We know this much: 'High Water Everywhere Part 1' and its B-side, 'High Water Everywhere Part 2', were released by Paramount Records in April 1930. Three years earlier, in April 1927, the Mississippi River broke through a levee in Mound Landing, Mississippi, about 20 miles north of Patton's hometown of Greenville. That same spring, the Delta had been pummelled

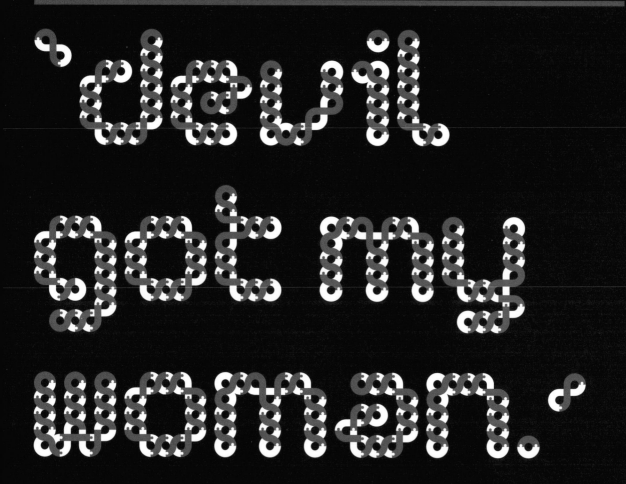

'devil got my woman.'

Amanda Petrusich

by a series of spectacular weather events – tornadoes, earthquakes, and hammering, merciless rains – and the river's levees were understandably taxed, trembling under the weight of a pulsing, thrusting, overfed river; when they finally acquiesced, a massive wall of brown, muddy water – some reports claim it was well over 20 feet tall – ate up much of northwest Mississippi, blanketing 27,000 square miles of land in water. According to John M. Barry, author of *Rising Tide*, the unleashed river carried in excess of three million cubic feet of water each second; as Barry notes, even attempting to harness a river as brawny and robust as the Mississippi required a certain amount of hubris, which, in this case, backfired. The flooding didn't let up until August; by then, at least 250 people were dead, maybe more.

In the summer of 1929, Patton – who was itinerant in the manner of all classic blues singers – was temporarily stationed in Jackson, Mississippi, where he became in-volved with Henry C. Spier, a white music-store owner who acted as a talent scout for a few major record companies (Spier is singularly responsible for launching the recording careers of a handful of blues luminaries, including Skip James). Spier arranged for Patton to travel to Richmond, Indiana, to record in a studio owned by Gennett Records, for sessions underwritten by Paramount. (Palmer describes the space as a 'barnlike frame building just a few feet from a railroad track', and notes that it also housed a pressing plant, which meant that 'the freshly pressed records could be con-veniently dispatched by rail, but recording had to stop whenever a train approached.')

On Friday, 14 June, Patton recorded fourteen tracks at Gennett studios. As Palmer explains, there's a decent chance Patton was drunk – '. . . most companies gave "race" and "hillbilly" artists liquor to loosen them up,' he writes – but Patton's performance is still riveting, all rage and rasp. His first batch of records sold well enough that he was invited to record at Paramount's main studio in Grafton, Wisconsin.

In the 1910s, the Wisconsin Chair Company, a modest, Port Washington-based furniture factory, had begun assembling small wooden phonograph cabinets under contract from Thomas Edison, and the leap to producing actual phonograph records didn't seem so far-fetched: in 1918, WCC opted to dip into the still burgeoning record business, founding a small label, which they named Paramount (it bore no relation to the American movie studio that was founded in 1912). After four floundering years as an unremarkable pop enterprise, Paramount launched its 'race records' series in 1922.

Between 1922 and 1935, scores of African-American jazz and blues artists, many from the south (Charley Patton, Blind Lemon Jefferson, Ma Rainey, Blind Blake, Son House, Skip James, Jelly Roll Morton, Johnny Dodds and others), trekked to Grafton, a small, predominantly white, town on the shores of Lake Michigan, about a hundred miles north of Chicago. According to Alex van der Tukk, author of *Paramount's Rise and Fall*, locals were visibly (and vocally) distressed by the sudden influx of African-American artists. Resident John Grams told van der Tukk: 'They were scared. When the artists arrived from Milwaukee with the interurban or streetcar and they got off, the kids would run. They had never seen black people.'

The Grafton studio was located on the second floor of the building across the street from the pressing plant, at Twelfth Street and Falls Road; van der Tukk claims the building was a 'rustic, muddy red wooden structure often described as a barn'. It housed a piano, a guitar, a few wooden chairs, a parabolic microphone, an amplifier and a speaker.

In October 1929 Patton recorded 'High Water Everywhere Part 1' and its sequel, 'High Water Everywhere Part 2', – a harrowing account of the 1927 Mississippi River flood – in Grafton, along with twenty-four other songs. 'The whole round country, Lord, river has overflowed,' he wails in 'Part 1', voice loose and rich, over a three-note, open-G-tuned guitar melody. There's a vague bit of percussion – Patton smacking his guitar or thwapping his foot on the ground – in the background. 'The whole round country, man, is overflowed,' he snarls. Patton sounds angry and indignant; it is the way we sing when we are singing about things that are out of our control, things that feel too large and too devastating to also be true. Patton knew that a few minutes gazing out at the Mississippi is enough to convince anyone that they don't know one single thing about rivers and the way they move: even when it's not breeching its levees, the Mississippi looks like the kind of thing that could swallow you whole.

In musicologist Dick Spotswood's notes for Revenant Records' *Screamin' and Hollerin' the Blues*, an epic, seven-CD compendium of Patton's work, he observes that Patton was 'Paramount's most prolific recording artist for 1929, an indication of the confidence that the company had in his sales potential'. Still, even though he was a commercially viable blues artist, a physical record of Patton's work has not endured, or at least not in its purest form. As Edward Komara writes, in the same set of notes, 'Listening to Patton's records today is challenging, given the battered state of many of the surviving discs, the provincial nature of Mississippi before World War II, and the changes in music since his 1934 death.'

Despite the considerable flow of talent into Grafton, Paramount was notorious for its poor sound fidelity and shoddy pressings, and in 1935, the label was swallowed up by the Great Depression, remaining dormant until it was purchased and briefly revived in 1942. When the Grafton plant first closed, part of its remaining dead stock was sold off as wholesale lots, although exactly what happened to the bulk of the company's records – and their metal masters – is unclear. Rumours abound: some claim that the factory burned 78s for fuel or used them to patch holes in the walls, but the reigning theory is that disgruntled Paramount employees, upon hearing of their termination, furiously hurled stacks of albums into the Milwaukee River. In 2006, the PBS television series *History Detectives* directed a professional scuba-diving team to the bottom of the waterway, to scour the silt for precious Paramount remnants. The divers didn't unearth any 78s, although they did note that a dam adjacent to the factory had been removed in 2000, thus permanently disturbing the riverbed – meaning, had any records or masters been sitting at the bottom of the river, they would have long since washed away.

Consequently, exactly how many copies of 'High Water Everywhere' were pressed, how many were sold, and how many remain is tough to definitively ascertain (Nevins guesses that there are about fifteen copies still in existence). All anyone knows for sure is that if you find one, you'd best hold it close to your chest.

While we wait for the rest of the guests to arrive, Heneghan and I dip crackers in the small tub of houmus he's set out on his coffee table. I admire his walls, which are covered – rather literally – with framed pieces of sheet music, hung inches apart to ensure maximum capacity. Heneghan is always self-effacing about his collecting habit; he recognises the practice as pathological and his interests as outmoded. Still, he fancies himself an amateur historian of sorts – which, given the rarity of 78s, is not entirely unreasonable – and is also convinced that, on some level, having interesting things around him makes him a more interesting person. 'When people come to my apartment, some walk in and get really silent, and I can tell they think it's creepy,' he says. 'And I think, OK, your house is like the Ikea catalogue, and so my stuff seems really strange. But I'm a little uncomfortable when I go to some-one's house and it looks like the Ikea cata-logue. This is the most thought you could put into the stuff you want to be around?' he asks, voice rising, incredulous. 'Give me that, give me A, B, C and D, because they're on the same page? To me, that's why George Bush is president. That's why everyone eats at McDonald's.'

Even though he rarely frames it as such, collecting has clearly become, for Heneghan, a functional way of rebelling against mainstream culture – like getting an AC/DC tattoo or jamming a titanium post through your septum, packing your apartment with old records and sheet music is a semi-public

way of establishing a counter-cultural identity, of rejecting a society that feels homogenised and unforgiving. Heneghan frequently speaks of collecting as a form of submission, as a way of giving in to basic urges and desires that other people stifle, and when he does, it's not without a certain amount of pride.

Heneghan earns his cash as a freelance video technician, setting up cameras for television shows and concerts, and, if pressed, will gently grumble about the nature of the work. He's particularly disgusted by the extent to which backing tracks are employed by pop stars paid mounds of cash to sing their songs live; he considers the entire enterprise an epic charade. 'It sounds like the album because you're listening to the album,' he spits. When he's not working, Heneghan is performing with Eden; together, they comprise John and Eden's East River String Band, a beguiling two-piece old-time outfit featuring John on guitar and Eden on ukulele and vocals. When they play, they sport period-appropriate garb and strum antique instruments (Heneghan collects old guitars, too). Each time I've seen them perform – at bars and small downtown clubs, mostly – they've enthralled the room with their charmingly antiquated odd-couple rapport. Today, Heneghan tells me he's been endeavouring to get their newest self-released album, *Some Cold Rainy Day*, issued on 180 gram 33⅓ vinyl with a gatefold cover (a cardboard sleeve that opens like a book, revealing additional artwork inside), but ran into a snag when the kid who answered the phone at the pressing plant didn't under-stand what gatefold meant. 'I finally had to ask, how old are you? I told him to find the oldest person who worked there and to ask them,' he says.

We eat some green grapes. A few minutes later, Heneghan buzzes in Sherwin Dunner, a jazz and blues collector who works with Richard Nevins at Yazoo. He sits in a chair. 'I notice that your Starkist lamp has a different shade than mine,' he says, surveying a Starkist Tuna-brand promotional lamp perched on Heneghan's bookshelf. He and Heneghan have identical carrying cases for their 78s, each marked with a little plaque that reads 'Music Appreciation Records'. Dunner sets his box of records on the floor. The handle has been reinforced with duct tape.

Dunner has been amassing 78s for years, and, like Heneghan, understands collecting as a way of insulating oneself from a culture that's not always especially welcoming (and, incidentally, a culture that is increasingly accelerated). 'It's the way you cope with feeling like an outsider, feeling alienated from pop or mainstream culture, which has gotten more and more controlled and oppressive and dehumanised. So you create your own world, using whatever you think has meaning or aesthetic value. It's a world that can save you from the modern world. Collectors are disconnected from society, in a way. Their passions are not part of the mainstream,' he says.

Both Dunner and Heneghan are fervent, focused music fans with comprehensive knowledge of the various sub-genres of early American music, and, accordingly, their collections are more functional than decorative; these records are not squirrelled away in glass cases or sitting silent in locked boxes. They're handled with care but they're *handled* – frequently and with enthusiasm, played for friends and in private. Con-

sequently, Heneghan has little interest in 78s that are so severely worn they no longer play properly. 'A guy I knew wanted $15,000 for a nearly unplayable copy of "Devil Got My Woman". I can play an old scratchy record and enjoy it, but this was almost not a record any more,' he groans. 'See, that would be crazy. But that's not to say that's not a fair price for that – he probably ended up getting twenty or thirty grand for that record.'

Unsurprisingly, both men also express deep vitriol for anyone who doesn't share a similar keenness for the music – like, say, some of the more investment-minded 78 collectors, who procure records because of their potential for financial appreciation. For Heneghan and Dunner, such fetishistic thinking fails to acknowledge the wealth inherent to the songs themselves.

'That's a level of collecting that I despise,' Heneghan says. 'The guys who just buy [a record] because it's worth something and they're speculating that it's going to be worth more. But with something like 78s, there's so few of them available in the first place, and if [Sherwin] gets a good record, I may be envious or whatever, but I don't feel like, "Oh, that's so horrible." There are other people who get a record and it's like well, that'll just sit on a shelf. No one's enjoying it, it's out of circulation, no one can hear it. With some of these records, there are so few copies [remaining] that really, *no one can hear it*,' Heneghan seethes. 'There's just something really despicable about that mentality. Those people tend to be the most, you know, "That's mine now, I got that before you could get it." '

Heneghan, accordingly, is generous with his records: he's periodically approached about loaning songs to documentary films

Amanda Petrusich

The Essential Companion to *Rip It Up*

TOTALLY WIRED: POST-PUNK INTERVIEWS AND OVERVIEWS

SIMON REYNOLDS

IT STILL MOVES

LOST SONGS, LOST HIGHWAYS & THE SEARCH FOR THE NEXT AMERICAN MUSIC

AMANDA PETRUSICH

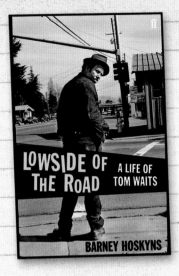

LOWSIDE OF THE ROAD   A LIFE OF TOM WAITS

BARNEY HOSKYNS

FABER POP CULTURE ESSENTIAL READING

'Reynolds has shed dazzling light on a neglected era of music' Adam Sweeting, *Sunday Times*

Simon Reynolds

RIP IT UP AND START AGAIN

postpunk 1978–1984

HANG the DJ

AN ALTERNATIVE BOOK OF MUSIC LISTS

Edited by Angus Cargill

NICK KENT THE DARK STUFF

SELECTED WRITINGS ON ROCK MUSIC 1972–1993 WITH A FOREWORD BY IGGY POP

'I COULD TELL YOU STORIES ABOUT NICK KENT THAT WOULD UNCURL THE HAIR IN YOUR AFRO' MORRISSEY

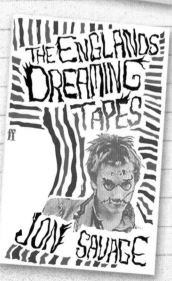

THE ENGLANDS DREAMING TAPES

JON SAVAGE

Praise for England's Dreaming:
'How about – the best book about rock and pop culture ever?' NME

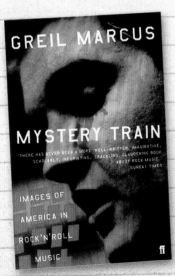

GREIL MARCUS

MYSTERY TRAIN

'THERE HAS NEVER BEEN A MORE WELL-WRITTEN, IMAGINATIVE, SCHOLARLY, INFURIATING, CRACKLING, GLADDENING BOOK ABOUT ROCK MUSIC.' *SUNDAY TIMES*

IMAGES OF AMERICA IN ROCK'N'ROLL MUSIC

'There has never been a more well-written, imaginative ... gladdening book about rock music.' SUNDAY TIMES

ff

(he's just given Cleoma Breaux and Joseph Falcon's 'Fe Fe Ponchaux', a Cajun song from 1929 of which he has the best known copy, to the BBC), and routinely posts requested tracks on his public MySpace page. If you manage to land an invitation to his home, he will play you anything you want to hear.

Three more guests arrive and settle into chairs. Dunner and Heneghan realise they own two different 78s festooned with identical white stickers foreswearing future commerce (the stickers read 'DO NOT SELL AT ANY PRICE' in careful, hand-written blue block letters). Considering that both 78s were purchased with the sticker already there, we wonder if their author changed his mind, or – the more likely scenario – if the departed's estate wasn't terribly concerned with his posthumous wishes for his precious little discs.

Heneghan begins playing records. As soon as the needle slumps into the groove, the room goes silent, reverent: although I've passed plenty of nights communing with music in private, I have never listened to records with friends this way, and the experience – communal, social, deferential – is immediately soothing. Although no one speaks much, it still feels like we're engaged, like we're all doing something together – different, in a way, from a live show at a rock club (where everyone's yammering, frantically thumbing text messages into their phones or ordering beers) and infinitely removed from the isolating practice of listening to a portable music player. After each song ends, discussions spark: is it two guitarists or one? What kind of open tuning? Is Charley Patton hitting the guitar with his thumb? Is the G-string missing? At one point, Heneghan pulls out an old acoustic guitar and demonstrates

his understanding of how a particular song is played; he nibbles on his lip and taps his foot, his whole body taut and engaged. He's almost glowing. I start to think that maybe his hobby is not so sick, after all.

⌘

In April 2006, Yazoo Records released *The Stuff That Dreams Are Made Of*, a double CD of rare and previously unreleased blues and country tracks from the 1920s and 30s. Most of the songs included are highly coveted and largely unavailable tracks – hence the title – and were hand-plucked by label head Richard Nevins, who mined his own stash as well as the private collections of a handful of eminent blues and country collectors (including Spotswood, Joe Bussard, Don Kent, Chris King, and Dave Freeman). The cover, an illustration by Robert Crumb, shows a bearded, frenzied-looking middle-aged man wearing glasses and a sweater vest, clutching a 78 and sweating. Two thought bubbles floating to the left of his moist brow read, 'After forty years, at last it's mine!' and 'Nice clean copy too . . . Look at the luster of those grooves!' Cubes of records – similar to Heneghan's – loom in the background, and a stack of audio equipment sits off to the side. The collector looks anxious, fretful, possessed. He doesn't seem like the type of dude you'd want to hang out with on a Friday night.

In the album's liner notes, Nevins offers up a spirited essay about the absurdity of and passion inherent to record collecting. He describes the contents of *The Stuff That Dreams Are Made Of* as 'super rarities and unissued gems that would cause even the most advanced collectors to sit up and take

Amanda Petrusich

notice – one might consider many of the tracks to be as revelatory in their domain as the Dead Sea Scrolls were in theirs'. Nevins artfully skewers the cult of collecting, cheerfully recounting examples of his own fanaticism: '. . . a building I was living in caught fire in the middle of the night and hearing a neighbor screaming I jumped out of bed into a room filled with smoke and followed my first impulse, which was to grab a box of scarce records and only then attempt to flee. The firemen saved the day, but only decades of time brought some semblance of sanity,' he confesses. (Heneghan will later tell me that it's not uncommon for 78 collectors to prepare a panic box – a crate of ultra-rare records that's packed and ready to be seized in the event of an emergency – although he himself has resisted the urge to assemble one. 'I can't let myself think about that stuff,' he says.)

In his notes, Nevins also narrates the story of a rainy night forty years ago, when – while approaching a North Carolina cabin whose owner was rumored to possess rare 78s – he walked into an electric cattle fence, was severely shocked, collapsed into a mound of cow shit, stood up, stumbled on, and ultimately landed a then-rare copy of the North Carolina Cooper Boys' 'Daniel In the Lions Den'. 'I guess you could say that was a record to die for,' Nevins writes. 'In this case, almost literally.'

In the hours before I first meet Richard Nevins, while he's driving from his home in New Jersey to my Brooklyn apartment, I become extremely concerned with whether or not he will think I have cool stuff, and elect to spend most of the morning rearranging stacks of books and records, positioning random, flea-market bits and pieces into impeccable little vignettes. I turn my Elvis bust lamp so that it is facing the front door. I reconsider and rotate the base so that Elvis is staring at the television. I wedge a pair of plastic gold aviator sunglasses over Elvis's orange face. I tug them off and put them in a drawer. I survey the space, squinting and critical. My general understanding is that Richard Nevins has very little use for or interest in contemporary culture, and, accordingly, I do my best to bury anything that might reveal my habit of using a cross-trainer while listening to Gwen Stefani singles on my iPod. I have specifically purchased a six-pack of Coca-Cola in small, old-fashioned glass bottles. I stick the first disc of *Woody Guthrie: The Asch Recordings* into my CD player, fold my hands, and wait.

'Let's just say I've always been an inveterate collector, but it's much, much more temperate now,' Nevins insists, after he's arrived, surveyed the space, and nodded to the stereo (Nevins, of course, states a preference for Guthrie's earlier, pre-Folkways work). He relaxes into my sofa and pours a beer into the smallest drinking glass I own, which he specifically requested. 'It's sort of analogous to filling out a crossword puzzle in your spare time,' he muses. 'It's no longer, "I gotta get it, I gotta have it." But the passion for the music has only increased.'

Nevins, who has known Heneghan for several years, appears to regard Heneghan with a mix of admiration and tender, knowing pity, and he naturally assumes his default role as the chiding elder statesman of the group. 'John is out of his mind. I can't think of a more off-the-wall, over-the-top collector than John. He's just crazy. When I was John's age, I was that way too,' Nevins says. 'But if you're older and you still maintain that [level of fanaticism], there's something awfully wrong with you.' (Later, Heneghan responds: 'He constantly tells me I have a serious problem, but it's usually when we're at his house, and I'm looking at all his stuff. It's probably because he can afford it and I can't,' he laughs. 'He's only done because there's so little left that he doesn't have. That's the truth.')

'If you have any sense of your own mortality as you increase in age, you give it up,' Nevins continues. 'But the other aspect of it, the listening – I hear more subtle details, more nuances [in the music] now. That's a complicated discussion about me and my brain, personally,' he says. Nevins also vows that electric-fence hopping is no longer a viable leisure activity for him. 'I sat around arguing with this woman about a stupid record for an hour or two. Any rational person would have gotten back in the car, stopped at a bar, and gotten a drink right away.' He shrugs.

Nevins has been collecting for as long as he can recall, and is adamant in his belief that collecting is born from a neurological impulse, and, consequently, is more a bio-logical imperative than a lifestyle choice. When I ask him if he remembers when and where he first starting collecting, he insists it was the maternity ward. 'When I was a little kid, the mail would come every day before school, and by the end of the day my parents would have gone through it and put it in a little wastepaper basket,' he continues. 'I would come home and go through it. I saved it and put it in categories. This is what every collector loves – putting things in categories. They love to arrange stuff. I graduated from that lunacy to tearing out pages of old magazines that had been discarded, saving

automobile ads, different categories of ads. The impulse was there. I had two brothers who never collected anything, ever. It's totally wired into your brain. It's not a reaction to society. You see the same exact pattern, all throughout the ages, in all different societies.'

Regardless of how or why collectors come into the habit, the practice itself tends to be skewed dramatically to the male – record collecting, in particular, is almost exclusively the terrain of men. No one is entirely certain of why. 'I think one reason is that women are predominantly right-hemisphered, and that's why they're not as inclined towards collecting, whereas guys are predominantly the opposite,' Nevins proposes. 'Women will collect, but it's not the nutty kind of collecting, where they've got to have it and they'll drive 500 miles to get something. It's nice – it's twenty-four salt-and-pepper shakers on a shelf. And that's it, they're done,' he says. Sherwin Dunner agrees that the impulse to collect is probably a genetic proclivity. 'Is the male wired as hunter-gatherer and the female as nurturer?' he muses in an email, before adding: 'Although that nurturing seldom gets expressed as "Yes, Honey, those are beautiful nineteenth-century belt buckles you've spent our nest egg on."' Indeed, record collectors will often speak, in low, anxious tones, about ravaged marriages or relationships that were sacrificed at the altar of shellac. As Nevins writes in *The Stuff That Dreams Are Made Of*, '. . . Another guy's wife of 22 years, who he appeared to love even more than his collection, left him – all she wanted in life was a house and a child – and they were sitting on a fortune in the vast collection. Then they divorce and the idiot collector loses half his stuff anyway, five times more than her simple requests would have cost!'

Heneghan is lucky that Eden is mostly bemused by his habit. 'I don't care,' she laughs. 'One time, he told me he was going to stop so he could save some money. He deleted all his record-buying mailing lists and stuff like that. He was like, "You've got to stop me, you've got to stop me." But I'm not really like that, so I tried for a few weeks – "No records, no records." Then I looked at the computer, and he'd been buying stuff – PayPal was open, you know?'

'I think she thinks it's completely insane, on some level,' Heneghan tells me later. 'I think most women – anybody who's rational, really – thinks that each one is the final one. You know, "You got what you wanted, isn't that great?" The first time she saw me go through the process, she was really happy for me, and then she was confused – "You mean you're looking at another record?" "Oh yeah, yeah, I need this one too." She always thought it was going to be the last one,' he says. 'Then she started to realise that it's always going to be like this. She was kind of freaked out.' He shrugs. 'But I never lied about it – I never tried to cover it up.'

Heneghan, for the most part, has mixed feelings about his own collecting. 'I look at myself and think, "I really shouldn't need any more of this stuff." But I can't fight the urge,' he says. 'It's an addiction. I say all the time that I feel like a drug addict. The only thing I can say about it is at least I'm *not* a drug addict. Everyone secretly wishes they could stop. I've tried to stop [collecting] a bunch of times. I spend a lot of money, but it's not even the money so much. A part of me thinks, "If I could just get rid of all this stuff, everything would be over." I mean, the rest of my life I'm going to wake up wanting Skip James's "Devil Got My Woman". Part of me wants to not want that. That's the rational side. Then I think: "What would I do?" I would be so sad. It would be nice not to have to be obsessed [with 78s], but, you know, it's not the worst habit in the world.'

I ask Heneghan what he thinks might happen if he acquired a playable copy of 'Devil Got My Woman'. 'I don't know,' he answers. 'I don't know what would happen. That might be it. I might stop collecting.' He pauses. 'I might go crazy.'

RICHARD KING
'We love the smell of napalm on a Monday morning'
Interview with Optimo

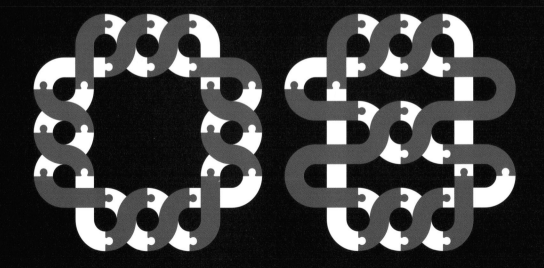

For over a decade Optimo Espacio has not only defined the sound and feeling of Glasgow's city centre on a Sunday night, it has stretched the perception of what a nightclub can be. To do justice to the wild, filters-off set lists at Optimo, the club has to be experienced for itself. The nights are intense, wild and happy; Optimo is a space where the experience of music is beautifully heavy.

As well as being its creators and resident DJs, JD Twitch and JG Wilkes have curated, goaded, teased, spewed and ached Optimo into a sensibility that combines music, pleasure and fun with deep feelings, unironic good times and trusting people's intelligence.

So did you meet at Pure?

JD Twitch I think we met when I was doing Pure and I lived in Glasgow, but I would go through to Edinburgh every week, and for a few years we used to run a coach. At that point, clubbing in Glasgow, there wasn't really that much going on, so all the people in Glasgow would go to Edinburgh, which was pretty revolutionary in itself.

JG Wilkes I met you briefly on the bus one time. I remember you getting on the bus with your records 'cos it made a few stops. We were all on the bus, and used to pick Keith up. It'd be a full single-decker through to Edinburgh, for a rave.

To listen to techno in the proper environment?

JD Twitch & *JG Wilkes* Yeah.

JG Wilkes It was a pretty mind-blowing club, Pure.

JD Twitch I mean, it was just a really horrible building, just a box, with the biggest sound system, literally – probably – on the planet at that time. It was without a doubt the loudest club. We toned it down after a few years.

JG Wilkes You couldn't even see the sound system but it got louder as you went up to the front – it was just black boxes —

JD Twitch Pitch black, full of smoke and rave lighting, before rave lighting had become a cliché. The people we did the club with owned a lighting company and they just used to fill it with as many lights as they could.

JG Wilkes They were from a rock background.

JD Twitch Which is why the sound system was like Swans had been playing there.

JG Wilkes They applied that kind of idea to it.

JD Twitch It was instant, you never did a warm up, it was, like, instant, straight into madness.

JG Wilkes There was, like, this group of disco hippies who were kind of whacked-out techno guys who would literally whip the crowd into a frenzy, wouldn't they? They were total freaks.

JD Twitch It was all sorts. It was from, you know, Belgium rave albums to, like, Strictly Rhythm to Chicago house. I mean, in hindsight people imagine it was this raging banging techno club, but it was all sorts from all the strands, like Shut Up and Dance, early UK hardcore to deep house —

JG Wilkes Piano house, Wild Pitch stuff, really deep stuff.

JD Twitch And then mind-bending acid rock.

JG Wilkes You know, regular.

Hawkwind?

JG Wilkes Aye, aye, you know —

JD Twitch Yeah, just smoke and strobes, more strobes than you've ever seen, and it was just at the exact right time, when obviously Ecstasy arrived and we were just really lucky to be in the time and the right place and we happened to be the only people that were into this music up here.

So we did a few collaborations which weren't very successful and then I got offered the opportunity to start Sunday night, and I thought, well, I want to do this with someone, so from knowing Jonnie, I thought he would be the perfect person to do it with.

What was the thinking behind the Sunday night?

JD Twitch We could do whatever we liked, so this concept had just always been there . . . I like all this other music. Everyone knows me as this techno DJ. I'm pretty bored with this and, more to the point, maybe I'll stop DJing – here's an opportunity to do something that's completely self-indulgent, doesn't really matter whether it's successful or not. So long as there's enough people to pay the bar staff, they'll be happy. They were all very supportive. Most clubs, unless you're successful instantly, you're out the door. But they had a lot more confidence in the night than perhaps we did.

JG Wilkes Yeah, there was a point when we were gonna wrap it up, actually. You know, there wasn't enough people going. We loved it, you know, but there wasn't enough people there and to be fair the owner was like, 'There's something good about this night, I think we should persevere.' It just blew up then. The first generation of people that came were basically our mates and a handful of people that happened to wander in . . . but all at once, it was literally an overnight change from one week to the next. For months it had been like 50, 60 maybe a 100 people on a good night. Literally one week there were 400 and it stayed like that.

What do you put that down to?

JD Twitch Maybe just people's curiosity. It seemed like people just hadn't got it before. People would come down, a few people loved it but everyone else would be like, 'Ooah fuck!' and they'd get really angry 'cos I wasn't playing techno. I was supposed to be this local techno hero and I'd betrayed . . . which I kind of always . . . I hate purism. I hate that purist attitude, so it just seemed that everything gelled.

JG Wilkes They were spitting venom at Keith . . . I think sometimes when people can't understand something they want to be critical of it or it sometimes makes people angry.

JD Twitch The first time we took it to Edinburgh, some guy physically grabbed me, he goes, 'If you come back to this city with this club, I'm going to kill you, you've totally betrayed what I . . .' This is ridiculous, this is a nightclub!

JG Wilkes I don't think I ever really remember us deciding exactly what we were going to do, we'd just put a whole lot of things into the middle and would try things from week to week.

JD Twitch And it was all about us having fun, that's all it was really all about. There was a restaurant in the west end of Glasgow and the manager or owner put up a noticeboard saying all staff must refrain from going to Optimo . . . 'cos so many people were calling in sick on every single Monday.

JG Wilkes There's people who'll stay 'til 4 or 5 in the morning and go in to work. There's no passing trade with Optimo, it's not like a Saturday night out and you're in a bar and you're like, 'Fuck, now we'll go to a bar and have a few drinks,' and you roll in there . . . it's like, people just come from their house, they've decided they wanna go and maybe they have changed their shifts or something around at work so they can go.

JD Twitch When we first started it was kind of like . . . a lot of people who came had never really been clubbers before, and you kind of had two crowds . . . all these people that had maybe never been clubbing before came. One, because there was live music. Two, because we would still play things with guitars and they could relate to that. There were people who liked that, but you also got a whole generation. I think it's all changed now, but then you got a whole generation of club people that had never been to see gigs, it had just never registered on their radar, so you were introducing these two disparate groups of people to something they hadn't ever experienced before.

JG Wilkes I think that that's true. I know Keith and myself would've probably started going to concerts when we were probably 14 or 15 and . . . but I do think that back then when we started the club there were probably people there would have never seen a live band and they'd never been to clubs.

JD Twitch Which I think now would be very unusual.

'get a few disco betties down.'

Richard King

Gaining a worldwide reputation for being something of a party, Optimo has inevitably been misinterpreted as being full of angular haircuts, hipsters and unnecessary bifocals.

JD Twitch The biggest misconception is always by people that've never been, that have an idea in their head of what it's like; but more than that, they have an idea of what the people that go there are like. They think it's full of people that are, like, out of *Skins* or *Nathan Barley* or something.

JG Wilkes It's not a particularly fashionable place to go at all. Someone was standing in the middle of the dancefloor last week with his trousers round his ankles . . .

You're named after a Liquid Liquid song, did you realise that something similar was going on outside of Glasgow, particularly in New York?

JD Twitch When we started, for me anyway, it was pre-internet . . . I didn't get on to the internet until '98, '99. It was a lot harder to find out what was going on elsewhere, but apart from that we weren't really looking. It was just from buying records . . . obviously as a record buyer you started noticing all these things come out and it's, 'Oh, these people are in a similar place . . . on a similar wavelength.'

JG Wilkes I remember James Murphy was doing the sound for The Rapture . . . it was the first time we met him. You know he came along and did the desk for The Rapture and actually made them sound brilliant under very difficult conditions.

JD Twitch I think it was just really great to discover there were other people out there that were thinking the same things, had been in love with the same kind of music that had been forgotten.

JG Wilkes Yeah, I remember talking to him about liking Killing Joke and disco.

When you put the bands on was there a policy of who you booked or was it just your own internal logic?

JG Wilkes I remember Keith was saying let's book Whitehouse at the club and I looked up at the calendar and I was like, 'It's a Bank Holiday Sunday,' and it's like when you get a few disco betties down and all that . . . and I phoned you back up and I was, that's a Bank Holiday, and . . . that's fucking genius . . . you know, if you ever wanted an insane night . . .

JD Twitch I remember these two totally working-class Glasgow girls – 18, 19, looked like they were in the wrong club; looked like they would never be into what we were doing. This girl comes up just as Whitehouse has finished and I go, 'Oh here we go, she's gonna give me a load of abuse for what the fuck was that about,' and she was, 'That's the best thing I've ever heard in my life. I've never heard anything like that ever. Where can I buy their CD?' On the other hand you'd have people that you'd think would be really into it just getting so angry.

JG Wilkes But it ended up in a total pain in the arse because they had some psycho stalker guy, trying to stalk all their gigs. And he phoned up, like, Glasgow district council and said there's this Nazi band, and I had CID phone me up . . . 'Erm, you run this night Optimo don't you? And you've got this Nazi band,' and I had to explain to this policeman what they were about, and he was like, 'Can I just ask you, who did you vote for in the last election?' . . . I was . . .

Your Boss!

JG Wilkes Yeah!

Have you had any other run-ins with the Strathclyde Constabulary?

JD Twitch We have, Jonnie had one, I think we were showing our —

JG Wilkes We were showing some edits, some Richard Kern films, which we'd taken parts off and put colour washes over, slowed down and stuff like that. The guy who does our lights, Adrian, he'd put in a DVD of some like really, pretty challenging stuff, like —

JD Twitch By mistake —

JG Wilkes By mistake. It was the wrong DVD or tape he'd put in, and it was Richard Kern's hardcore series – this piece called the sewing circle, which is like —

JD Twitch This woman decides she doesn't want to have sex with men any more so she has her genitals sewn up. And someone complained to the police about it. First they emailed me and they'd never been in the club before, they came in and they just said this is wholly inappropriate. I apologised and said the intention hadn't been to show it, but anyway, you know, we have the right to show

it if we want, and she got really, really upset about it. We had this long exchange, and finally she goes, 'Well I think you need to be saved from yourselves,' and that was the last I heard of it. The next thing the police got in touch.

JG Wilkes The licensing police and all, they wanted to search the club, and I had to go in for an interview with the CID. They had the DVD there, and it was a female superintendent. I was thinking, 'This is gonna go down the art–porn debate here, and it's not gonna work. The best thing I can do here is just say, "It was a mistake, it never should've got shown, I'm really sorry about that."' And they had watched the whole thing, the police, before I got there.

JD Twitch And in the meantime I emailed her back: 'I can't believe you took this matter to the police,' I can't remember what I said, but I definitely didn't accuse her of being a Nazi. But she went back to the police and complained about this too, at which point the police started to realise this woman is a nutter basically.

JG Wilkes The police were getting sent all the emails and so I was trying to get out of this very, very difficult corner, but they were getting a picture of this woman – that she was maybe a wee bit unhinged.

JD Twitch The police ended up saying, 'Don't do it again, don't have any more contact with this woman,' but the police sergeant who Jonnie watched the film with then asked at the end of the interview, could he borrow the DVD, he wanted to go over it again.

JG Wilkes But it was funny as well because he was going through the file, and he had on file about the Whitehouse gig, and I was like, oh there's a really bad sort of picture emerging here in front of the police of this sort of fucked-up thing we're doing on a Sunday night.

Optimo however, have always tried to give 'fucked up' it's own nuanced definition . . .

JG Wilkes Every few weeks we'll do an instal of some lighting gear and we'll maybe have a sort of an idea what we're gonna do. At the birthday party we had a mirror ball installation, there was 24 mirror balls in the club . . . so we'll do one thing well rather than . . . we've done a few parties where there's been a sort of theme to it. We did an *Apocalypse Now* party this year, which was great. We just did a poster that said —

JD Twitch 'Apocalypse on tonight' —

JG Wilkes No, it just said, 'We love the smell of napalm on a Monday morning', in the *Apocalypse Now* typeface so it was just —

JD Twitch So a few people guessed and a surprising number of people turned up.

JG Wilkes In combat gear.

JD Twitch An amazing number.

JG Wilkes But the club, it was like . . . there was just fucking trees and branches everywhere. Sandbags. There were dead bodies – we had actors in who were just lying there dead underneath the tables.

JD Twitch There's this huge table by the bar and this guy was looking at it just thinking it was like a dummy . . . and it's real.

JG Wilkes Orange smoke everywhere. We had pyrotechnic guys with metal bomb tanks.

JD Twitch So every few minutes there'd be like the loudest explosion . . . when people came in the club we had smoke machines behind the doors pumping out smoke . . . all the doormen were dressed as GIs.

JG Wilkes Bamboo cages with people in them!

JD Twitch Sound effects, helicopters!

JG Wilkes Total mess.

Did you charge the same to get in?

JG Wilkes Yeah, aye aye . . . people were like, 'What the fuck is this mess?' There's just stuff everywhere, sandbags, ammo guns . . . went on the web and found out all the different machine guns and rocket launchers that they used in Vietnam and I found some of those Hollywood Edge sound effects so we had, like, you know —

JD Twitch State of the art.

JG Wilkes The music would just stop and Keith would have it all set up . . . there'd be a battle for five minutes . . . explosions . . . fuckin' machine guns . . .

JD Twitch Everyone's going around going, 'Why why?' . . . 'Cos it's fun! These guys had come up from Manchester for the first time and were asking, 'Is it always like this?'

We did a whole thing where the theme was like *2001: A Space Odyssey*. It was amazing. By sheer chance it was the same week that Arthur C. Clarke died and we did it in a different space that no one had ever really been to before.

JG Wilkes Yeah, and we had a friend of ours as well who gets involved in all the production of these things and there was a monolith, lots of video monitors.

JD Twitch And he'd built all these, you know like, Hals, modules of the computer, and they were like all round the club and it was mainly done with projections . . . the music was space-themed and again a surprising number of people came dressed —

JG Wilkes Fuckin' goldfish bowls —

JD Twitch Monkeys.

You must be playing now to people in their 20s and teens. Do you ever think, 'Fuck we're an institution now . . . '?

JD Twitch It's kind of interesting I mean . . .

JG Wilkes Fuck, we're a pair of old spunkers.

JD Twitch I think it bothers us a lot more than it bothers . . . no one ever seems to, like, mention it that comes to the club. Sometimes you're thinking, 'Jeez, we're pretty old.'

JG Wilkes Bona fide old spunkers yeah. We

try and deal with it with as much dignity as possible. What is challenging, I think, is as long as we've done it there's always been a new kind of generation that have come along and fallen in love with it, and the last couple of years it hasn't happened. It's noticeable that the number of people that are coming, it's in decline because I think today's 18-, 19-, 20-year-olds probably aren't into what we do

JD Twitch At the moment I spend my whole life wondering what I'm gonna do next.

Nightclubs are pretty seductive places aren't they? Do you think you've got a reputation for being hedonistic?

JD Twitch I think it's maybe a little bit undeserved . . . I think that's changed over the years. When the club first started, the people that went were incredibly hedonistic. It's a lot less now, I think the current generation is probably less hedonistic.

JG Wilkes Yeah, I think so.

JD Twitch Perhaps that's a good thing actually.

JG Wilkes It was really, really messy at times you know . . .

JD Twitch But nightclubs are. I mean they're hedonistic places, a place where escape is prevalent: anything can happen, anything's possible . . . like you say, they're very, very seductive places, but as far as I know, they're the best fun you can ever have.

Mash-Up

Manchester-born Kevin Cummins has an international reputation as one of the world's leading photographers. His iconic portraits of rock musicians as diverse as Joy Division, The Smiths, Manic Street Preachers and David Bowie have graced magazine covers, galleries and bedroom walls the world over and are included in the collections of the National Portrait Gallery and the V&A among others. Kevin has published three critically acclaimed monographs to date and a fourth: Manchester: Looking for the Light through the Pouring Rain *will be published by Faber and Faber in September 2009. He has lived in London since 1987 but retains strong links with the north-west of Engand.*

In 2008 I travelled to Jamaica to shoot a travel guidebook for Insight Guides.

The brief I gave myself was to eschew the standard brochure imagery and look for street colour. I wanted to find the kind of pictures that would excite me and encourage me to visit the island. I was immediately stuck by the amount of impromptu celebratory wall murals around Kingston. This was a city that many Jamaicans had warned me of, telling me that it would be too dangerous for a white man to visit. More specifically, a white man toting a bag of obviously expensive camera equipment.

That wasn't my experience. Once the Jamaicans I spoke to knew what I was doing they went out of their way to help me. One person took me to the outskirts of Kingston to show me some of the murals on these pages. Well, he sat in my rental car drinking my Red Stripe while I drove him there.

I tried to imagine how it must feel to be so excited by Sean Paul's new album that you immediately went out with a couple of tins of Dulux and painted a massive picture of him on the side of your house. If only that happened in Manchester; it would have cast off its reputation as Engels' 'Hell upon Earth' much earlier. Unless that is, you were similarly excited by the new waxing from Simply Red or something.

I love the simplicity of many of the paintings. There's an innocent exuberance about them. Especially in the not quite fully developed picture of Marcus Garvey.

It was difficult to find a street without at least one painting of Bob Marley. But I hadn't realised that Beenie Man was similarly revered. My favourite murals were the paintings of Jamaican sporting heroes, but you'll have to buy the guidebook to see those. Or better still: visit Kingston and discover them yourself.

Big up uno dem.

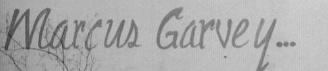

Marcus Garvey... king Selassie I

SEAN PAUL

SPICE

JAMES YORKSTON
Perfect Button Drumming

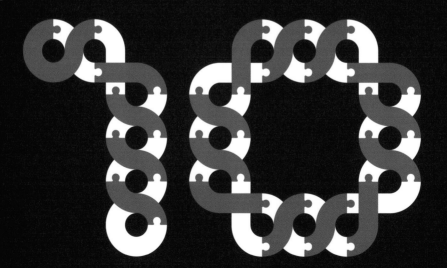

I find myself in a small bar in the port of Rosslare, Ireland. I have a show with the band up in Dún Laoghaire the next day and have come over via Pembroke from Cardiff, where I'd had a solo show – I thought it may be romantic to take the ferry and avoid the stress of flying. The barmaid is telling me how she hates it here, how the constant influx of tourists and travellers using the port makes for messy evenings and obnoxious customers. She tells me she used to run a bar in Kerry, but moved over here for the money, was going to see out her contract and hot-foot it back home. There's a table of guys acting like monkeys, literally, in the corner. Idiot-dancing on the tables, grunting, the lot. Hmm. One of the guys comes over and starts talking to me in an ambiguous English accent – asking what I'm doing here and such. I lie, of course, telling him I'm on my way to Cork where I've taken a job. He asks why I've come from Scotland via Wales, the long way – to avoid drunk Englishmen, I reply, with much whisky bravado and little wit. His accent changes to thick Welsh and he offers me a drink, looking a bit embarrassed about his jovial chums as they sing some song about a *Maid Called Mary-Jane*. He seems OK, actually. Just a guy on his way somewhere – We've just had Bill's stag weekend, he tells me, pointing him out. Ah. Good old Bill. I wonder who's marrying Bill, currently displaying himself as the oxen slumped at the back, wearing a stained Irish rugby shirt and fake orange ears. Good luck to them both though, I say. I decline my Welsh pal's drink and leave the bar, looking for some food. There's a nasty-looking pizza place I walk straight past but find myself returning to twenty minutes later, having walked around Rosslare getting colder and colder in the November wind and found nowhere else open. No cheese? I ask, and wait outside. It's around 11 p.m., I guess, and the massive ferry I disembarked from is around 100 yards in front of me, lights ablaze and filthy white, looking like floating polystyrene Christmas debris, its oil trail rainbowing slightly under the port-illuminating flood lights. The smell here is sea and diesel and the noises mostly industrial – cranes loading stock, guys shouting in the distance, unidentified bangs and clangs, lorries and coaches passing. There's a group of lads walking around and as I wait outside the pizza shop one of them breaks ranks, approaches and fires a football directly at my head. It misses and rolls down the slope towards the dock. 'Ah ye feckin eejit, you should have stopped it,' says the guy, now chasing after the ball, his pals laughing at him. I return to my food, gather things up and head off to my B&B. As I struggle to get the key into the door, the landlady appears and says, 'You can't eat that in here.' 'Oh,' I reply. 'No,' she says. So I sit on her front garden wall and eat the stale dough and wrinkled veg on a tomato-sauce-coloured pizza. I can hear her watching *The Generation Game* on TV through the window. It starts to drizzle.

Next day, I slowly make my way up the coast to Dún Laoghaire. The train carriage is old. Retired rolling stock from the UK, I guess, patronisingly. My seat is shiny from compressed chewing gum, I have a migraine and am reading a Grassic Gibbon compendium when I should be attempting to write something. Sitting opposite me is an old lady, sooking her teeth. I put on some headphones, close me eyes and try to sleep.

When we arrive, I make my way to the B&B, around two miles out of town on the main road. 'Ah there's only one of you, but I've beds for five reserved.' 'Ah don't you worry, the other guys are coming later on,' I say. 'We'll be fairly late – is that OK?' 'Ah yes, that's fine.' Good. All sorted. I order a cab and make my way into town.

The guys have arrived and are setting things up. After sound check, we sit around in the bar and catch up. There's no news. Nothing has happened. 'How was Cardiff?' they ask – I'd forgotten all about it. Hmm. It was OK. I got into a bit of stick for mentioning I liked their bridge. Apparently it's an English bridge and the tolls go to

Westminster, so it's not to be spoken of. Ah. We sit around and flick matches at each other, watching a Manchester United match that's being shown live on the TV. The sound is down and the puggy machine and the guy playing it are providing the commentary. 'Ah fuck,' he says, repeatedly, while the puggy zips away, out-foxing him.

⌘

That evening, I'm watching the first band and the bar is full. The girl at the back of the stage is playing a long low whistle, her fingers hardly reaching the holes and the occasional bird squawks emerging further evidence of her unease. The crowd clap along merrily, mostly out-sized, out-of-season Germans, delighted to be experiencing this authentic Irish ram-jam. The whistle player looks around 12, but she's not the youngest. Beside her is a wee brother, around 10, playing a very quiet bodhran and beside him a tiny wee lassie of around 8 who's scraping away on a fiddle. Their three elder 'siblings' seem to be taking the musical strain, with guitar, tenor banjo and a bonnie lass on fiddle. At the side of the stage a largely unkempt larger lady is surveying her brood with a mixture of pride and veiled threats. Certainly, the children don't look happy – I imagine they'd rather be listening to Elvis than falling their way through indeterminable jigs and reels. Still, grey Ma-Ma, with her off-white jerkin and straggled hair, divides her gaze equally between her offspring and the braying, applauding, loose-mouthed crowd.

I sit at the back with one of the band. I know the venue reasonably well, having passed through here many a time in my youth and am enjoying the whole spectacle. I admire the talent in the elder fiddle player and wryly smile at the missed notes, slipped beats and resigned scowls on the rest of them. I keep getting jostled by an elderly Irish gent with a thick grease on his black hair and a big gap between his buck teeth, who's grinning as though he's just discovered Planxty playing in his back tavern. Hmm. 'Very good,' he says – very good indeed – and he claps along wayfully woefully out of time – 'They'll grow up to be something special,' he nods. I disagree. No, I reckon they'll flee the coop as soon as possible and leave the bodhrans languishing in a cupboard somewhere, or perhaps a pawn shop, alongside the 1990s beat boxes and £79 Fender-esque Stratocasters. I wish I'd been bought up in a musical family like this, that way I may have rebelled and found myself quite happily working in a bank. Instead, I find myself waiting for the Irish Family Robinson to finish their set so I can get on stage and woe the crowd into submission with my tall tales of what never actually happened.

They do encore after encore and I eye my watch happily – this place has an eleven curfew and it's fast approaching ten now. If I'm lucky, I'll get away with playing for less than an hour, then I can retreat to the bar again, if we get a lock-in. Over in the corner I see our accordion player, Reuben, slapping his thighs and laughing like a daftie as the elder violin executioner slides on a slip jig and falls off her seat, bringing the crowd to a rapturous applause. They decide to end the set there. Ah well, time to go to work. I walk over and congratulate them all on their fantastic musicianship – the look of resigned fatigue in their eyes matches mine almost completely and I wonder just how far they've

already come to be feeling so bullet-holed by the whole music thing.

The bar is rapidly emptying, much to my pleasure and dismay. I had hoped, somehow, that all these tourists were actually here to see me and the band, but, of course, no. They were drawn in by the fish restaurant next door and the real live Paddy family entertaining in the snug. I ask for another whisky and wait until the stage is cleared, then we move on. Our bass player is standing by the side, ready, with a bottle of wine all done and another just opened. I untangle my inexpensive bag of leads and set up, turning around to see – ooh, perhaps two or three dozen folk who may be actually here to hear us and around half a dozen straggling German tourists, resplendent in bright yellow waterproofs and thick-rimmed glasses. I imagine they think we are a traditional Irish band. After all, guitar, double bass and accordion – we could be.

They leave halfway through the first minute, waving as they go, politely. I don't blame them. The rest of the bar is quiet though, listening, which is a good sign. We do a medley of five songs – it's a way of battering a crowd into submission, so even if they hate you, they're so pleased you've finally finished they can't help but applaud. I think we get added points for endurance, also. Happily, it seems to go down well and my mood lifts slightly. Halfway through the next track, I look at Reuben and he's grinning wildly and lifting his big old boots up and down in an approximation of the timing of the song. I think – I'll have to ask him to stop wearing those boots, they're extenuating his personal rhythm choices – but then I realise it's maybe me out of time, as Doogie starts thumping the strings on his double bass aggressively as if to say, 'Aye and mind that we're onstage with you Jamesie and dinnae just go off playing mental,' so I bought it into place again. A good show though. We had a few requests – including 'False True Love' which we merged into 'I Feel Love', such is our outlandish humour. By 11 p.m. it became apparent that there wasn't a curfew as such and things were just expected to roll on. I was talking nonsense on stage again – the story about my dog eating a rat whole, comparing Doogie to Alison Moyet, the usual drivel. A few of the Germans had come back in and were clapping along merrily. It was fun.

The owner bought out his pipe, despite the smoking ban, and that starts it off. Soon everyone was reaching into their top pockets and the whole venue became the lum that I remembered from my youth. Doogs decided this meant he could have a long cigarette, so he rolled one up on the shoulder of the bass while I told a story about the time I worked in Butlins and had to cover up the pool with tarpaulin – to hide the elephant that had slipped, cracked its head on the side and drowned. A dead elephant is a big beast, even in a swimming pool – perhaps more so, due to the amplified visuals – magnified visuals, I should say – that come with the rippling of the water. We were waiting until the end of the season before it could be removed. Until then, we just kept on pumping it full of chlorine, trying to keep the smell from escaping. I had a whisky, bought for me by some kind Irish lady, who despite, or perhaps because of, my protestations, got me some Irish whisky – which I cannot stand. Still, it was a gesture which I appreciated. There's no gig finer than one with waitress-service whisky. There's no gig finer than when you're in danger of falling off the back of your seat with laughter at some eejit from the crowd who's taken it upon himself to stand up and sing 'Bright Eyes', 'Burning Like Fire' or whatever it was, lifting his shirt to show his flubby tummy and being brought back to earth with a bump as his slightly more sober pals grip on to his chalk white, inky T-shirt and pull him down with a 'Sit Down Ye Big Tit'. 'Play some Pogues?' I know no Pogues, though I do know how to end the set with a song about Jesus himself coming out of the ground and striking a farmer down for ploughing on Christmas Day, so we choose that path.

Packing up, I see it's twenty past midnight, which is a fine long set we've played. The audience actually grew in size, although it could just be they doubled through my cheap-joke slurring vision. We sit around a table and talk nonsense. I cannot think after a show like that. I guess a different part of my brain is used to dredge out lyrics of songs I haven't sung in years and that, in combination with the liquor, causes a slight delay in reverting back to the conversational. The owner of the bar seems happy as an egg and delivers our fee gleefully. I ask our merch/driver guy Dave how we've done and he replies, 'Aye no' bad Jamesie, three T-shirts, a dozen CDs and that jug you stole from the Holiday Inn.' We pack up, call a lang cab and get driven to the local B&B. It's well by 2 a.m. when we arrive and the auld wifey seems a bit shocked, but I explained to her – remember I explained we were going to be really late? Well, it's just as I explained – we're really late. She seemed happy. I guess it all made sense to her. I got into my room and threw my guitar on one of the twin beds.

The shower-room was tiny and had little packets of heavily scented soap as decoration. There was a sign above the shower saying 'No Smoking In The Bath'.

⌘

Next gig was in Belfast. Always pretty happy to be playing up there. My first Belfast show was supporting John Martyn. That tour had been going pretty terribly for me – I was a reasonably cack-handed guitarist at that stage and my songs were fairly unformed – of course, not much has changed, etc., etc. However, by the time we got to Ireland, I'd somehow managed to get a wee bit better. I guess just being on stage night after night somehow polished things up. Same bad guitar playing, same awkward songs, just . . . I guess they were shinier. Better realised. Anyhow, the first thing I heard when walking onstage in Belfast was somebody shouting, 'Is he drunk yet?' – referring to John Martyn, of course. It was a nice welcome. A fun 'ach, we're not too serious and we don't really give a fuck' welcome. Later that set I attempted a traditional tune, that I introduced with: 'This is an Irish folk song.' 'We'll be the judge of that,' came the reply. Ha.

So, we're in the upstairs of an old pub just off the Dublin Road. This, I feel, is most definitely the pub circuit that people talk about. Standing in the corner there's an old-looking guy, dressed in crow black, eyeing us nervously. I recognise him as being an American singer I'd played with once in London. Hey Adam, I say, How are things? What brings you here? – he looks a little shocked – it's Adrian, he says, and I'm here playing this evening with you. He's not the guy I thought at all. Ah right, I say. He must be a local support. He asks me how I've been and I look at him again thinking, maybe I do know him. I say, fine thanks, and go looking for a bag or some other kind of distraction. The promoter walks in and I ask him what the score is with this fellow and he says, 'Ah yes, he lent you a guitar once in Dublin, says he knows you and is doing the whole tour with you.' My memory is a little blocked these days, I have no way of remembering the number of people you meet on the road. So, I ask him, 'So, you're doing all the shows?' He says, 'Aye.' So, I say, 'So – are you driving?' And he replies, 'No, I'm with you, has this not all been sorted out?' It hasn't. It has not.

It becomes a three-band bill. I introduce Adrian to Kenny, who's playing the main support. They get on pretty well and we have a big enough van, so there are no problems. Welcome onboard.

During the gig, an eejit stands in front of me and says, 'Play the laarng tune play the laarng tune,' over and over, like a stupid broken nodding dog. It throws me a little, usually I'm used to people asking for requests, but his insistence is dull.

We play it. It goes down well. We leave the stage. He tries to speak to me and I shut the dressing room door in his face, like a real pro. Next time I'm in town his mate will say, 'Fancy going to see JY?' And he will reply, 'No, that guy can suck my sack.'

After the show, I go to the cocktail bar over the road from the hotel with Dave and bluff our way past the security, despite the fact I look like an old old man alongside the already instilled clientele. The music they're playing is horrible chart techno and we can hardly hear ourselves talk. It seems to be a young, rich man's bar, with thin football players in black-tie outfits and their long blond partners. I'm dressed in the classic old, well toured shirt and scaffy breeks combo and our Dave looks as though he's been off camping somewhere muddy. The waiter hands us a cocktail menu and scoffs off.

Next morning, we get in the van and drive off, heading to Galway. Galway is a place I've always been fond of, simply through repetition and recognition. I'm sitting up front beside Dave, in a bit of a dwam. We're listening to 'The Black Saint and the Sinner Lady' and talking nonsense, when roadworks approach. Before I know it we've slowed to 10 and Dave looks at me as if to say, 'Eh?' All around the van there are workmen shouting at us and throwing plastic cups. Dave is a fool. Dave has driven us into the workman's area beside the motorway. We laugh a bit and I point wildly in the air, as if we're chasing an eagle. The paper cups stop and the momentous distraction proves long enough for us to regain our place on the motorway, just behind an old lorry full of black smoke that it politely coughs out every few hundred yards. We stop at a garage on the border and I buy some horrible thick painted bronze sunglasses, plus some handwoven slippers and a blue and yellow tea-cosy-style hat. There are sandwiches for sale that I could never consider eating, even in the event of fire.

Before we reach Galway we stop at an old abbey, which has long since gone to ruin. We get out of the van and trek away in different directions, each as eager as the other to put some distance between ourselves. I meet Doogie in the turret, smoking a rolled up cigarette, he's staring into the distance and lifting himself up and down using his toes. I

think – if he jumps off, this will become an entirely different trip. I was here once before when I was supporting some bigwig. One of the bigwig's band members followed me into an abandoned room and tried to turn me against the rest of the band. The trumpeter was a drunk. The bass player was false. The drummer was a fat lazy fuck. The driver was a shitter. I was bored then and wanting to go home. This time, it seemed like an entirely different place. I stood at the side and watched this massive bull watching me, chewing it's cud and breathing noisily. It had angry black eyes but didn't seem to pose much of a threat. Bulls are bulls. When I was a child I got chased across a field by a bull when I was picking blackberries, I only just made it to the gate, the rest of my family laughing merrily. I guess, the bull wasn't that close – in fact, it may not have even been a bull – it could have been an angry cow. Later, when I was in my teens, I ended up herding Highland cattle on one of the Fife farms. They're not so brave, I thought. Just big, and angry from the flies.

The Galway show was a disaster. The venue had changed from a nice sit-down place – where you could place your drink on somebody's table while you played and just keep going on – into an anonymous black hole, the same as you'd find in any city anywhere around the world. The stage was 5 feet off the ground so the crowd had to wrench their necks up if they fancied seeing you play. Unless they watched your knees. Afterwards, we go drinking and drinking, to the upstairs of the venue, which has changed into a disco and is full of youngsters, running around drinking watery lager. Pretty soon we're all dispersed and I find myself with a couple of American singers who happened to be along. We have a time. As much as I drink I can never escape whatever it is that makes me drink. The best I can do is hide from it for a few hours. The problem is, I enjoy the taste of alcohol too much. Not the beer, not the whisky, the actual alcohol. I think we all do. If there was only Good in the world, alcohol wouldn't be a problem – we could use it to clean our tape heads and fuel our moon buggies – but, the Evil comes along and makes it oh so easy to swim in. Happiness comes with forgetfulness. At around 4 a.m. I'm walking around Galway harbour, listening to the sound of parties in distant houses and staring at the slowly rippling black water. I'm thinking about the Arran Islands and J. M. Synge, I'd love to make it over there one day. Although I know it'll be the same as Sherkin Island and Cape Clear – islands off West Cork I knew well in my childhood – pleasant tourist boat rides and days out. I've lived in tourist towns all my life – St Andrews, Edinburgh, now the East Neuk – they're lovely places all and I don't begrudge the attraction that brought me there appearing to others. As if the Arran Islands would have any of Synge's words left in them anyhow – they'd be long gone, slipped into the sea. Hmm. I remember as a teenager, visiting Cape Clear, I hitched a ride on a tractor when I was trying to get from one of the castles – the Castle of Gold maybe – back to the harbour, for the ferry home to Baltimore. I got on the old potato cart at the back and was shaken to buggery by the roads. After a few minutes I discovered to my horror that I had appeared to have wet myself – my crotch was soaked through – I guessed the furious shaking of the journey had somehow caused me to lose control. The tractor stopped at the school

and I got off and walked, ashen-faced, but smiling, not wanting to draw attention to my dilemma. Then, in my pocket, I discovered a can of Coke that had overturned on the journey and emptied itself on to me. I was pleased that I was still capable of bladder control, but disappointed to find that Coke never really dries – it just gets sticky and gloopy and attracts wasps. I had an uncomfortable ride on the tiny ferry, the *Miss Josephine*, back to Baltimore.

At 5 a.m. I climb on to a Japanese trawler that's anchored at the harbour. I find a seat and bob up and down merrily for an hour or so, watching the sun come up. It's a happy time and I feel very content. A Japanese man appears at a hatch and tells me to fuck off, so I stand up, walk off the gangplank on to the harbour and fuck off, back to bed.

⌘

No surprise to anyone, I wake up feeling pretty rough. We have a drive down to Limerick. We drive through a small town and stop off for a short break. I find a small bookshop and walk in. It seems fairly well stocked and I'm having an interesting browse, when, to my horror, the man behind the counter starts to talk to me. I hate this, more than anything. The last thing I want to do in a shop is talk to someone. Especially a bookshop – maybe if I was in a fridge shop it'd be OK. I turn around and it's a young guy. He looks Belgian, if that's possible. He has thick black hair, beard and rimmed glasses combo. Is that Belgian? He looks Belgian. He's not though, he's American, or perhaps Canadian. I bluster something out about W. G. Sebald and his eyes light up – however, very quickly he makes it clear that Sebald is HIS author

RECORDS   AND   PEOPLE

monorail music

12 KING'S COURT, KING STREET, GLASGOW G1 5RB
0141 552 9458 WWW.MONORAILMUSIC.COM

and he needs to examine what rights I have to be talking of him. He reels off the names of all Sebald's work, paying special attention to very tiny details and asking me about them. I'm lost in a hungover dwam and finding him hard to follow. I don't like this man. When he gets to the end of his list of obscure facts he asks, 'So, what is it you're actually looking for by Sebald?' – as if to say – 'Don't tell me you haven't read everything already?' I make something up – that photo book he did in collaboration with the German lady, I say – where she contributed the pictures and he wrote short stories around them. There's a grain of truth in the story, as he did put out a terrible book of awful poetry alongside unforgivably bad images. The shop man stands up and starts to shout – and I mean shout – I'm wrong, he says, there's no such book, waving his arms around as though there's a wasp flying in his face. The book man's quite wee – about 5 foot 4″ – apologies if you're wee like him, I don't mean it in a nasty way, but he seemed to forget he was wee and what's more, he had a problem with it. He wasn't as powerful as when he was sitting down. I tell him the book was from an independent publisher, whose name I couldn't remember. Fuck this, I think and walk out quickly. His face has gone red. There was a good-looking book by Benedict Kiely there and I wish I'd braved the guy out, but really – stuff him. If he's reading this, aye yer a wee black-haired mothball of a man so ye are.

I go into the bar next door and have a BBC – a double Bacardi and Coke. More Coke. I don't spill this one. I was introduced to the joys of the BBC a few years ago and it's my one nod to alcopop land. I leave and get back in the van.

⌘

I'm resigned to the fact that I always seem to love the morose and dead pan – those authors who you just know are so well aware of their own mortality that everything else – life and its living – seems pointless. Brautigan and W. G. Sebald, Bukowski, also. I always connect his writing to Ivor Cutler, strangely enough – something about how unconcerned they both seem to be about their writing fitting in with what's around them – although I find Bukowski got less interesting as he got older, or maybe it was as I got older, whereas with Ivor Cutler it was the opposite. Sebald though was an absolute gem. Sadly I've only managed to keep one of his books back unread – so, one day, I know I can take it from the shelf and start. It's like that lottery ticket my pal Tom UNPOC buys once every six months but never checks to see if it's won – until the last day before it expires – keeping it's potential value intact. Similarly with music, I've never even attempted to listen to Neil Young – every-thing I hear is pretty good – I know that one day, I'll be able to sit down and delve into this amazing back catalogue. Until then though...But the new musicians – some-times I feel so much guilt when I find I absolutely love a fresh band or a hot young singer, as it means, nine times out of ten, that nobody else will. That's good taste for you. The other side of the coin is – Ah, James, you have to hear this new guy, his name is Felix Maboabbie and he's better than Nick Drake and John Martyn combined – with a touch of John Lennon. And you know what, they are always, always utterly shite. Frequently, they sound like an Oasis tribute band, or like a photocopy of Drake–Martyn–

Lennon – there's one song in a *Pink Moon* style, one in a *Grace and Danger* and one in a Lennon. I prefer Jack Lemmon and that's no flippant comment – well, maybe it is actually, but I do prefer Jack Lemmon. I'll always watch him. He had such a good face. John Lennon and the Beatles – of course, they're the greatest band in the world ever, but they only have about three songs that actually excite me and make me want to listen more than once. Which ones? 'Walrus', 'Sir Walter Raleigh', 'She's So Heavy'. There's probably a couple more, also. The thing I do actually like about them is Ringo's perfect button drumming, which is the very thing you're not supposed to like. Hmm. It causes a bit of grief, not bowing at their altar, but that's fair enough. I've never got Fleetwood Mac either, but people seem less concerned about that.

⌘

We arrive in Limerick and the venue looks tiny. Back room of a pub, I imagine. And when we get into the room it is just that, except the back room seems to hold around 1,000 people. I think, in my naivety, gosh, we must be really big in Limerick. We're not. Twelve people turn up. They're a nice twelve people, though, and we have fun. After the gig we watch a boxing match, a big white guy fighting a big black guy. One of them is British, but to be honest I don't really give a fuck for supporting either so I sit at the bar and talk to the barman. He's another wee guy, slightly smaller than the bookshop's wee man. The barman's trying to hide his height by wearing heels and a bouffant quiff. He manages reasonably well. We talk about Seamus Ennis and that crazy concertina shop in Cleckheaton that resembles the Tardis. Every now and then the whole bar erupts with a yyyeeerrssss or an ooopppphhhh. Ugh. He tells me that he has a plan to beat the smoking ban – he's going to open a pub on a barge. He tells me that he plays a bit of guitar but nothing really. I feign interest and he disappears for a while before returning with a cassette (!) of his playing, with a bar mat for a cover. It's pretty odd, but he looks serious as he hands it over, so I take it and thank him. A week or so later, when I eventually get home, I put it on. It'll be a cross between Dick Gaughan and Joseph Spence, but ultimately it's the way he slides between notes that gets me – sort of like a pedal steel player, but obviously not. It's really amazing. Raw recording, peaking on the meters, distorting randomly. Mostly Irish traditional tunes, that I can pick out anyway. On the cassette, the only name written is BOAG, but I have no idea what that means... Listening to it, I feel my music is such a huge horrific falsehood, as it should just be guitar and voice, but it's collapsed all around by cornets and drumbeats. I feel guilty that I haven't the guts to release such an unadorned album, yet alone hand it out to complete strangers in bars. Good luck to him. I leave the pub and walk around looking for some food or a nice bar or anything really. Limerick used to get called Stab City when I spent time in Cork, so I still have this hangover fear that I'll be jumped by some bozos in Pringles, but nothing happens. I find a small quiet bar called O'Driscoll's and settle down for the remainder of the evening. No one tries to talk with me and there's no television.

⌘

Early next morning I take the bus over to Tralee. I have no romantic associations with Tralee, I never enjoyed the terrible horrible programme when it came on and I have no reason for going other than to see an old friend who has set up a bar there. The journey takes forever and the bus is cold, sheltering us from a thin rain. Opposite me there's an old man with a thick black wool coat, bald head and wispy white beard, carrying a set of pipes. He looks pretty derelict. My guitar's in the van so there's no reason for him to see me as a fellow musician, but he still stares over at me occasionally. I worry if he's the ghost of Willie Loman coming back to haunt me; showing me who I'll be in twenty years' time if I don't get it together and write some pop songs or, better still, give up completely. We get talking and it seems he's from Cobh. We talk about living near the water and I tell him I'm a musician – I knew rightaway – he said – you spotted the pipes and you dress like you've never worked a day with your eejit earrings and baldy head ah ha ha. He cackles away, but I'm in a light mood and we get on extremely well. He's off to play at somebody's wedding. They like him to dress like an old one, he says. It brings good luck. I don't believe him for a second – his jacket is his jacket, same as mine, there's no cabaret here. We have pipers also at weddings in Scotland, I tell him – and we all get spoken to in a language hardly anyone understands, at least in the central belt. It's all nonsense I say, this grumpy Scots piper welcomes in the congregation, then any conversation is drowned out by a CD playing yon Willie Stewart wifey. Aye, she's no' welcome here, I can tell you. Tralee arrives and we go our separate ways. I take a photo of him and shake his yellow hand. The photo doesn't come out – I don't think this is because he's a ghost. More likely because the sun was at an awkward angle.

I take out my phone and call my buddy Pete. He's in and I'm thirsty so I head straight over. The taxi takes around 90 seconds and I feel a complete fool. The driver no doubt feels the same. I walk into the pub and Pete's there, behind the bar, playing a Steven Jesse Bernstein CD over the tannoy. We shake hands grinning and exchange small talk, there's not much going on he reckons. It's cold. November is a cold time. I ask him if he's settling in to Irish life and he just smiles and looks out of the window. 'Aye James there's cocks and asses here just the same as in Edinburgh.' It sounds slightly ominous, so I raise an eyebrow and ask where I should put my jacket. He has to go out, so I sit in the corner and sip at a peppermint tea. After a while a wave of sleep hits me and I'm dozing, the side of my head cold against the window, listening to the rain's slight taps on the window.

I decide to stay the night – I can get a bus to Cork tomorrow, I'm told. That's me sold. I had a B&B booked in Mallow, but that's not a place I knew and had no desire to take another bus journey that day. Mallow will have to wait. I take a taxi out to a vegetarian restaurant I'd heard of, but it's closed, so I sit in the cab all the way back, feeling pretty stupid again. The driver is silent and as I get out finally, I ask him what's wrong – he replies that his wife is dying of cancer and that she's only a few months left and there's nothing he can do.

I see Pete again in his bar and get a drink straightaway, before finding some food. I wish I could have said something to the driver that would make a difference, but my big mouth slammed shut. I wish I could have said something meaningful about God or somesuch, but . . . All I did was tip him and ask for a receipt. What a clown.

Pete has some live music on later – I'm half expecting the piper guy from the bus, but it's not, it's a young trio, playing concertinas. The bar slowly fills and by 8 p.m. it's awkward just standing up. I find a place by the wall. Good old place by the wall, eh? I am squashed into submission by two middle-aged ladies and a middle-aged gent with a hawky nose. One of the players is his son, it seems. He's very friendly though and, noticing I'm by myself, maybe, begins to talk away. He mentions that he's a successful businessman and he's spent his whole life in a very starched environment, in nice suits and crocodile shoes, first-class lounges and sushi restaurants. He tells me it took him a long time to accept that his son wanted to be a musician, what with his pierced ears and wolf T-shirt. I begin to realise what a mess I must look to him, with my creased shirt and baggy jumper and lazily uncut hair and token beard and scaffy £6 shoes and and and. 'Still,' he says – I'm loosening up now – 'you'll never guess what I did the other day?' 'I have no idea,' I reply, thinking maybe he got a tattoo or his nipple pierced – but no: 'I bought a pair of open-toe sandals' – then he nods at me wide-eyed, as if to say, 'No, really, it's true, believe it or not,' and sups away at his stout. His son starts to play and he's really good. He's slipping between the notes and the rhythm like a good uilleann piper – in fact, it reminds me of Willie

Clancy, without the oddly out-of-tune incidentals. Maybe I could join in and play those bits. I'm transfixed and utterly happy, despite the shelf on the wall cutting into my ribs and the perfume from the wifey beside me making my drink taste like a lavender toilet freshener. I make my way to the bar and find a slot between the peanut dispenser and an old guy called Jack who's wearing long false teeth that don't fit so well. He spits quite often during conversation, so I try and keep chatter to a minimum. He tells me he keeps greyhounds that he was left in his brother's will and I was welcome to one if I pleased. I wonder if they are his brother's teeth. In fact, I know they are. You, sir, are wearing your brother's teeth and what's more they don't fit. It's a fine night. Around midnight it all closes down and everyone leaves bar me and Pete. We have a whisky and he asks me about the Edinburgh Festival. I don't miss it, he says. Not at all.

⌘

Next morning I have to get the bus to Cork, which only takes four hours or so. Ugh. I take some painkillers and shut down, uneventfully, until we arrive in Cork. Rainy old Cork. I walk over the bridge and up the hill to the venue. The band haven't arrived so I sit in the corner merrily, reading *The Speak of the Mearns*. I love touring in winter, something about the weather making even the grottiest of hotels seem warm and inviting. Something about people being happy merely to be inside, so that's half the job done. The band arrive and we exchange greetings. They had a nice day off, spent half climbing up and down a hill in the rain and half drying off in a pub. They tell me a story about a ball of wasps they found at the top of the hill – or mountain, as it has become. Apparently there was a swarm, all fighting to get to the queen, I imagine. It seems a little out of season to me, but there you go – also – I should point out – I know nothing about wasps. I remember one time our bass player bought a duck for cooking, but left it in a cupboard of the B&B we were staying in by mistake. I got a bill through the post a month or so later – apparently the duck's fats had begun to drain and it had stained the downstairs ceiling. They sent me a photo as proof, but I didn't pay the bill – I figured – maybe, just maybe, they should clean the cupboards once in a while.

The promoter appears and I ask him what's what. Good news, he says, we've had over 120 tickets go. That's pretty good, I think. How much were the tickets, I ask? Ah, they're free – it's part of the Jazz Festival. Ah. Hmm. Who else is playing? It's just you and your fine buddies, grand.

And the Cork audience is good, once more. I like audiences with a bit of life to them – some heckles and requests and whoops and whisky and stories and anything really. Gifts. Cards. Best gifts I've been given have been sketches and pictures folk have drawn during the gig and handed over. I've also had Marmite, books, Christmas cakes, a jumper, once (I think they'd found it on the floor outside the venue – our driver Dave took it and used it to wipe the windscreen), all sorts. Worst thing is bad CDs of acoustic Oasis covers. That's a bad present, no thank you very much. We got some mugs once, in France somewhere, and some socks in Stockholm. The socks were a treat. Any clean clothes on tour are a treat. Mugs are also handy. I did a show once in Stockholm where the airline lost my luggage and to make matters worse, I was given a really nice bottle of Hembränt by the promoters. I wasn't allowed to carry it on the plane back, and as I had no luggage, I had no way of storing it, so I left it with the happy-looking moustached customs man. No presents in Cork though, but a lively audience. Play 'St Patrick's Day' – I have a song, 'St Patrick', that is *so* slow and without chorus, but the title – or at least I guess it's the title – always causes folk to call out for it – even though they always get the title wrong – 'Play "St Patrick's Song/St Patrick's Day"' – so, we do. It's long and without chorus, but there's a melancholy in the air and it sits just right. A good show. I laugh all the way through at some drunken women who are dancing and chatting noisily. They must be so drunk to dance to this, I think, they'd be happy dancing to a wasp.

Afterwards we decamp to a local bar where we meet up with some local legends, who are only too keen to talk and drink. They all look like middle-aged bookkeepers, I think, before realising the look is familiar. We talk about hurley, the game, and Michael Hurley, the singer. I've played a few shows with Michael Hurley here and there and am a huge fan of his music – he's one of these artists that seems to have released at least half a dozen genuinely great albums (and at least half a dozen not so great) yet he plays in venues smaller than my own (!) and to fewer people – in the UK at least. When I do a show in Nottingham, say, or anywhere where there's a dribble of punters rather than the long-hoped river, I always think of Michael Hurley. I stand on stage thinking, 'It's no bloody surprise there's no one here, you love Michael Hurley's music and there's no one at his gigs, maybe you should model yourself on someone more popular, like Jack Vettriano' – but then, when I sit down to write some new songs, as soon as a chorus pops up I feel ill and knock it back down again. I guess you have to live with yourself. Plus, Jack Vettriano – come on! I blurt out something about my childhood summers in West Cork and we're off talking about Leap and Clonakilty and all sorts. It was a different country then, I say, patronisingly, all B-roads and nuns, fucked old cars and Poitín blind tramps. Or maybe I have a selective memory. Fair credit to them, they keep talking and don't ignore me for the overbearing drunk American tourist I remind myself of. The evening finishes very

quietly, a last orders and an orderly queue to leave. Not quite the lock-in I was hoping for, but it was a school night and my companions turned out to be schoolteachers. Outside, it had turned wet and windy. A horrible wet, that ran down my coat on to the thigh of my trousers, where it seeped in instantly and jagged like a hard cold piece of cardboard insistently into my legs. Hmm. The band had disappeared, so I walked down the hill, over the bridge and towards the railway station. The bridge – ugh! – with the wind. This is shit, I think to myself. Tomorrow we go home, home will be good. A taxi arrives, going the wrong way. I hail it and get in before barking out directions. We're going the wrong way, said the driver. Yes, said I.

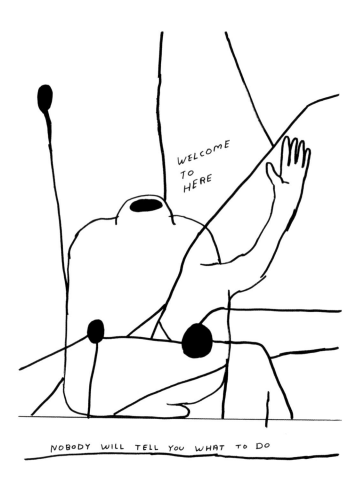

WELCOME TO HERE

NOBODY WILL TELL YOU WHAT TO DO

James Yorkston

Switched-On

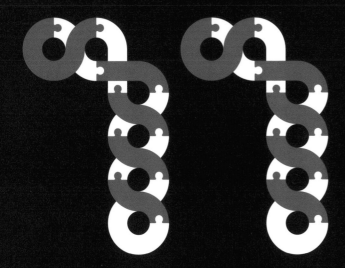

BUCHLA 100 (1963)

EMS VCS3 (1969)

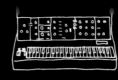

MINI MOOG (1970)

ARP 2600 (1976)

TASCAM
PORTASTUDIO (1979)

ROLAND TR-808 (1981)

ROLAND TB-303 (1982)

ROLAND SH-101 (1983)

RZWEIL K250 (1984)

YAMAHA DX-100 (1984)

AKAI S900 (1986)

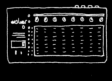

YAMAHA TX -812 (1987)

AKAI MPC 60 (1988)

CUBASE ON AN ATARI ST (1987)

PRO TOOLS ON A MAC (1991)

DS1 EVOLVER (2002)

ELEKTRON
MONOMACHINE (2004)

FUTURE
RETRO REVOLUTION (2004)

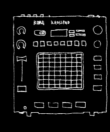

KORG KAOSS PAD (2006)

NOVATION
REMOTE ZeRO SL (2006)

Switched-On

Given the phenomenal amount of writing on music it is strange that any writing on the technical aspects of its creation is confined to an inner circle of musicians. Is the production of music really such a difficult thing to comprehend? Can it truly be such a boring subject? Given how the evolution of electronic music in particular is practically dictated by the form and function of these tools, it's yet more peculiar that, beyond a smattering of buzzwords, critics have been unable to talk about it with more than a fraction of the attention that they invest in describing its abstract qualities, discussing its relationship to contemporaneous philosophical currents or plotting its sociocultural context. Given the commercial audience's progressive disenchantment with electronic music over the past decade, it seems the moment is ripe for a dispassionate critical engagement with its production practices. To do this is to undertake a task similar to that practised by the artist David Hockney in his 'Secret Knowledge' project in which, with unadorned northern charm, he illuminatingly described how Florentine and Flemish Masters used mirrors and lenses to paint their pictures.

Halcyon Days

Since 2000 we have witnessed a dissipation of the elemental power of electronic music. A unique synergy led the '90s to be a golden era for the form. We experienced a confluence of technological, pharmacological and social factors that saw the avant-garde strains of '80s popular music (electro and synth-pop) blossom into a rainbow of musical variety. Recognisably new forms of music seemed to arrive by the week as we plunged headfirst into booming possibilities. The sheer quantity of releases within a genre such as hardcore jungle between 1991 and 1993 attests to the rabid explosion of interest in what had previously tended to be a fringe music. People's emotional investment in their particular scenes was so great that it is hard to fathom the intensity of feeling in the drear light of 2009. This pulsating force of energy still emanates from the grooves of those old records with their almost simplistic power. However, it was more than simply a case of music being the vessel of this energy, the means of production were in a sense 'right', and better suited to channel that energy than the sterile compositional environments of today.

Romplers

It is interesting to reflect that this tidal wave of seemingly futuristic music, originating in Detroit and Chicago, was in fact impelled by profoundly retrograde tendencies. Towards the end of the '80s synthesisers were becoming sleeker and better able to reproduce 'proper' musical sounds. It was, after all, the original intent of synthesisers to 'synthesise', to accurately mimic other instruments. To this day one can still purchase books like Welsh's analogue synthesiser 'cookbook' which instruct one how to emulate the sound of brass or strings with subtractive synthesis. To many of the earlier generations of synthesiser users the electronic sound of their instrument was a hindrance to be overcome, not a sound to be celebrated in its own right. Early 'romplers', keyboard samplers that manipulated pre-recorded sounds, were seen to be a massive step forward towards accurate synthesis. Machines like the Kurzweil K250 (1984) produced by the company of Raymond Kurzweil, a fascinating character who had previously invented OCR (Optical Character Recognition), the flat-bed scanner as well as the text-to-speech synthesiser, were unequivocally seen as leading the way to the future.

Conversely instruments such as the infamous Roland TR-808 (1981) and TB-303 (1982) were old hat because they were seen as producing poor sonic imitations of drums and bass lines. However, their charm lay, perhaps not so much in their now hallowed 'analogue' nature (for instance a great many Detroit records were made using digital FM synthesis), but in their wonderful control surface. These instruments had lots of knobs and tweaking them could produce an immediately gratifying effect. In stark contrast the latest machines of the day often had forbidding interfaces and were 'black boxes' when it came to trying to reconfigure their frequently staid, respectable presets.

Presets Not Necessarily the Enemy

It's a common argument to lay the blame for the ills of electronic music at the foot of producers' supposedly lazy tendency to use presets. Ed DMX, noted for Nu-Electro records such as 'Make Me' as much as his forays into cerebral electronica like 'The Collapse Of The Wave Function', showed me round his East London studio. Ed was quick to point out how much mileage was got out of the presets on his humble Yamaha TX-81Z rack. On an equivalent Yamaha FM synth (all children of the DX-7), the DX100, none other than peerless artiste Derrick May caned the 'Dynowurlie' preset for 'The Dance' while Doug Lazy relied on the 'Solid Bass' preset for the magnetic bass on 'Let It Roll'. Both patches are available on the TX-81Z, as well as the famous 'Lately Bass' which R'n'B Producer Babyface used so much it became his signature sound. Babyface went as far as having two of the units, one detuned, which he'd trigger simultaneously for a thicker sound. Ed was philosophical on the issue of presets: 'At the end of the day it's all about taste.'

However, in instrument design convenience tends to go hand-in-hand with musical inflexibility. Ed described trying to write his own patches for the TX-81Z (he demonstrated a Fender Rhodes patch he'd painstakingly created) as 'like painting your hallway through the letterbox with a paintbrush tied to the end of a stick'. For creativity in music to flourish, there need to be certain structural parameters that are flexible. This can be as simple as having assignable knobs on a particular machine, or as thoroughgoing as the means by which various machines can fluidly interact with one another.

My favourite example of the inherent fluidity of the older wave of musical hardware is from an interview A Guy Called Gerald gave to Peter Shapiro in *The Wire* (October 1996) describing his studio workflow: 'In the early days I'd hook up the SH-101 [an early Roland Synthesiser] to one of the triggers on the 808 because the 101 has its own internal sequencer which can be triggered. I'd write a bass part into the 101's sequencer and I'd use a rimshot on the 808 to trigger the bass sound. Then I'd have a sequence already done in the 303 and I'd hook that up to the sync in-and-out on the back of the 808. All you'd have to do was press play on the 808, which was like the main brain of the system, it would trigger the SH-101 at the same time as the 303.' Ingenious.

Rather than artists having to inquisitively and intelligently crack open the occasionally forbidding interfaces of these electronic devices in pursuit of their aural image, the instrument-building industry has second-guessed musicians, and has progressively 'locked down' the process. This market-led drive towards convenience has trammelled musical possibilities. In the past, and more so in the days of Buchla boxes and the EMS VCS3s (ancient modular and semi-modular synths), creating electronic music was vastly more complicated, painful even, a true labour of love and devotion, but by means of practical magic all that energy found its way into the music.

Virtualisation

At the centre of this drive towards convenience has been the computer in the form of the desktop PC. It seems as though every process that musicians and technicians have asked the computer to perform it has done more quickly, more efficiently, with a greater degree of cleanliness than by previous solutions. Concomitantly the evolution of electronic music has been one dominated by the process of 'virtualisation'.

The first synthesisers, or analogue synthesisers, as they have come to be known, used voltage-controlled oscillators to create their source material. These sonic signals were shaped by a series of other modules in the same way that the throat and mouth shape the sound of our own vocal folds, in a process called subtractive synthesis. The first wave of electronic music we are familiar with is characterised by an unfettered approach to sound generation. Unless recorded and marshalled by tape-edits, they spooled out interminably over the vast canvases of twenty-minute tracks at the hands of players like Klaus Schulze or worked freely like glorified organs (albeit with fascinating textures) by jazz alumni like Herbie Hancock.

Sequencing

According to the recent documentary about the synthesiser manufacturer EMS, *What the Future Sounded Like*, the introduction of sequencing was first pioneered by British engineer David Cockerell. Cockerell later went on to work for Roger Linn on the Music Production Centre (MPC), hip hop's pre-eminent tool. In synthesisers sequencing was initially handled by analogue means, for instance by a dedicated module within an analogue synthesiser. This meant too that one machine's control voltage could trigger another. Differing companies developed their own sequencing languages; A Guy Called Gerald for instance worked purely with Roland machines for this reason. All this changed in 1983 when a cross-industry group headed by US engineer Dave Smith devised the MIDI format, which meant that across the board, all the music industry's machines would work together in harmony.

MIDI

The significance of MIDI to our story is that it decentralised the control of musical instruments. Where once, when huddled over one's Moog, one would have been at the metaphorical coalface; now, wherever the MIDI signal was originating from became the compositional nerve centre of an array of machines. The transition to the sequencer's organisational dominance is clearly audible in the clipped electronic music of the '80s and equally in the stark rhythmic patterns of that of the '90s. The first sequencers were stand-alone boxes often made by the same manufacturers as the synthesisers themselves (Korg, Yamaha, Roland, etc.), but it became clear that this was a task that a regular desktop PC could perform equally well.

Computer Music

While there is a distinguished history of computer music independent of this drive towards automation, dating from the pioneering work of Max Mathews at Bell Labs (honoured in the name of MAX audio software), that of the Dutch composer Gottfried Koenig and fledgling experiments at Pierre Boulez's IRCAM, this early music seems to have had little bearing or influence upon the subsequent barbarian-style invasion of hordes into the domain of computer music seeking convenience.

Initially software on desktop computers, like the earliest version of Cubase (1989) on the Atari ST computer with its inbuilt MIDI port, were simply running MIDI sequencer programmes – not exactly doing away with dedicated hardware sequencers like the Roland MC500, but giving them a run for their money. However as consumer-level computers increased in power they were able to take on the task of recording, editing and playing back digital audio.

Consequently the DAW (Digital Audio Workstation) was born, the most famous example of which being Digidesign's high-end Pro Tools Software (and its associated hardware). In 1991 Pro Tools combined its audio editing with the capability to also sequence MIDI, this was in essence 'the killer app'. When in 1993 Cubase became Cubase Audio, offering the same combination of MIDI sequencing and audio editing, the DAW exploded across the market. The first casualty was multi-track recorders like the Tascam Portastudio (which recorded on to C90s!) but also eventually 2" 24-track recorders. However, in spite of the DAW's ability to handle recorded audio, dedicated hardware samplers like the Akai S900 (1986) continued to thrive, but only until the introduction of software samplers like Tascam's GigaStudio in 1996.

Once Cubase, or Logic, or MOTU, or Ableton Live, or FL Studio (aka Fruity Loops), or Cakewalk or whichever more-or-less interchangeable DAW found itself in the hot seat, at the centre of the music production environment then the same 'virtualisation' quickly extended to the last remaining element of the equation: the synthesisers themselves. For many musicians off-board synths were nothing more than a pain in the ass. There's the tedious process of having to rout signals, resulting in a weave of cables, and issues caused by improperly synched synths. Hardware (and especially old analogue synthesisers) also has a tendency to break down. Everyone from old lords Kraftwerk to young bucks like Plaid could be read in interview in the mid-1990s celebrating the new order of soft synthesisers.

Soft Synths

Soft synthesisers were initially frowned upon for their lack of character but were adopted quickly enough. One approach with this instrument has been to build up large libraries of recordings of a particular instrument, be it a vintage Oberheim synthesiser or, in the case of the Vienna Instruments company a Bosendorfer Imperial Grand Piano, and have them triggered via a piano-style interface. This approach is very similar to that embodied in romplers. For a period soft synths engaged in a laudable forward-looking pursuit of new sound using digital algorithms; however, recently the drive of the software community seems to have settled around creating supposedly perfect emulations of older, often analogue synthesisers. Moreover, it appears that the irony of this situation is lost on many musicians. Companies such as Arturia turn out celebrity-endorsed versions of legendary war-horses like the Roland Jupiter 8 and the ARP2600. Naturally there are modern soft synths that are designed with something like purity of intent, like Vember's exquisite Surge, but these seem to be increasingly in a minority.

There is a more healthy strain of computer music embodied in modular software systems, such as MAX/MSP, cSounds, Pure Data, Composers Desktop Project or Reaktor, where the emphasis on an understanding of coding forces the musician to embrace the fundamental quality of the computer-as-instrument, but by and large the computer as an environment for creating music can be seen as being largely detrimental to the power of music. Furthermore detractors argue that the process of working within the computer in this kind of software can result in a music which is too 'granular', focused on the kind of incremental shifts in texture and tone which only a composer locked away on his own for days at a time with his own sound can really appreciate.

Analogue Forever?

The backlash against the prescriptiveness of DAWs is evident in the swollen cult that analogue synthesisers have recently come to enjoy. With an analogue synthesiser, by virtue of there being at root a tangible element to sculpt (the sound of the oscillator itself), there is a sense of the enterprise being grounded in fundamentals. A number of companies have actually started building analogue synthesisers once again, with a degree of success, most famously Dave Smith Instruments (the aforementioned engineer) with his Desktop Evolver and Mopho but also enterprises like Cornwall's Analogue Systems and Germany's Doepfer.

DAW Music

Criticism of all-digital music often settles upon some mythic quality absent from the sound. There is often a case for describing DAW music as being like an 'audio trickle', though it is not necessarily owing to any fundamental quality of digital audio as manifested in the 44.1 khz encoding one hears on a CD. Putting the semi-rational fetish of analogue signals aside, we must recognise that it is still possible to make dynamic electronic music on a computer. Looking deeper it's more true to say that the very interface of the DAW, the manner in which it encourage musicians to work, is the problem.

The fundamental visual paradigm of the DAW, one pioneered in Cubase, is the first thing at fault. The user is encouraged to view music as if it were a giant sandwich of vertically arranged elements stacked upon one another. The tendency this encourages is one of interminable layering. A number of artists, including (perhaps surprisingly) Autechre, have criticised the way that the visual paradigm of these programmes, their 'data representation', and the way you can 'see what's coming up' messes with a proper engagement with sound itself.

Throughout the 1990s and into this decade, perhaps the one truly vibrant culture of electronic music, hip hop, has clung to the outdated tool of the MPC. Producers like Timbaland have feted this hardware sequencer-cum-sampler with its punchable drum-pads and distinct absence of lavish graphical interface. While no magic bullet for quality music, at least the MPC is focused around the musical 'event'. Conversely the computer interface encourages not the rawness of the event, but rather the act of tweaking all parameters to perfection.

Control Surface Crisis

The keyboard and mouse might suffice for word processing but as far as tools to manipulate music go, they're sterile. Brian Eno, who has long held this opinion about computers, has recently sung the praises of Korg's current Kaoss Pad series of sound controllers which generate reverb, echo and effects according to one's finger's movement across a touch-sensitive pad. Indeed with increasingly sophisticated MIDI controllers being made by hardware manufacturers like Novation, designed to make working with soft synths a more physical activity, there is a sense that the musical instrument industry is trying to think out of the box. Small companies like Elektron, Future Retro and Jomox also continue to try and make innovative hardware.

It is interesting to note that this crisis of the control surface doesn't just apply to musical instruments. NASA engineer and synth enthusiast David Cornutt remarked recently: 'Consider modern aircraft design — even a 777 doesn't physically have enough room in the cockpit to provide discrete controls for all of the aircraft's parameters.' There are cogent arguments being made on forums such as Vintage Synth that the key to the future of electronic music lies more in the attention to the interface than in any specific sound-generating properties of the instruments themselves. Surprisingly hardcore synth heads seem comfortable with the idea that it is the interface which yields a distinctive sound as much as which Oscillator, Filter or Modulation Matrix is being employed. In many ways it's a shame that the rash of crazy MIDI interfaces developed in the late 1980s in response to the then nascent MIDI technology (like the Buchla Lightning – two wands that look like the sticks waved by airfield staff) didn't prove more popular than the dominant keyboard paradigm.

Critique

Music critics have never hesitated to tell

musicians what works and what doesn't on what must appear to musicians to be a purely subjective basis. Perhaps it is equally unfair to suggest technical approaches that might yield better results! Naturally the reader might wish to take for granted this writer's disdain for the computer's environment and the supposedly limitless possibilities it offers, but I believe the key to making interesting electronic music seems to be either to avoid the pitfall of working entirely within the computer domain or to pursue a path like dubstep artist Burial, who cuts and pastes his music together in Sound Forge, relying on the shape of waveforms (and no sequencer) and making choices that go against the grain of the technology. There is also a genius to artists who seize on a very few particular instruments and hone the way they use them, for instance Juana Molina and her delay pedal or DJ Shadow, who made the whole of *Endtroducing* on an MPC 60.

Flying Lotus

According to Flying Lotus, the wildly innovative Los Angeles-based post-hip hop artist signed to WARP records, on the subject of technology in music he's 'the worst guy in the world to talk to', but given that he's created a highly distinctive music while working with a narrow range of tools I'd have to disagree. Indeed when I put it to him that as far as creativity goes it's all down to one's limitations, he volunteers that 'when it becomes focused on technology it takes it away from its core essence.' A Google search of the term 'flying lotus synth' brought up a cornucopia of journalistic slang: 'liquid synths', 'butter synths', 'dynamic synths', 'floaty synths', 'mercurial synths', 'hard-edged synths', 'maniacal synths', 'silky synths' and 'dusted synths'. All of which somewhat embarrassingly foregrounds the occasional paucity of music journalism.

Flying Lotus in fact uses an old Fender Rhodes (less a synthesiser than an amplified glockenspiel or celesta, an instrument often used by jazz fusion artists in the 1970s) and a Moog Little Phatty, one of the rejuvenated Moog company's brand new analogue synths. While he'll often record himself jamming on these two and record the results, he says he's more likely to either sample a record – 'I think you'd be surprised at the amount of samples I use' – or work up something from his laptop with his Novation MIDI controller. A snapshot of the Flying Lotus Studio online is pored over on forum threads (visible are a TR-909 drum machine, a Boss SP-303 sampler, a KORG KP3 Kaoss Pad and an old Roland Space-Echo effects box), but although he confesses to suffering the dreaded musician's lurgy, gear lust ('Every week I go and see if there's some shit I can buy'), more often than not it's 'a great idea until I bring it home and end up not using it'. By any standard it's a minimal set-up of instruments, an unusual one and clearly a rig he knows inside out.

Thanks to Flying Lotus, Ed DMX, Marcus Scott, Rob Hill, David Cornutt, Vintage Synth *and* Sound on Sound *websites.*

CHRIS KILLEN
Paul Simon Gives Chevy Chase the Finger
A Short Fiction

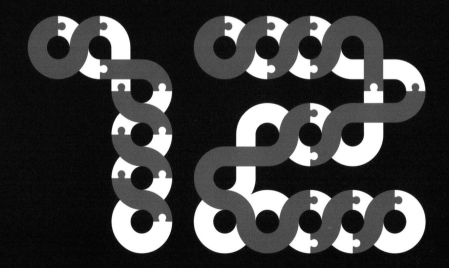

Paul Simon wakes up and gets out of bed. It's some time after 1 p.m. Paul Simon had a late night. He went to the casino with Chevy Chase and lost between $200 and $400 dollars. Paul Simon goes into the kitchen and pours cornflakes into a bowl. Paul Simon has a flashback to the casino: he is taking off his Rolex and mouthing off at the croupier and putting his Rolex on to the blackjack table and demanding chips for it. Chevy Chase is near the roulette, looming over it, about 7 feet tall in a white suit. Paul Simon pours milk into the bowl of cornflakes and carries it into the lounge. He sits on a salmon-coloured leather chair. His feet don't touch the floor. Paul Simon picks up a controller and presses a button, and the Yo La Tengo best-of CD *Prisoners of Love* starts playing throughout the house. Paul Simon sits on the salmon-coloured leather chair and listens to Yo La Tengo and closes his eyes as his cornflakes become soggy. Paul Simon wishes he could somehow saw himself free from the rest of his life, and go into a flotation tank and just listen to Yo La Tengo forever. He would eat using a tube and soup, maybe. Paul Simon puts the bowl of cornflakes down on the salmon-coloured tiled floor and hops down off the chair and goes over to a coffee table. He picks up the Yellow Pages and flicks through for the Fs, for 'Flotation Tanks'.

⌘

It's a Sunday. Paul Simon has nothing to do. Paul Simon has already gone for a jog, and read the classified paper, and put a lasagne in the oven to bake. The phone starts ringing. Paul Simon picks up the phone.

'Yes?' he says.

'Paul!'

'Chevy,' Paul Simon says.

'Paul! I've just had a fantastic idea!'

Paul Simon makes a face to himself. 'Go on,' he says.

'We should do a music video together,' Chevy Chase says.

'We already did that,' Paul Simon says. 'We did that twenty years ago.'

A long pause. Paul Simon listens to the sounds of Chevy Chase's apartment – street noise, a TV, something that sounds like dried leaves being shaken around in a bag.

'Well, we should do it again,' Chevy Chase says, finally.

'Maybe,' Paul Simon says.

They talk for a while longer – Paul Simon

trying to slip out of the conversation and Chevy Chase somehow managing to keep introducing new topics and Paul Simon-specific questions – until Paul Simon notices an appropriate moment to hang up.

'Fucking hell. My food's burning,' Paul Simon says. 'I put a lasagne in the oven.'

Chevy Chase starts to say something else, maybe something to do with the lasagne, but Paul Simon hangs up the phone. Paul Simon goes over to the oven and opens the door. A cloud of black smoke goes into Paul Simon's face.

'Fucking hell,' Paul Simon says.

⌘

Paul Simon is in the flotation tank. The song 'Our Way to Fall' by Yo La Tengo is playing. Paul Simon is thinking about a relationship, which is now over. The relationship feels very over to Paul Simon. Other times the relationship has felt a bit over, but with the secret possibility of it starting again. This time it doesn't feel like that at all. Paul Simon's remembered relationship feels a lot like the song 'Our Way to Fall' by Yo La Tengo. Paul Simon wishes he was in Yo La Tengo. He wishes that he'd written the song 'Our Way to Fall', so that he could email it to the person who he was in a relationship with, and when the person listened to it they would feel a mixture of nostalgia, sadness and awe at Paul Simon's song writing ability. They would listen to it three or four times and then start crying and feel like they needed to get in immediate contact with Paul Simon. Maybe they would email him, or better, they would be overcome with the extreme urge to call and try to work out what had gone wrong in their relationship, and within five minutes

Paul Simon and the person would be back in a relationship again. The song finishes, and 'From a Motel 6' comes on. Paul Simon wants to listen to 'Our Way to Fall' again. He pushes open the door of the flotation tank. He climbs out of the flotation tank and water drips off his body on to the salmon-coloured tile floor. Paul Simon slips over twice on the way to the CD player. He's naked. It's about four in the afternoon. When he reaches the CD player, he skips the track back to 'Our Way to Fall' and then presses the repeat song button. Paul Simon is standing near a large, clear-glass patio door. He looks out into his garden. There's a child in the garden, holding a rainbow-coloured ball. The child is frozen in terror. The child looks at Paul Simon's naked body and then runs off down the garden and disappears through a hole in the bush.

⌘

Paul Simon gets lost on the internet. He's not written a new song in maybe seven or eight months. The last time he tried to write a song, it sounded so bad that he said 'Fuck America' out loud and put his electric guitar very carefully into his giant fish tank. The guitar wasn't plugged in. It's still in the fish tank. Paul Simon is on Facebook. He's just discovered that he has been deleted by the person he used to be in a relationship with. He feels inordinately depressed about being deleted. He's not sure but maybe he feels more depressed about being deleted than being told in person that the relationship was over. He tries to put himself in the position of the person who deleted him. He imagines himself looking at his own Facebook profile and thinking 'Fuck

America, I want nothing more to do with Paul Simon and his crappy songs, he hasn't put out a good album in over twenty years, anyway, and he's rubbish in bed' and then pressing the delete button. The song 'Our Way to Fall' by Yo La Tengo is playing on repeat. It's been on repeat for three days. The flotation tank is making a strange noise. Paul Simon gets up from the computer and goes and looks at the flotation tank. It needs to stay plugged in – to keep the water at a certain temperature, etc. – and is probably using a lot of electricity. Paul Simon goes into the hall, opens a closet, and looks at the electricity meter. He watches the numbers revolving on the electricity meter for a long time, then begins to need the toilet.

⌘

Paul Simon drives to Chevy Chase's apartment. It's Tuesday – 'Cards night'. Paul Simon feels a bit better about things. He's moved on to disc two of Yo La Tengo's 'Prisoners of Love' best-of compilation. He's unplugged the flotation tank. He's put on a white suit and pushed the sleeves up. He is sixty-six years old. 'Fuck the United States of America,' Paul Simon says joyfully, as he watches the white stucco apartment buildings zip past from his car. Paul Simon parks across the street from Chevy Chase's apartment. A bird is pecking around next to a bent-over palm tree. Paul Simon has $300 folded up in the breast pocket of his salmon-pink shirt. Paul Simon takes out his phone and dials the number for Chevy Chase's house. It rings for a while, then Chevy Chase picks up.

'Chevy,' says Paul Simon. 'Listen. I don't think I'm gonna make it over tonight.'

'What?' says Chevy Chase.

Paul Simon is smiling.

'Yeah, you see, something's come up. I have this other engagement.'

'Oh,' says Chevy Chase.

A long silence. Paul Simon has to bite his lip to stop himself from laughing into the phone.

'Okay then,' says Chevy Chase. 'Maybe next week?'

'Yep,' says Paul Simon. 'Maybe,' and hangs up.

Paul Simon wishes there was someone else in the car to witness what he just did. For the first time in his life he wishes a reality TV crew was following him around. For a moment Paul Simon considers the idea of proposing a reality TV program about his life, (*The Osbournes* meets *The Hills* meets *The Band's Last Waltz*) and then dismisses the idea. Paul Simon gets out of the car and locks it and crosses the street. He presses the buzzer to Chevy Chase's apartment. No answer. Paul Simon presses the buzzer again. He presses the buzzer five or six times. He tries to phone Chevy Chase, and hears the phone ringing in the apartment. No one picks up. Paul Simon eventually crosses the street again, gets into his car, and drives home.

⌘

Paul Simon is trying to make pancakes. He's following the instructions very carefully, but can't seem to make a pancake that stays together and doesn't stick to the pan. He has even cross-referenced his own pancake recipe with two others on the internet. Paul Simon is listening to a mix CD someone made him in 1999. The song 'He's Kissing Christian' by That Dog comes on. Paul Simon skips the song. The song 'Girl From

Mars' by Ash comes on. Paul Simon skips the song. The song 'Jump Around' by House of Pain comes on. Paul Simon goes back to making pancakes. When it gets to the lyric 'So if you come to battle bring a shotgun,' Paul Simon sings along and makes a shotgun gesture with his spatula. The child is in the garden again, kicking around its rainbow-coloured ball. The child comes and goes freely now, and is treating the garden as its own. Paul Simon almost feels like he doesn't have the authority to ask it to leave. Paul Simon hears a noise. He turns down 'Jump Around'. His phone is ringing. He looks at the screen. It says 'Private Number calling'. Paul Simon tries to think who could be calling him. He wonders if it's the person he used to be in a relationship with. Paul Simon decides not to answer the call. He turns up 'Jump Around'. He tries to flip the pancake and it falls apart. He scoops it into the bin with his spatula.

'I'm comin' to get ya, comin' to get ya, spitting out lyrics homie I'll wet ya,' he says.

⌘

Paul Simon feels sick with worry. He tries to listen to the song 'Our Way to Fall' by Yo La Tengo again, but whereas before it suited his feelings (nostalgia, failed love affair, small quiet feelings, sadness, longing), it now feels kind of mocking. Paul Simon's hands feel shaky. He feels sick. He's felt sick for two days. He can't really eat anything much. He's thinking the same four or five things over and over. One of the four or five things will pop up in Paul Simon's head, suddenly, and he will get a pang of worry in his stomach and feel sick. Paul Simon's nails are bitten and red. Paul Simon decides to start

smoking again. He's not smoked since the early 1980s. He gave up at a New Year's Eve party at Diane Keaton's house. Paul Simon drives to the 7-Eleven. 'Milkshake' by Kelis is playing in the 7-Eleven. He buys a pack of Camels. He gets outside and opens the Camels and puts one in his mouth. He realises he's forgotten to buy a lighter so he goes back inside the 7-Eleven. 'Milkshake' finishes and '50 Ways to Leave Your Lover' comes on. Paul Simon feels awkward and strange. He queues behind a drunk man who's buying cigarettes and a pastry thing. Paul Simon listens to the lyrics to '50 Ways to Leave Your Lover' and thinks, 'What a crock of shit.' One of the four or five things pops up suddenly in Paul Simon's head: I did nothing wrong, I was just a kind person and that still wasn't enough. I'm a useless human being. The drunk man leaves the 7-Eleven and Paul Simon steps up to the counter and asks the cashier for a lighter. The cashier gives Paul Simon a strange look and nods and hands the lighter to Paul Simon very reverently and says, 'It's on the house.'

⌘

The child has pitched a tent in Paul Simon's garden. The tent is zipped up. It's after midnight. It looks like the child has a torch in the tent. Maybe the child is reading a comic. Paul Simon is sitting in his kitchen, looking at the tent through the patio doors. Paul Simon wonders if the child's parents know where it is. He wonders if he should go out and say something. Since the child has started appearing, Paul Simon hasn't gone into his garden. Paul Simon wishes he was a child in a tent and not a 60-six-year-old American singer/songwriter. He wishes he could get into the tent with the child, but he knows that such a thing would be frowned upon. Paul Simon inadvertently thinks about Michael Jackson. He remembers a time at a party somewhere, shortly after Michael Jackson released *Bad*; maybe it was the release party for *Bad*. Paul Simon was a bit drunk, anyway, and desperately wanted to get into a conversation with somebody, anybody, about the album *Bad* so he could make a joke. He wanted them to say, 'So what do you think of the album?' so he could reply, 'Not bad.' He became fixated on the idea and then drank too many whisky-and-cokes and ended up going round saying 'Not bad' to anyone who'd listen, until his manager finally found him and steered him outside for some air. Paul Simon goes up to the patio doors and taps quietly on the glass. The child doesn't hear. About five minutes later the torch light goes out in the tent. Paul Simon has a sudden pang of worry in his stomach and feels sick and then goes to bed. In bed, Paul Simon holds his phone close to his face and looks at the number of the person he used to be in a relationship with. He hovers his thumb over the 'call' button. Paul Simon puts the phone on his night table and lies there in the dark.

⌘

Paul Simon drags the flotation tank out into his front yard. There are other things in the yard, too: the gigantic fish tank with the electric guitar in it, a bookcase, a gold disc, a wooden chair, some expensive suits and shirts, a VHS copy of *The Graduate*. Paul Simon faintly remembers a short story by Raymond Carver about a man putting all his furniture in his front yard and a young couple coming along. In the story, the girl dances with the man who's giving away his furniture. Paul Simon is hoping a young couple comes along. He wants to dance with someone. Paul Simon sits on the wooden chair and waits for a young couple to come along. It's early evening. Paul Simon can hear crickets and rustling palm tree leaves. A car pulls up. Paul Simon recognises the car as Chevy Chase's. Chevy Chase looks out of the window of the car. Paul Simon sits in the chair and looks at the car. Chevy Chase moves his hand up to the window and beckons to Paul Simon. Paul Simon gets up and walks towards the car, but as he gets closer he realises Chevy Chase isn't beckoning to him. Chevy Chase is making an obscene gesture with his hand and tongue and cheek. Paul Simon gives Chevy Chase the finger. He runs back up the drive, picks up the VHS copy of *The Graduate*, and throws it at the car but it misses and skitters out on to the street. Chevy Chase looks like he's laughing. He starts the car and revs the engine and drives away loudly. Paul Simon sits on the wooden chair and waits for the young couple to come.

⌘

Paul Simon stands in the shower for a long time. He washes the different places on his body over and over again. He sings the song 'Did I Tell You' by Yo La Tengo, but forgets some of the words and has to make them up. Paul Simon decides to get out of the shower and work on a cover of 'Did I Tell You' which includes his made-up words. He goes into his bedroom. His laptop is on. He looks at the laptop. He sits down on the edge of the bed and connects to the internet. He checks his emails. He checks his MySpace page. He checks Facebook again. He feels sick with worry and is almost sick onto his laptop. Paul Simon remembers that his guitar is out in the yard, in the gigantic fish tank, and probably doesn't work anyway. He goes to the window and looks down at the yard. The flotation tank is still there. The gigantic fish tank is smashed and on its side. The guitar is gone. The bookcase is toppled over. The expensive suits and shirts are gone. Paul Simon lights a Camel. He puts the laptop away and walks around the room, touching his head and face and neck. Paul Simon thinks about commerce, the music business, increased internet downloads, dwindling CD sales and the person he used to be in a relationship with. Paul Simon thinks about *The Apprentice*. Paul Simon takes his mobile phone off the night table and looks at it. No calls or messages. He scrolls through the numbers until he finds the name of his manager. Paul Simon is still thinking about *The Apprentice*. He phones his manager. When his manager picks up, Paul Simon immediately says 'You're fired,' and hangs up the phone. I'll call back later on, Paul Simon thinks, and tell him I was joking. He sits in the room and smokes Camels and feels sorry for himself.

Discover the Recipes You Are Using
and Abandon Them
Brian Eno in the Kitchen

Discover the recipes you are using and abandon them.

OBLIQUE STRATEGY, 1975

To understand Brian Eno's techniques in the studio, one of the worst things to do is to read up on how records are actually produced. Over the past few years, there have been several books on the role of the producer. Two of these books are *The Producer as Composer: Shaping the sounds of popular music* by Virgil Moorefield, which devotes almost an entire chapter to Eno, and *Echo and Reverb: Fabricating space in popular music recording*, by Peter Doyle. *Echo and Reverb* is far more successful in discussing Eno because the author ends his story in 1960, sidestepping the question of Eno's productions entirely. Moorefield is a professor of music; Doyle writes mystery novels. And so perhaps it's not so surprising that Doyle is better at explaining the art of production.

How do you understand a producer who has generated reams of words and yet claims that words are meaningless, who says he doesn't like to talk about the past but can't help referencing it in his rhetoric about the future, who fades to the background as easily as he rushes to the surface? In the liner notes for *Music for Airports*, Eno wrote that the record was designed to be 'as ignorable as it is interesting'. Eno, too, is as ignorable as he

is interesting. It seems like a fool's game to construct a narrative around someone whose entire *modus operandi* seems based upon denying any threads of narrative structure.

Frustrated by this, I put on *Taking Tiger Mountain (by Strategy)*, and as 'Mother Whale Eyeless' was spinning these lyrics flew out:

> Take me – my little pastry mother take me – there's a pie shop in the sky . . .

The proof was in the pudding. The answer was suddenly crystal-clear: I had to see how Eno worked. Not in the studio, but in the kitchen. (Not The Kitchen, the Manhattan art space that Eno frequented in the late 1970s.) This was not without precedent. In one of the most revealing and trenchant pieces of music journalism ever written, the late and great Minneapolis 'zine *Gourmandizer* ran an interview with producer Steve Albini in which he divulged the bonkers eating habits of the bands he worked with. The article ended with Albini's personal recipe for mayonnaise. On German television, there was a popular ongoing cooking show in which musicians were invited to make their favourite foods. For one episode, Blixa Bargeld of Einsturzende Neubauten dourly constructed an entire meal in black, centred on a squid-ink pasta with squid-ink sauce. This tells me more about him as a person than his most recent record did.

For a few years, I went through reams of old Eno interviews and writings and picked out every reference to cooking. Noticed: a definite tendency for improvising intensely flavoured (but not terribly spicy) dishes with odd combinations of ethnic ingredients, with a blatant disregard for recipes or notions of authenticity. Gobs of garlic. Lots of rice. A consistent use of thick Asian sauces, particularly black bean sauce and oyster sauce, in non-Asian dishes. Mixing oyster sauce with balsamic vinegar! Continuous references to eating rich truffle-based dishes, especially truffle risotto, with U2 and being nonplussed. An odd risotto recipe of Eno's which involves non-arborio rice, and the use of a rice cooker (?!) instead of the traditional constant-stirring technique. Unconventional drop scones made with 'cinnamon, peanut butter, vanilla, pumpkin seeds, sultanas, poppy seeds'. Eno's appropriation of African culinary ideas into his cooking is a bit too Bill Laswell for me sometimes – a 'West African composite with roast chicken and peanut butter sauce' that he once detailed in a diary entry sounded a little dull to me, be honest.

'I'm starting to think that all the world's problems could be solved with either oyster sauce or backing vocals,' wrote Eno in his diary *A Year with Swollen Appendices*, published in 1995. In Eno's interviews and personal writings, there are repeated references to food and to cooking. There are also references to cybernetics and gardening, among other things, but the food references are the most interesting. He writes again and again about cooking in his diary, and a few themes keep popping up. He is liberal, perhaps too liberal, with his use of garlic. He displays a penchant for using thick bottled sauces, particularly black bean sauce and oyster sauce, in dishes that don't seem to call for them. 'I'm sick of restaurants, and more sick of what they cost,' wrote Eno. 'Decided to take a more creative approach to eating from now on. Four clues: (1) less, (2) cheaper, (3) faster, (4) more portable.' The words are an echo of his compositional strategy circa 1974, paired with Robert Fripp – a 'small, mobile, intelligent unit', free to make their own rules separate from the soggy prog-rock of the day. After all, Eno is a man with a certain passive disdain for rules. To this day, he is possibly the only art-school graduate to take a leak in Duchamp's urinal and get away with it.

In 2000, Eno wrote:

> I'm quite a good cook! But my style of cooking is let's see what's in the kitchen, and think of something imaginative to do with it. Which is exactly the same idea one has as a producer. So as a producer you say, let's see what is in the studio, who's there, what they can do, what tools we have available, and let's see what we can do with it. The other way of being a chef or a cook, which is not the way I like, is to have a recipe, to get all the things that the recipe suggests. To carefully measure them out, follow the program, and then to end up with the expected dish. That's sort of the opposite of what I do. Both as a cook and as a producer.

Some of Eno's most memorable musical moments in the '70s were created with the aid of Fripp. Fripp, of course, was an ace guitar player and a total muso; Eno was a dabbler and an avowed non-musician. Some of Fripp's best guitar solos on Eno tunes emerged from Eno goading Fripp into making sounds that Fripp protested would clash dissonantly with the song, according to the conventional rules of music theory. But Eno insisted that they try it anyway, and Fripp found to his amazement that his odd guitar lines fitted the song's lines perfectly. In a way, Fripp was the oyster sauce in Eno's green-bean-and-balsamic-vinegar recipe – the element that shouldn't quite work but did.

I dug back into Eno's deep past to learn more about the recipes of his childhood, but came up mostly empty. My guess is that Eno's path to lifelong eccentricity began at age 11. In the archives of a defunct '70s rag about synthesiser technology and hairy prog bands, called *Synapse*, Eno talked about his kooky uncle:

> At the age of 11, I had this uncle – a real uncle this time – who's like the eccentric of the family, very nice man, and he had spent some years in India. So he had these kind of strange Indian ideas about things. He's quite eccentric, very strange, always trying out weird experiments at home, building ways of distilling liquor and stuff like that, and taming the strangest animals, like rooks. He was very important to me, because he represented the other half, the sort of strange side of life, and he was to me like all that music was as well. And I would think, 'Where's he

coming from?' as they would say now. I used to go and visit him regularly, once or twice a week, and he used to talk and introduce me to ideas.

At around this time, his uncle showed him a book of miniature Piet Mondrian reproductions. Eno was instantly captivated by Mondrian's coolly intersecting lines and clean rectangles in primary colors – so much so that he enrolled in art school to study painting. But it was the world of cassette tapes that fascinated him in school, the gooey analogue quality to them, the ability to record and re-record and create small, contained messes. To this day, I don't think Eno has ever quite created a record with Mondrian's flair for simplicity.

It so happens that Mondrian had severe problems with eating. 'He was terribly thin, and seemed to live mostly on currants and vegetable stew, because he followed the Haye diet,' recounted fellow artist Naum Gabo after his death. Mondrian attempted to eat scientific combinations of food, adhering to a rigid grid of what he could and could not eat. Eno, in comparison, can't even make rice without dousing it in black bean sauce and sunflower seeds. Even Eno's most spare ambient records display an abundance of layers and a baroque sense of eccentricity. But not too abundant – as he complained once in 1983 about the overblown pomp-rock of the '70s, 'rock became grandiose and muddy, like a bad cook who puts every spice and herb on the shelf in the soup.'

⌘

There was a missing link in my Eno–Mondrian food connection, I realised, and that missing link was Erik Satie, Eno's ancestor in modern ambient music. How could I have forgotten about Satie and his tortured relationship with food? Yes, we all remember the *Gymnopédies* – so beautiful, yes – but Satie was a class-A crackpot. This was a man who started his own church after quitting the Rosicrucians, called 'L'Eglise Métropolitaine d'Art de Jésus Conducteur'. For a long time, Satie subsisted on only white food (fitting, then, that one of his later works was titled 'Menus for Childish Purposes'), which matched his equally weird penchant for wearing grey velvet suits almost constantly. White food and Satie's music made intuitive sense to me somehow; there's this snowy sense of purity and a solemn, crystalline radiance to his music. Satie's most famous work is tidy and elegant – there's this pearlescent plastic quality to it that's sort of Apple Computer in a way. But have you ever listened to Satie and wondered, well, this is all very nice, very pretty, but there's something sort of evil lurking beneath this music? Something deeply weird along with that refined sense of melancholy? So back to Satie's tormented dealings with food – he 'never spoke while eating for fear of strangling himself'. Even his famous explanation of 'furniture music', the original foundations of ambient music as we know it, was framed in the context of dinner:

> You know, there's a need to create furniture music; that is to say, music that would be a part of the surrounding noises and that would take them into account. I see it as melodious, as masking the clatter of knives and forks without drowning it completely,

without imposing itself. It would spare them the usual banalities.

You could set up a whole Mondrian–Satie psychological continuum of eating in the context of Brian Eno's influences, though I'd say that Eno's attitudes towards food probably run more in line with another huge influence of his, the late Fela Kuti. I found this reminiscence by a Nigerian writer on his experiences at Fela's club the Shrine: 'I also recall with great fondness, the savory piquancy of the excellent Jollof rice and stewed fried meat sold outside of the Shrine. I recall nights during my University of Lagos years when we visited the Shrine area just for the food.'

Back to Satie's grim culinary universe. 'My only nourishment consists of food that is white: eggs, sugar, shredded bones, the fat of dead animals, veal, salt, coconuts, chicken cooked in white water, moldy fruit, rice, turnips, sausages in camphor, pastry, cheese (white varieties), cotton salad, and certain kinds of fish (without their skin),' he wrote in his *Memoirs of an Amnesiac*. I am not sure about the amnesia, but Satie probably had at least three personality disorders that could be identified if I had a copy of the DSM-IV handy. This odd French website I found, which celebrates 'Satie-inspired desserts' in a sort of proud French *Amelie*-ised version of the man (including a section titled 'Satie and the Joy of Eating', which would make you think the guy was munching happily on pear galettes while frolicking down the picturesque streets of Montmartre), offers more choice titbits: 'For me, eating is naturally a duty – a pleasant, festive duty – and I really want to perform this duty with exactitude and due attention,' wrote Satie. 'My appetite is good and I eat for myself, without selfishness or the urge to wolf things down. In other words, 'My posture is better at a table than on horseback – even though I ride rather well.' 'Exactitude and due attention' reminds me of Mondrian's strict attitude towards food. Now, Satie was French, of course, and Mondrian was Dutch, but it was in Paris that Mondrian had his massive mind-melting paradigm shift leading to the development of his signature rigid Neoplastic style. Interestingly, though, it was only after moving to Britain that Mondrian fully developed and refined his truly freaky eating habits! Which brings us back to Eno . . .

With Eno, it's all about balance and knowing when to stop. 'If you're an intelligent cook, you'll abandon the recipe at a certain time. You taste the dish and you realise there's the seed of an interesting new taste. So you work on that and forget you were making chicken Kiev, or whatever. You make something new.'

From The Bridge

SIMON ARMITAGE

The same bridge, in fact, where it had occurred to
Uncle Eddie that the so-called Manic Street Preachers,
for all their flame-grilled adjectives and sulphuric aftershave,
were neither frenzied, credible or remotely evangelical,
just as the so-called Red Hot Chili Peppers, for
all their encouraging ingredients, were actually
no warmer than a baby's bathwater and not in the
least bit tangy, whereas The Teardrop Explodes,
either by blind accident or through careful purpose,
had kept every promise ever made. Below him,
the soupy canal swallowed his last coin with an agreeable
gulp and slouched unknowingly and profusely onwards.

Wild Beasts and the New Vorticists

Our good friend the gentle giant Nick Scott (sleeve designer for *Limbo, Panto*) first brought the *Blast* journal to our attention for stylistic reasons. Our eyes fell from their sockets and on to the page. The brash and fragmented mediums brought together by the Vorticists suited our brash and fragmented collection of ten songs, like ten fingers fit into a pair of gloves. We are so much alike, both being English avant-garde cubist futurists who are not, and will never be, victims of traditionalism, caring, as we do, far too much for the cause to worry a great deal for the consequence. Finally we have a short-hand description of Wild Beasts. Although, let me assure you that the natural correlations between the Vorticist approach and Wild Beasts' own approach have, up to this point, been purely by exquisite chance.

As with any grand manifesto, especially an avant-garde one, interpretations are treated as putty to be sculpted into whatever form is most helpful to the reader. Just as certain songs may have entirely different meanings to vastly different people, yet are cherished equally, manifestos are a rally cry to those of like mind who see their own sense in the words. For this reason I make no apologies for manipulating the Vorticists' manifesto for Wild Beasts' own use.

Having first intended to wade in with heavy-weight intellectualism reinforcing the Vorticist manifesto, I quickly had to adapt to the obvious fact that my chosen sphere of lyric writing has rendered my long-hand approaches to writing a little limp, rather like an arm that has been slept on all night by a heavy, drunken body. Rather than wait in flapping discomfort to use the arm, I chose to sober up that heavy body and use it. So my contribution has become a series of short allegories, using the manifesto statements as titles. In conjunction with Tom's lucid treatise and Fiona Morley's stunning modern sculpture we have come to approach our piece much as the Vorticist's *Blast* journal did, using different mediums to express the same core values. We are our own Ezra Pounds, T. S. Eliots and Jacob Epsteins. We are three folk lucky enough to have been donated a dressing-up box by Richard King and, as anyone would, we have dressed up in our favourite play-clothes.

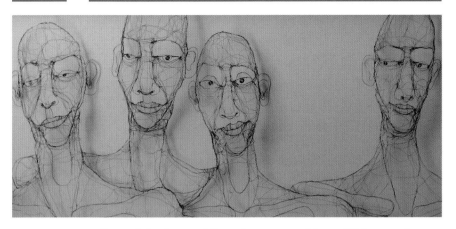

1 Beyond Action and Reaction we would establish ourselves.
action and reaction
two death-dealing snakes of matching species
maggot like slipping reel to reel around each other
locked in a deadly courtship dance
pissed on their own poison
sickly smit and badly love bit
mollycoddled creatures
grazing only for easy prey
grinning
the solitary snake climbs to the high branches
to be closer to the ether
beyond
peering down like a swinging grappling hook
sulking in the leafy shadows
smelling soft meat
nerve ends withering to pulp
bitter envy swallowed thick
poor solitary snake
he worships his prey
understands her needs
troubles after her
with a broken heart
her suffocating death
mirrors the finesse with which she lived
as he swallows hog whole
snakes of action and reaction crawling on their bellies
the empty carcasses

2 We start from opposite statements of a chosen world. Set up
violent structure of adolescent clearness between two
extremes.
Brothers must bully and torment one another
Through stunted jealousy and
Towering love...

Best friends and biggest rivals,
Who don't know their own strength
Go too far, if only to scare themselves.

One sibling is for intellect and the thoughtful mind
The other is for instinct and unconscious.
One brother savours
So the other must consume.
One rubs your burning belly
As the other pats your thinking head.
One loves Father more
And one can love only Mother.
⌘
Oedipal latitudes and longitudes
Breach across our chosen world
Making up the synapses to the fist
And the synapses to the heart,

Sometimes occupying
The same circuits.

3 We discharge ourselves on both sides.
Upon which glorious chariot does the climax ride?

With the soaring heart,
to be greeted by the plump uteri of Queens?

Or with the plummeting fist,
to be bastard fodder for the famine ground?

Answers on a postcard please.

4 We fight first on one side, then on the other, but always for
the same cause, which is neither side or both sides and ours.
We know our enemies as we know our lovers,
too well

Tom Fleming and Hayden Thorpe

Like the lines on their needy bodies
our fingers always trace back to that same tender point

We lust
as only consumed juveniles would recognise

Kissing with lips that pivot both of our bodies
as we pirouette down the plughole

Love's holy water and anger's rich blood
must eventually blur into one stocky colour

Feeling now how two boxers do in the final round
we sleep walk further into an unconscious twilight

Slogging on. Driven by cruel fascination and a deep-set heart spite.
But always, always, for the same side.

5 Mercenaries were always the best troops.
We will wave the flag for the family that provides for us
On special occasions you can see us pursing our lips
To look pretty for the camera
Then recoiling our death hoods. To blot ourselves out.

We can love only whole-heartedly
And give nothing but generously to our fosters
While forever threatening to turn tail and run
The instant our charity is questioned

Like the weak-kneed lice we are
We clingers-on must
Morph into more
Than we were to begin with

To keep on proving our love
We're compelled to absorb
And understand intimately the nature of our host
To suckle, and to be gratified

6 We are primitive Mercenaries in the Modern World.
The Modern World will wrap its baby in pristine bombazine
While we find more worth in his forgotten after-birth.

The Modern World will be crowning the new child King
As we are in the backstreet aborting our own.

The Modern World will be fully formed and over-grown
While we will still suffer a fluid puberty and misery.

The Modern World will renew its vows
When we speak ours only to ourselves, to hear how they sound.

The Modern World will be passing batons between the greatest of
    athletes
Ours will be butter fingered.

The Modern World will suck at the thirsty soil
We primitive mercenaries wait patiently with open mouths
To be nourished and cared for.

7 Our Cause is NO MAN'S.
We exist between borders, belonging in no-man's-land.
Framed as we are by the Holy Ghost of air
Held between two hands in prayer.
Devoted to no-man. You shall find us rejoicing
With hot tears in our eyes
Doing such irrational and godforsaken things
In such elegant ways
As to churn the bile in our bellies
Causing us to clutch each other's ruined bodies
In foul-mouthed frenzy.

Watch as we waltz through the filthy streets
To the abandoned houses of worship
Where infants wait to pluck thorns from our bleeding feet
Sunk like anchors into innocent white flesh.
Sucking at the marrows, where the milk of kindness is kept.

Our cause is our own,
And though no man shall suffer as we do,
Neither will they know our release.

**8 We set Humour at Humour's throat. Stir up Civil War
among peaceful apes.**
In consolation, when the iron bars are taken away...

Some pink-fleshed apes
will choose to remain in the zoo
having grown fond of their cage.

Tom Fleming and Hayden Thorpe

While others who do remember the forest
will use their warm legs to carry them
to their keeper's throat.

9 We only want Humour if it has fought like Tragedy.
How we laugh all the harder
At those moments when our cheeks
Should be buttery with sob

How similar our bodies look
When doubled-up in agony or
Unrelenting joy

How we are able, with big brains,
To learn the small differences
Between such states

How we are set apart
From more simple creatures

How summoning those fragments of funny
In oceans of broken glass
And knowing our own reflection in the shards
Are some of the most sophisticated skills
Civilisation passes on

How we drag our songs to the gallows
To examine those soft-fleshed subjects
That are most delicate and hidden.
For that brief flash, that snapshot
Of ourselves...

How we collaborate in our own de-pantsing
To do nothing else but laugh hysterically
At what we find underneath

How does any decent sport hold thrill
If not laden with so much violence and bravado?
It is in the losing fight when we feel most alive!

How vigilante mobs stir from their safe homes
To put peaceful wrongs
To violent rights.

10 We only want Tragedy if it can clench its side-muscles like hands on its belly, and bring to the surface a laugh like a bomb.
The grotesque is beautiful how prettiness never can be.
True, shocking beauty is alluring
Only for those with strong enough constitutions,
Whose crude immodesty lets them arrest
Their hands from their brow.

Ease on the eye is for men and women
Too lazy to love the ugly
As it deserves to be loved.

I say show those milksops the pock-scarred face of nature
And let it be celebrated!
Such vomit inducing examples will serve to remind you
That your sorry little life is only ever
Devastating and pitiful.

A laugh gurgles the guts
And a herculean grin
Is smeared upon your features.

Laugh my son, laugh like a mad bastard
At the absurdity of us all.

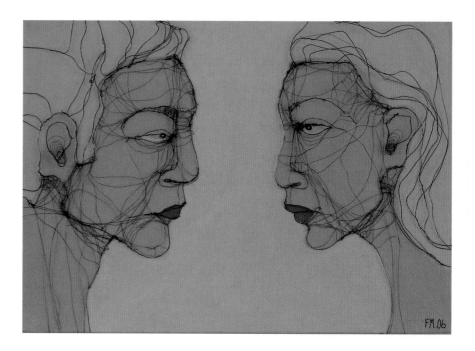

Tom Fleming and Hayden Thorpe

The 'Inky Fingers' blog appears twelve times a year on the website of the Observer Music Monthly, *where it builds – month by month – into a complete anatomy of British pop criticism. But the intentions of pseudonymous author Maggoty Lamb go far beyond the merely commemorative. By subjecting the bedraggled remnants of the once mighty UK music press (alongside its broadsheet, glossy tabloid and online inheritors) to the sternest of moral and aesthetical examinations, and projecting the results directly into the blogosphere, he/she aims to open up a new channel of communication between the impoverished critical discourse of the present day and the millennial dreams of the old school rock-hack. As well as establishing a repository for music journalism's finest traditions of unfettered idealism, syntactical overload, and industrial-strength sarcasm.*

This edited selection of entries covers the period December 2007–December 2008.

December 2007

—

Forensic perusal of the Christmas best-of lists is one of the great pleasures of the musical year. Seeing which obscure but not entirely brilliant album has overcome its incipient mediocrity to be controversially number two with a bullet in the Rough Trade Shops' top 50 ('Oh, you mean you haven't been listening to *The Novelist* by Richard Swift or [this year's choice] Patrick Watson's *Close To Paradise*? How can you possibly live with yourself?'). Marvelling at the sudden disappearance of records prematurely deemed to be classics on their initial release (Roisin Murphy, how quickly we forget). These innocent enjoyments of the festive season are to be cherished with the same intensity that earlier generations used to bring to the roasting of chestnuts

But this year a sombre shadow has fallen across this idyllic winter landscape. When last month's free *Q* CD managed to come up with a 16-track 'best of 2007' selection which contained absolutely no music by black artists (for all the considerable input of peerless Afro-beat drummer Tony Allen, The Good, The Bad & The Queen cannot really be classified thus, however much Alex James

might argue that Damon Albarn would like them to be), it was possible to view this as an isolated aberration. Looking at this month's editions of Britain's leading music magazines, however, that head-in-the-sand position gets increasingly hard to maintain.

Has there ever previously been a year when neither *Mojo* nor *Q* has had a single artist of colour in their respective top 30? I don't think so. Even *Uncut* can find room for M.I.A. But only M.I.A. Not, say, Dizzee Rascal, or Common, or Kanye West, or Rihanna, or the Wu-Tang Clan. And as for Orchestra Baobab, well, don't even think about it.

Now all of the above acts produced truly impressive albums over the past twelve months. But if the pasty-faced legions of indie or country-rock had marched onward to a year of unprecedented creative triumph, their absences might be entirely proper. So let's look at some of the alternative choices. Nick Lowe, The Shins, Bright Eyes, Andrew Bird, Linda Thompson, Efterklang and Pissed Jeans have all made it into *Mojo*'s top 30. Obviously these things are a matter of opinion, but with no disrespect intended to any of the artists concerned, it's not exactly the rock 'n' roll hall of fame, is it?

Scouring year-end lists for top acts you're

not that familiar with in order to check whether they are black or white is an uncomfortable experience for anyone who believes in the power of music to transcend boundaries of colour and creed. (Especially when the legendary rigour of the *OMM* blog fact-checking dept demands a phone call to the boss of The Cinematic Orchestra's record company to confirm that they are, as I always suspected, honkies.) Of course, it is nice to imagine a world in which all musical talent would be acclaimed and rewarded equally, irrespective of ethnicity, but such a planet would be a very different place from the one we actually live on, however much those with a vested interest in maintaining the status quo like to pretend otherwise.

Once you've rejected the transparently bogus notion of some monumental downturn in the creative achievements of black music, an alternative explanation has to be found for this bizarre outbreak of year-end apartheid. In a piece in this month's *New Yorker*, the critic Sasha Frere-Jones suggests one. As a rule Inky Fingers is contractually obliged to deal only with articles you can hold in your hand, but in this case a web-link is the least those sufficiently culturally self-assured enough not to have subscriptions to *The New Yorker* deserve: http://www.newyorker.com/arts/critics/musical/2007/10/22/071022crmu_music_frerejones?printable=true

The basic thrust of this very long article (with apologies for any subtleties that may have been lost in translation) is that having enjoyed Arcade Fire the first time he saw them, on second viewing the author begins to find their obliviousness to what rock journalists of the 1970s would have had no compunction about calling 'the groove' to be

indicative of a disturbing trend within the disparate musical kingdom that unites beneath the tattered banner of 'Indie'. He identifies this tendency as a willing, if not self-conscious, rejection of those attributes which have historically been associated with black music (warmth, sensuality, rhythm) in favour of a kind of Caucasian autism.

Now Frere-Jones is a gifted music-writer – especially knowledgeable and committed in the fields (hip hop, grime even) where his magazine's coverage might be expected to be at its weakest – but this article is not one of his finest moments. Not because the propensity he describes does not exist, but because it is nothing new. As any veteran of the halcyon days of the mid-'80s will tell you, a large faction of musicians within the cadre that used to be called alternative until it became the mainstream has *always* – at least in the pre indie-disco epoch – rejoiced in its right to disdain rigorous beat-keeping and conventional notions of musicianly expertise (though God knows, Bogshed were funky).

If *The New Yorker* does not have the solution to the 2007 year-end whitewash mystery, where is an explanation to be found? Perhaps Morrissey's recent spat with the *NME* would be a good place to start. As this is the subject of endless (and endlessly diverting) speculation elsewhere, I am not going to reflect on it for long. Except to say two things.

First, that the assessment of the *NME*'s decline in Morrissey's extended rebuttal statement is one of the most astute pieces of criticism in the history of pop literature (anyone who doubted this had only to see the way the paper's editor vindicated his disgruntled cover-star's criticism of his 'cheers mate, got pissed last night, ha ha' approach by prefacing the next week's unusually grown-up

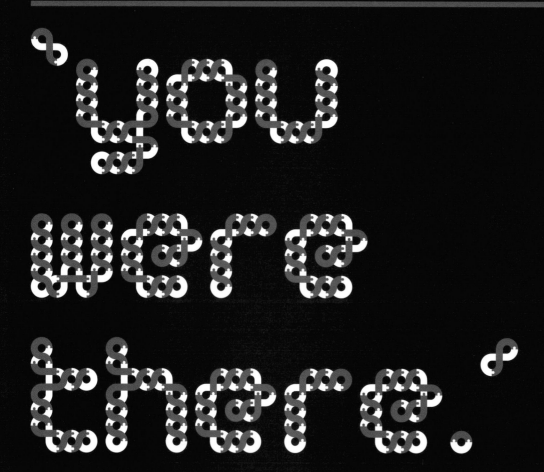

'you were there.'

letters page with the condescending proviso 'when a mate suddenly says something that makes you uncomfortable, you have to respond'). Second – and warming to a literary theme – it is intriguing to note the extensive parallels between the Morrissey/*NME* face-off and another recent 'racism' furore: the one involving Martin Amis.

Both cases revolve around a crumbling but still grandiose pillar of the '80s counter-culture (it wasn't just the sixties that had one of those, whatever those baby-boomers might try to tell us) with a new album or book to promote. Both began when wilfully provocative statements about matters of great contemporary import were deliberately taken out of context by self-appointed guardians of liberal opinion.

Under attack from a motley selection of adversaries – in Morrissey's case, assorted out-of-their-depth *NME* hacks; in Amis's, a bizarre alliance of crusty Old School Marxist Terry Eagleton, writer of TV terrorist dramas Ronan Bennett and a seemingly deranged Chris Morris (whose uncharacteristically clumsy interventions in this debate are only explicable in terms of un-requited love affairs with either Islamic fundamentalism, or Martin Amis, or both) – both singer and novelist have sharpened up their acts considerably. The spectacle of Amis and Morrissey resolving the careless ambiguities in their original positions, rediscovering their respective polemical mojos, and swatting their would-be tormentors aside with a magisterial flick of the quill, has been an intensely gratifying one.

However, it is in the unspoken assumptions of the 'anti-racist' position that the awkward truths of this situation are really to be found. The weird totalitarian undertones

(as opposed to the loveable populist ones who sang 'My Perfect Cousin') of both Bennett and Morris need not detain us here. But the awe-inspiring hypocrisy of the *NME*'s position certainly warrants closer attention.

For all the relentlessness with which this once authentically more-radical-than-thou publication trumpets its 'Love Music Hate Racism' campaign, its writers' own choices send out a very different message about the paper's credentials in this area. No, M.I.A. is not the lone non-white representative in the paper's top thirty albums of the year. But the two black faces who join her – Lethal Bizzle and Bloc Party's Kele Okereke – both secure admission to the *NME* pantheon only via their willingness to partake in (and in Kele's case, to administer) the white-bread sacrament of indie rock. Perhaps next time the paper's editor is about to pontificate about the evils of racism, he might ask himself how many hip hop artists he put on his cover in 2007.

At the start of this decade, when the British music industry decided to marginalise the thriving home-grown UK garage scene, via the disastrous strategy of calling all records made by black people 'urban', and everything else 'pop', certain prophets of doom sensed a conspiracy afoot. Seven years on and – with a little help from Michael Parkinson – their most apocalyptic projections have been surpassed. In a country where Jamie Cullum represents jazz, and Joss Stone and Amy Winehouse are our best-known soul voices, it now seems as if only white performers are allowed to have careers singing black music.

The specialist British music press needs to take a step back from the conveyor belt of deadlines, demographics, and circulation anxieties, and ask itself serious questions about the role it has played in this process of ghettoisation, and whether – to borrow for a moment the antique language of agit-prop – it wants to be part of the solution, or part of the problem.

Reading this month's *Mojo* cover-story (or non-story, as she didn't actually turn up for the interview) on Amy Winehouse, it's certainly clear that something needs to be done. After poignantly describing La Winehouse singing 'a song for her husband…the man she's so desperately in love with: a man currently being held in a prison cell' Paul Elliott goes on to depict her thus: 'Illuminated by a single spotlight, the tortured artist is laid bare in a moment of transcendental intensity.'

Apparently, 'This is an image that carries echoes of Winehouse's heroine Billie Holiday.' Well, up to a point. At least in the same way that *Harry Potter* 'carries echoes' of Tolkien. Or the fictitious plays of Ernie Wise 'carried echoes' of Anton Chekhov. Billie Holiday was a musical genius whose extraordinary body of work encapsulated the agony and the ecstasy of one of the twentieth century's great liberation struggles. Amy Winehouse is a talented suburban stage-school graduate (I know she got chucked out, but you don't have to stay in those places for long) who seems to have a death-wish.

These two artistic phenomena are not the same, and it's about time people stopped pretending they were. It is especially unsettling to see a magazine with *Mojo*'s unrivalled reputation for furthering the appreciation of a broad spectrum of musical endeavour (cf. this month's lovely free Stax soul cover-mounted CD) peddling this kind of garbage. But a change, as Sam Cooke pointed out, is

definitely going to come. These things always move in cycles, and there is a powerful impetus for natural justice within pop's still thriving eco-system.

January 2008

—

Before we get down to the exciting business of analysing which of this month's next big things might be 2008's Kate Nash, and which will be its Circulus, there is a bit of outstanding business left over from 2007.

First, a few words in praise of *The Wire*'s end-of-year issue. Not only does this trusty institution trump all other specialist round-ups by actually coming out at the end of December, it is also the annual best-of list most likely to single out an ensemble called Kiss the Anus of the Black Cat as having made 'one of the most interesting records of the year'.

I especially love the beleaguered, even apocalyptic tone of the 'Writers' Reflections'. Only while reading the line, 'On a dark January night here in Washington DC, the chill of Presidential inauguration was dulled by the responding heat of Monotract' does the sick truth hit home that the issue currently delighting me is actually two years old. But that's the great thing about *The Wire*: for all its earnest avowal of rupture and dissonance, it is actually this magazine's rare sense of continuity and tradition which keeps loyal readers in its ascetic spell.

Fast-forwarding to this January's '2007 Rewind' spectacular, even the usually upbeat Simon Reynolds begins his recollection of the highlights of the past twelve months 'Against the backdrop of blank bleakness', while someone called Adrian Shaughnessy whets our appetite for his nostalgic look back with the following summary: 'A year of green-flecked morbidity and environmental foreboding.' Someone buy that man a Girls Aloud album.

Of those with a more positive outlook, Louise Gray's personal highlight – 'Watching a colony of Greek bats dip and dive above Laurie Anderson's head in the gathering dark of an open-air concert staged in the Odeon of Herodes Atticus' – is probably this issue's most transcendent piece of lifestyle-based one-upmanship. Although Edwin Pouncey certainly deserves some kind of honourable mention – not so much for setting himself the challenge of first finding and then listening to the complete works of terrifying avant-jazz eminence Anthony Braxton on vinyl, but for actually finding this 'a sublimely pleasurable and educating experience'.

All of which brings us (and just in time, some might say) to 2008's bumper crop of highly fancied newcomers. There is something rather inspiring about the sheer abundance of new names on display this year. It seems that the more nay-saying and doom-mongering goes on in and around the music industry, the more eagerly gangs of fresh-faced innocents strive to get entangled within its rusty mechanism.

A few Januarys back, Starsailor were all we had to look forward to. The great thing about 2008's myriad young pretenders is that they all have the kinds of names you'd give new bands if you were making them up yourself. Joe Lean & The Jing Jang Jong, Black Kids, Eli 'Paperboy' Reed, Foals . . . Essentially these are the pop equivalents of the made-up names Alan Partridge's sports report gave the rival mounts in the legendary horse-racing episode of *The Day Today*. It will be exciting to see how many of them will still just be names by the end of the year, and how many of these performers will have acquired enough extra layers of collective character – in the same way that, say, Oasis or Blur have (but Elbow, sadly, haven't) – that you need to think twice to remind yourself that the words they've chosen to represent themselves also have other, simpler, meanings.

Comparing the rival new faces of 2008 coverage in *Mojo*, *Q*, and *NME*, it is encouraging to see the first of these magazines doing its job properly by picking out people no one else has mentioned, like the aforementioned Eli 'Paperboy' Reed – 'Bostonian king of rhythm & soul' (whatever that means) – and promising LCD Soundsystem-approved house enthusiasts Hercules & Love Affair. Highlights of the *NME*'s similarly expansive top eleven include Yo! Majesty – Domino Records' first ever lesbian hip hop duo from Florida (remember folks, you read it here second) – and sardonic major label enthusiasts MGMT.

Q's list is, predictably enough, the stodgiest and least interesting of the three. (Anonymous-sounding Scouse foursome The Troubadours are introduced with the not-so-enticing tag-line 'If you like The La's and The Coral, try this', while the horribly named Glasvegas are described as 'The Jesus And Mary Chain meets Phil Spector'.) I thought the whole point of the Jesus And Mary Chain was that they had *already* – in musical terms at least – met Phil Spector). In the latter magazine's defence, it should be noted that *Q* is also the only one of this month's music titles to feature Mariah Carey's answers to readers' questions ('If you're a guy in my house, you're going to be on your knees fixing something' being my favourite response).

As competition for dwindling stocks of potential purchasers continues (to borrow the catchphrase of *Masterchef* ingredients expert Gregg Wallace) to 'just get tougher', the need to demonstrate mastery of upcoming trends becomes ever more pressing. This anxiety has now spread outwards from the specialist music press to what used to be called Fleet Street – and beyond – with potentially perilous consequences.

I think it was *Elle* that recently described feisty and worldly-wise South London ingénue Adele as having 'A catalogue of heartbreak to rival Leonard Cohen's'. Those are pretty big shoes for a 19-year-old Brixtonian to be asked to fill. No doubt she'll give it her best shot, but such is the deadening effect of all this pre-emptive hyperbole that it is now possible for people to feel they have already had enough of Adele's music (or indeed that of her fellow new year's handicap front-runner, Duffy) before they've even heard it. In this context, it is the responsibility of the critical community – and even using those three words (not 'of' and 'the', the other ones) in such close proximity feels like it's asking for trouble – to stop overloading up-and-coming acts with unreasonable expectations before their first albums have even hit the shelves.

In a cultural climate where the language used to describe the sounds people make seems to be slipping its moorings in the marina of actual significance, it's intriguing that one of this year's biggest creative growth areas should be spoken word with musical accompaniment. Such is the vogue for off-kilter narration that it surpasses not only the current upsurge of onomatopoeic band-names (How many Ting-Tings does it take to change a Holton's Opulent Oog?), but

also the sudden glut of Afro-pop (or, at least in Vampire Weekend's case, Paul Simon's *Graceland*)-influenced indie bands, as 2008's most beguiling subliminal trend. And that took some doing; the second of those other developments being especially welcome, if only for how foolish it's made *The New Yorker*'s Sasha Frere-Jones look.

It's not just poetically inclined East Londoner George Pringle who's carrying the torch here (although she has certainly got something – even if it is only the capacity to compress into a single verse everything that's most untrustworthy about people who live in Hoxton by choice). There are also winningly articulate Laughing Clowns-influenced psycho-geographers One More Grain to be considered. And let's not forget the boozy soundscapes of Gerry Mitchell and Little Sparta – gleefully colonising the previously unmapped buffer state between Arab Strap and Sir John Betjeman.

March 2008

—

Up to this point, it has seemed best not to consider *The Word* as part of the research sample for our monthly investigations into the psychic well-being of the British music press. That decision has not been taken with the intention of making the hard-pressed coterie of erstwhile EMAP executives who put the magazine together feel bad about themselves (they are prey to enough anxieties as it is), but to encourage them to believe in their dream.

As *The Word*'s 'director' David Hepworth explained in his anguished summary of the first half-decade of the title's existence in the recent fifth-birthday edition: 'When we launched this magazine . . . it was our intention to cover TV, film, books and technology as well as music.' Yet when faced with the dilemma of where the magazine ought to be racked in supermarkets, its publishers opted (perfectly sensibly) to throw in their lot with *Classic Rock* and *Mixmag* – rather than, say, *New Scientist* or *The Puzzler* – on the grounds that 'nobody was likely to buy the magazine who wasn't interested in music'. And now *The Word* has 'Music Magazine of the Year!' on its masthead (is that exclamation mark ironic? I think perhaps it is. I think it is an exclamation mark which encapsulates the abandonment of an ideal), it seems reasonable to assume that the die has been cast.

The funny thing is, there would be no reason to see this tightening of editorial focus as in any way problematic, if it weren't for the feelings of impotent fury it apparently inspires in the magazine's top brass. After all, if you consider the respective (sadly, long gone) heydays of both *Rolling Stone* and the *NME*, these two publications derived the intellectual momentum and moral authority to establish a broader cultural agenda entirely from their pre-eminence in the well-ploughed field of rock criticism. And yet, when Hepworth addresses the music-led iconography of that elusive and enigmatic entity – the regular *The Word* reader – he does so with a hostility that borders on outright hatred.

'Your heroes are probably cultish and slightly off-centre,' Hepworth virtually hisses. 'One of your defining characteristics is the desire not to appear obvious.' Are these bad attributes in a reader? I don't think so. And yet his magazine's failure to attain the commercial objective he had set for it – to help him and his colleagues, in his own

words 'get rich' ('If I had a premium whisky I would put my money into sponsoring *The Word* podcast,' Hepworth wheedles later on, '. . . By the way you haven't *got* a premium whisky have you?') – seems to have turned him bitter.

In the course of an otherwise perfectly interesting and well-written encounter with kora master Toumani Diabate, in which Hepworth is privileged to be granted access to the celebrated nightlife of the Malian capital, Bamako, he refers to 'slim white aid workers doing the international dance of the smug'. Perhaps it's just me, but in a battle for moral superiority between physically fit charity employees enjoying a dance on a well-earned night off, and a veteran pop hack jetting out to the world famous The Hogon nightclub on record-company expenses, I fear there can only be one winner. And it's not David Hepworth.

The Word's other former *Whistle Test* presenter Mark Ellen puts a more personally appealing gloss on the dark cloud of self-doubt which hangs over the magazine's fifth-birthday edition. 'It's wise to adopt a self-lacerating view of your own capabilities,' he warns, 'if you want to survive the storms of contemporary publishing.' And while the blizzard of self-criticism which ensues makes a bracing and welcome change from the neurotic assertiveness of, say, the twenty-first century *NME*, I'm not sure if it actually leaves us any the wiser.

Devoting a whole page to 'The 20 Worst Bits of *The Word*' is undeniably a bold move, but apologising for having once put Dido on the cover ('the worst bit of *The Word* ever,' it says here) seems counterproductive, as well as unchivalrous in the extreme. Especially as the excuse offered for that particular editorial lapse (apparently Travis had 'put their album back a month') merely opens up a still more daunting vista of cosmic mediocrity. Indeed, it is possible that the attempt to establish a false dichotomy between Dido and Travis holds the key to the crisis of confidence with which this magazine seems to be afflicted.

If there is one sacred cow that *The Word* badly needs to slaughter, it is the idea that the expression of a preference – any preference, but especially one for Travis over Dido – is somehow of interest in itself. In the halcyon days of *Smash Hits* (one of the three most important DNA strands in the magazine's ancestral lineage, alongside *Select* and *Mojo*), it was fun to ask people what their favourite kind of cheese was, as the posing of such questions reminded us that the dark old days of political engagement and caring about anything were behind us, and now we were living in the eighties.

A quarter of a century on, however, as we teeter perpetually on the brink of the blogosphere's all too accessible abyss of unmediated likes and dislikes, a magazine which hopes to persuade people to pay money for it on a regular basis has to offer something a little more substantial. So when Mark Ellen identifies the 'Word of Mouth' section – in which a series of not especially eminent people tell us whether they have 'found any good books, films or records lately' – as 'the point of the publication', it seems like he is selling the whole enterprise short.

Is this really what all concerned hoped for when they waved goodbye to their fat corporate pay-cheques to reconnect with their mojos (although not their *Mojos*) by coming together in a single room to put together a glossy magazine with a fanzine mentality? In my ideal world, *The Word* would not be a gated retirement community with only the occasional sympathy call from a highly paid BBC employee to look forward to. It would be a heroic and almost ludicrously risky mid-life experiment – a little bit Tom Cruise in *Jerry Maguire*, a little bit Tom Good in *The Good Life*, and a whole lot Peter Finch in *Network*.

It would cut down on the unbelievably sycophantic two-page interviews with Mark Kermode ('My sacred areas are *not* negotiable . . . Everyone who doesn't agree is *wrong*.') and bump up the commendably pithy demolitions of Alex James's performance on *Question Time* ('Anyone who saw it wanted him strangled.'). The fact that these two diametrically opposed articles were written by the same journalist (Rob Fitzpatrick is his name) is evidence first of how deep is the split in *The Word*'s personality, and second of how close to hand its salvation might lie.

May 2008

—

With which major historical event do you find it easiest to associate Coldplay? The Diet of Worms? The Irish Potato Famine? The Scramble For Africa? The Molotov–Ribbentrop Pact? As nonsensical as these suggestions are, none of them is quite as ridiculous as the one the band themselves have come up with.

On the cover of last week's 'new look' edition of the *NME*, readers yet to acclimatise to the drastic change in editor Conor McNicholas's byline photo (out go the wind-machine and Scott Baio's old hair, in come the kind of glasses Jodie Marsh wears when she wants to look like a big reader) were obliged to face up to an even more radical redrawing of their intellectual parameters. Those lucky enough to have seen the musical *Les Miserables* will remember the plucky Gallic urchin who sings the poignant street-fighting anthem 'Little People' before meeting a tragic end in a hail of monarchist bullets. Well, Coldplay are dressed as him.

The idea of Chris Martin and co. posing as French revolutionaries is a provocative one for a number of reasons. Let us set aside for a moment the nagging suspicion that had they actually taken part in Robespierre's answer to the Glastonbury Festival, Coldplay's role would surely have been as victims of the guillotine, rather than foot soldiers of La Marseillaise. It would be churlish to condemn this band from an inverted snob's perspective when they have given us so many other much more persuasive reasons to hate them. (After all, if you're going to write Coldplay – or Radiohead or Blur for that matter – out of your rock 'n' roll script, purely on the basis of an accident of haute-bourgeois birth, you're going to have to do without The Clash, The Rolling Stones and Santogold as well.)

I for one have always been deeply offended by the way all four of their outfits are invariably styled to be slightly different yet remorselessly complementary – paying lip-service to the concept of individuality through slight tonal and textural variations, without ever actually having the courage to fully commit to it. And by extending this transcendently bogus styling methodology to their appropriation of the rags of a revolutionary army, Coldplay have somehow rendered themselves even more sartorially despicable.

'We designed the clothes ourselves,' claims Chris Martin – a man not previously regarded as a directional fashionista – before back-peddling prudently: 'Someone else made them, but we customised them.' If you look very closely at the first picture on the inside page, it is possible to discern compelling evidence of just how extensive Martin's personal contribution to this drastic image revamp might have been. The left cuff of his artfully distressed band-jacket is adorned with approximately two square inches of multi-coloured star stickers. Whether these had to be flown in from Milan or were simply borrowed from Apple's pencil-case, we will probably never know.

Either way, James McMahon's article – grandly titled 'Talkin' 'Bout A Revolution' (and the Tracy Chapman reference pitches it about right in terms of the extent of the musical upheaval involved) – abounds with similarly stark instances of creative underkill. Among the pointers we are given to Coldplay's new direction is the revelation that their specially prepared studio in Primrose Hill is 'across the road from a council estate' (so that's the urban audience taken care of), and has a picture of P. J. Harvey on the wall. Not since the news broke that Maeve Binchy writes beneath the malevolent eye of a life-sized portrait of William Burroughs has there been a similarly blatant instance of repositioning through Blu-Tack.

Unless you are one of the three or four people in Britain independent-minded enough not to have already downloaded it for nothing, *NME*'s free giveaway of a 7-inch vinyl copy of the first single 'Violet Hill' will have been of no more than sentimental value. But there is something grippingly

PERFECTING SOUND FOREVER
THE STORY OF RECORDED MUSIC

BY GREG MILNER

From Thomas Edison's claim in 1915 that he could perfectly capture the sounds of a live performance on his phonograph – to the most advanced digital tools used today – through all forms of music in all sorts of places – it's all in this book.

What makes a perfect recording, is a perfect recording even possible, and indeed, should a recording ever attempt to be perfect? You'll never listen to recorded music in the same way again.

GRANTA
www.granta.com

Available from all good bookshops ⊙ £20.00

insidious about the way Coldplay have laid claim to Oasis's musical and geographical territory at the same time (the imagined realm of Violet Hill presumably being fairly adjacent to the actual North London neighbourhood of Primrose Hill, where this album was made, and where Liam Gallagher likes to go jogging).

To be fair (which is of course this column's ultimate objective), 'Violet Hill' does have a nice little piano coda at an end – almost (though not quite) pleasant enough to erase the memory of that horrible pub joanna Martin played on Kanye West's supernaturally disingenuous 'Homecoming'. The bonus b-side 'A Spell A Rebel Yell', meanwhile, sounds a bit like an early '80s Peter Gabriel b-side, but not in an entirely bad way.

Aficionados of genuinely drastic change will find it between the lines of the *NME*'s Coldplay exclusive rather than in the actual quotes. I'm not sure at exactly what point it became first acceptable and then *de rigueur* for journalists working at this paper to subsume their individual personalities within the title's corporate identity by referring to themselves as 'The *NME*' in interview scenarios ('*NME* has been invited . . . *NME* politely declines', etc.). But those discerning the dead hand of 'Brand Manager' Steve Sutherland in this paradigm shift will probably not be too far off the money. Either way, its inherent absurdity is neatly encapsulated by the moment when Chris Martin demonstrates his capacity for charm by complementing a particular aspect of his interviewer's physiognomy, and editorial dogma decrees that this exchange should be rendered as Martin 'informs *NME* that *we* [my italics] have a "beautiful nose" '.

A Royal We from IPC: now that's what I call a new rock revolution. From an environment in which cocky young fanzine editors could hone their own style to a fine point of acerbity and egotism before striking out into the mainstream media, *NME* has become a kind of pet cemetery of writerly ambition. And when media-studies students of the future look to identify a precise moment when the paper finally surrendered its role as a proving ground for the Fleet Street columnists, Harry Hill script-writers and Radio 2 DJs of the future, this one will probably do as well as any.

June 2008

—

If *Mojo*'s Sex Pistols cover had a fight with *The Word*'s John Martyn cover, would the picture of Crosby, Stills, Nash and Young on the front of *Uncut* be the winner? This is just the first of a series of tricky philosophical questions raised by a close reading of this month's UK music magazines.

Does *Mojo*'s revelation of John Lydon's abiding love for Steeleye Span – meeting Maddy Prior was, Lydon confessed (throwing in a suitably archaic syntactical reversal to clinch the deal), 'one of the most wonderful things I ever have done' – atone for not even mentioning his upcoming high-profile court case, sparked by the erstwhile Johnny Rotten's showbiz tantrum about inadequate five-star hotel accommodation? Is it worth ploughing through a whole issue of *The Wire* just to find out that Wu-Tang overlord RZA based the structure of his excellent soundtrack to Jim Jarmusch's *Ghost Dog* on Stravinsky's *Peter & The Wolf*?

Even for those (and I must admit I am one of them) whose answer to the second of those rhetorical inquiries is a resounding

'Yes', it is hard to feel optimistic about the evolutionary progress of British popular music when the *NME* identifies the three essential albums of the moment as being by Coldplay, Spiritualized and Weezer, and a recent issue of *Q* gave three stars to obvious landmark new releases by Portishead and The Last Shadow Puppets, but four to The Rolling Stones' concert film and a Stereophonics live show. So it's nice to be able to announce two new ventures promising to bring an extra dimension to domestic pop discourse.

The first of these, a new 'online music portal' called 'Nationwide Mercury Prize Recommends' will have to work hard to overcome an informed usership's initial scepticism. While no one denies that the Mercury Prize (whose shortlist will emerge next month to the usual ecstatic cries of anguish) provides an excellent annual gambling opportunity, there are – to say the least – question marks over its decision-making pedigree. As consumer recommendations go, 'From the people who brought you M People's *Elegant Slumming*, Roni Size's *New Forms* and whatever the first Gomez album was called' probably raises more questions than it answers.

The problem for the Mercury Prize has always been the need to simultaneously shore up its own institutional status while gratifying the vanity of particular juries by keeping the public on the hop. Occasionally (as with Dizzee Rascal's *Boy In Da Corner*) these conflicting requirements have led to a truly inspired surprise selection. More often (see examples above) the overriding desire not to be seen to be making an obvious choice leads to an aggressively mediocre compromise whose underlying message is

'How dare you attempt to compromise the collective individuality of this panel by expecting us to actually pick the album we all know in our hearts is the best?' Whether or not that is a secure aesthetic foundation for an online portal, only time will tell.

This summer's other new pop publishing initiative comes with far more auspicious antecedents. The first edition of *Loops* – a biannual collaborative endeavour between Domino Records and Faber & Faber – is not scheduled to come out for a full twelve months. But its editors' advance promotional proclamation sets out their stall somewhere between *Mojo* and *Granta*, quite reasonably playing up the illustrious reputations of both participating organisations, while not putting undue emphasis on Lightspeed Champion's horrible cartoons, or that terrible book about rock lyrics and Greek mythology Faber published a few years back.

The idea of 'a haven for adventurous long-form music writing of every sort' is inevitably an appealing one to those who are lucky enough to fulminate about their favourite records for a living. But the question *Loops* will have to answer to its readers' satisfaction is whether a 'haven' is really the environment likely to bring the best out of people who – it might be argued – are already spoilt enough by virtue of having a job which enables them to get paid actual money to write about music they have been sent for free.

Looking back across the marvellously chequered history of rock journalism, doesn't most of the most memorable stuff seem to emerge from circumstances in which the four-way tension between writer, subject, reader and publication was running at its highest? In attempting to edit out the crackling static of commerce, not to mention the wow and flutter of deadlines and release schedules, there's a danger *Loops* might create the kind of sterile atmosphere often ascribed by learned critics such as Jack White and Neil Young to the digital recording process.

In their struggle to foster the right kind of mentality for a new music magazine – which is a sense of common purpose that stops short of being a house-style – *Loops'* editorial advisory board could do a lot worse than take a look at the recent anniversary issues of two very different but similarly enduring titles. While DJ bible *Mixmag's* Twenty-fifth Birthday Spectacular was wrapped in a costly but hilariously unglamorous *Vanity Fair*-style fold-out cover (Sven Vath's skinny tie and the scary gurning of Underworld's Karl Hyde were probably the images that it will be hardest to erase from the mind here), 'Worldwide roots music guide' *fRoots* celebrated its three-hundredth issue by changing its already confusing title to *fƺoots*, which looks more like a price-tag in a French department store than the name of a magazine.

The superficial contrasts between commemorative methodologies could hardly be more striking. *fRoots* gathered together a group of veteran writers including (get this, ladies) 'Colin Irwin in a crisp white shirt and jeans' around a kitchen table 'set with sheets of blank A4 . . . sharpened pencils . . . and bottles of sparkling water'. *Mixmag* gave decadent nightclub hosts Mike and Claire Manumission the chance to look back upon their own highlight of its first quarter of a century: 'that picture of Derek Dahlarge after Jon (Carter) stuck a dildo on his head with superglue'.

Yet beyond the yawning cultural gulf which separates the two publications, significant common ground could be clearly discerned. If knowing who you're speaking to and what you're trying to say to them is the vital first step to a magazine's long-term survival, using that knowledge as a license to expand those boundaries – rather than an excuse to retreat behind them – is the only way to really flourish.

Whether this means *Folk Roots* (as it then was) outraging morris-dancing die-hards with a Thomas Mapfumo cover story in 1985, or *Mixmag's* recent decision to risk the wrath of the turntablist establishment by putting two bands on the front in successive months (even accepting that those bands were The Klaxons and Hot Chip), the message for *Loops* is clear. If it wants to be more than a short-lived vanity-publishing exercise, it needs to work out exactly who its readers are going to be, and start thinking up ways to piss them off.

August 2008

—

A year ago, the first edition of this column promised to engage only with music journalism that was available in the theoretically antiquated but irrefutably glamorous medium of print. But the advent of www.thequietus.com – a website nobly devoted to providing a home for refugees from the Atlantis-like lost world of the early nineties rock press – has forced a reappraisal of Inky Fingers' objectives.

In today's fast-moving media landscape, it is vital to move with the times. As the great Caribbean polemicist C. L. R James might have put it, what do they know of *Uncut* whom only *Uncut* know? And for those who feared the closure of first *Sounds* and then *Melody Maker* meant they'd missed their last chance to ponder exactly where Ted Mico ends and Tommy Udo begins, the coming of *The Quietus* will be both a revelation and a source of emotional succour

This latest offshoot of the *Drowned In Sound* internet quasi-empire was, it says here, 'Born out of a frustration with the mainstream music press and a yearning for the kind of personality-driven writing that once violently engaged the reader.' When confronted with the words 'a frustration with' in situations of this kind, it is often a good idea to substitute the phrase 'an inability to secure employment within' and see if the sentence still makes sense. It does? Good, then let's read on.

'*The Quietus*', it says here, 'has spent the first half of the year pulling together an impressive cast list that reads like a greatest hits of music journalism from the past thirty years.'

Well, perhaps not quite like a 'greatest hits'. In fact, if there is a sustainable analogy for *The Quietus*'s contributors' list to be drawn from the world of the stopgap compilation release, it is probably the b-sides and unreleased tracks collection. Looming large among these journalistic relics are names such as 'Ex enfant-terrible' (truly a capsule description that chills the blood) Taylor Parkes, and 'Gold Blade frontman and writer' John Robb (and if that is the order in which this redoubtable ex Membranes mainstay turned pithy-soundbite-contributor-to-TV-list-shows expects posterity to rank his achievements, then who are we to argue?).

While the aggressively iconoclastic tone which characterised the *Melody Maker*'s original death throes grew mighty tiresome first time around, in the current almost hysterically uncritical critical climate – where the mildest of raised eyebrows with regard to the supposed once-in-a-lifetime genius of say, Bon Iver or Fleet Foxes, tends to be greeted as an act of profound aesthetic heresy – there is actually quite a lot to be said for it.

The absence of any kind of career safety-net – whether that takes the form of regular work at the BBC, or a freshly signed contract for a seventh volume of nauseatingly self-indulgent adolescent memoirs – seemed to add a welcome extra edge to some of *The Quietus*'s early album reviews. The occasional whiff of critical cordite makes a welcome change from the smugness and complacency which prevail all too often in the pages of, say, *The Word* (very much the propaganda of the victors, in terms of the early '90s music press diaspora).

Compressed rage and distilled sour grapes have always had an important role to play in rock journalism. And it was invigorating to see worthwhile but flawed albums such as Tricky's *Knowle West Boy* and The Bug's *London Zoo* – handled with kid gloves elsewhere – getting a slightly more stringent going over in the site's first few weeks.

The Quietus certainly shouldn't worry too much about never actually getting that promised Metallica exclusive (judging by how boring the one in this month's *Q* is, they didn't miss much). And so long as they don't get too bogged down in running rose-tinted retrospective features on 'the day David Stubbs got arrested with the KLF', (has it occurred to anyone that the real motivation behind Bill Drummond's latest campaign to 'end all recorded music' might be how horrible his old records sound?) this motley crew of old-stagers may even enjoy a glorious Indian summer.

Even as this optimistic prognosis makes the journey from mind to fingertips, news breaks of the sad demise of *Drowned In Sound* and *BSkyB*'s joint venture (a corporate tie-up of which I must admit myself to have been unaware, but I suppose someone had to be paying for *The Lipster*, and it might as well have been Rupert Murdoch). Early indications are that *The Quietus* 'will continue as an independent operation'. Perhaps Piers Morgan might be persuaded to put his hand in his pocket.

Last week's *NME* provided ample evidence of just how urgently new blood is needed in British rock journalism's ailing body politic (even if that new blood takes the form of old *Independent* Radiohead interviews by Andrew Mueller). And not just in the disturbing shape of the following half para at the start of Gavin Haynes' interview with The Hold Steady (another one of those bands about whom it is currently not safe for critics to entertain a critical thought): 'Craig Finn is a shepherd. Except he doesn't carry a staff and stand on hillsides. That's just boring. He's actually the most exciting kind of shepherd: a metaphorical one.'

The real alarm bell (and not the kind that rings to warn schoolchildren of a fire, thereby saving hundreds of innocent young lives. That's just boring. But the most exciting kind: a metaphorical one) was sounded by the double-page spread which rejoiced in the headline 'What Now For Dizzee?'

'A collaboration with Calvin Harris has seen Dizzee Rascal become a major league star', an ominous sub-header alerted any readers who had been away on holiday for more than the past eight weeks, 'but at what cost to his credibility – and to his art?' Before we can even begin to address the disingenuous absurdity of this rhetorical inquiry, it will be necessary to elegantly side-step the question of when it was that the *NME* last expressed concern about the 'credibility' of any of its rapidly vanishing demographic's favourite bands, never mind their 'art'? (My guess would be some time around 1982, but apparently there's one rule for The Verve and another for performers in the grime/hip hop/R'n'B idiom, so let's not allow this subsidiary issue to detain us.)

With the latest set of ABC sales figures revealing a 17.4 per cent decline in sales year on year, and Morrissey orchestrating a campaign of great resourcefulness and cunning in pursuit of legal redress for last year's ill-fated cover-story, you might think *NME* would have more pressing matters on its mind than whether Dizzee Rascal can 'survive' the unprecedented (and entirely deserved) chart success of 'Dance Wiv Me'. But apparently not.

Writer Barry Nicolson doesn't even have the courage to take responsibility for this utterly bogus show of phoney concern himself, but calls upon such 'experts' as Hattie Collins of 'UK hip hop bible' (and there was I thinking it was just a glossy fanzine given away free in jeans shops) *RWD* to make his non-points for him. 'There are definitely more credible [that word again] artists Dizzee could have chosen [than Calvin Harris],' asserts Collins, nervously. 'I don't know if the grime scene faithful will be too happy about it.'

Readers with reliable information as to exactly when it was that Dizzee Rascal last allowed his creativity to be constrained by the feelings of 'the grime scene faithful' are advised to keep it to themselves. In the meantime, let us break this situation down to its essentials.

On the one hand, we have a maverick East London MC who ever since the start of his career has shown an almost visionary determination not to be boxed in by other people's expectations. Who has shared stages with (among others) Jay-Z and Justin Timberlake, Matthew Herbert and the Red Hot Chili Peppers, Arctic Monkeys and Babyshambles. Who has survived not only a life-threatening multiple stabbing but also (potentially far more injurious in career terms) winning the Mercury Prize. Who has made three brilliantly diverse, intense and critically acclaimed albums, and sampled Captain Sensible's 'Happy Talk'. Whose one problem at this stage in his career seemed to be that he was banging his head against a glass ceiling at daytime radio and consequently in terms of actual record sales. And who has just spent an entire month at number one with a huge summer pop hit which he was able to put out as the debut release on his own Dirtee Stank imprint after his usual record label (the usually astute XL) passed on it.

On the other hand, we have the *NME*, which has a problem with Dizzee's creative collaborator Calvin Harris. Or can't forgive the Rasket for making his own luck. Or lost a feature on the day before press-day and had two pages to fill at short notice. Or (perhaps most likely) all three of the above.

'We certainly don't begrudge Dizzee the commercial success,' Barry Nicolson insists, not all that convincingly, 'but it says something worrying about the self-confidence of black British music that he's had to hook up with Calvin Harris to get it.' Does it really, Barry? Does it really? As they ponder the transcendent bad faith of that conclusion, readers may well ask themselves which of the two relevant parties they are more inclined to feel sorry for – the young British rapper, enjoying unprecedented crossover success entirely on his own terms, or the once great music paper, fallen on extremely hard times.

October 2008

—

First, an apology. There are so many important moral issues raised by this month's mainstream music publications that the in-depth analyses of *Art-Rocker* and *Plan B* which numerous Inky Fingers correspondents (not all of them co-editors of the former magazine) have been demanding will just have to wait a little while longer.

Second, a few words of unqualified praise. It is a rare thing for any newspaper or magazine to respond to a bad set of circulation figures by making a deliberate shift upmarket. But that is exactly what *Q* – not a title historically known for its willingness to take risks – appears to have done. The classy new typeface bids to establish a previously unremarked kinship with *The New Yorker*. Longish profiles of Will Self and Barack Obama ('Like U2 or the Rolling Stones,' the latter piece asserts reassuringly, 'Obama has been filling stadiums across America and around the world.') telegraph an audacious sneak attack on the unclaimed middle ground between *Uncut* and *Prospect*. And AC/DC's Angus Young is an exemplary choice of cover star – especially following so hard on the road-calloused heels of Metallica (anyone would think these people were taking Metal seriously), and with *Mojo* apparently stuck on an endless circle-line trip from the Beatles to the Clash and back again.

Inevitably, as with any redesign, there is the odd teething problem. Readers with fading eyesight may wonder whether the savage migraines induced by the almost-too-small-for-comfort typeset are worth incurring just to read 200 more of Rob Fearn's words about the new album by Keane. And the usually reliable Michael Odell's attempt to re-launch the 'Who the Hell does . . . think he/she is?' interview slot at the front of the magazine (this used to be *Q*'s signature feature, when the charismatically unsteady hand of Tom Hibbert was on the tiller) is too busy hedging its bets to actually take a proper gamble. Once you've opted to give a platform to the famously grandiloquent Will Self, it seems a bit churlish to take him to task for using too many long words. What's next – Girls Aloud's Sarah Harding getting a hard time for being a dirty stop-out?

But the one really jarring note in this unusually fresh 'new look issue' is sounded by Britpop authority and long-term *Q* stalwart John Harris's column about 'life in pop's dumper'. 'One of the more unpleasant downsides of writing about music,' Harris explains, is having to have conversations with musicians he first encountered on the way up, when their careers are headed in the opposite direction.

Perhaps before making this observation, he should have paused for a moment to consider how those on the other side of these awkward exchanges must feel about them. What does he expect the unfortunate victims of pop's ever-shortening career-cycle to do – crawl away and die? Then again, if the only other choice is being patronised by a regular panellist on *Newsnight Review*, I'm sure there's many a no-longer-quite-so-hotly-tipped indie band who might consider the cold comfort of the grave to be a blessed sanctuary.

The point at which this article's subtle tint of inhumanity really becomes a fluorescent glare is when Harris decides to include the Young Knives (alongside 'My Vitriol, The Von Bondies and good old Starsailor') in his list of formerly going concerns that 'the force is no longer with'. Those who used to read his fortnightly column in the front of the Friday *Guardian* will remember that Harris's personal fondness for these fogeyishly attired XTC-lovers was perhaps – next to the Kaiser Chiefs' status as the most significant British rock band of their generation – his most frequent recurring theme. And yet here he is callously consigning them to the dustbin of history with their second album barely cold on the shelves.

It is one of the many great unfairnesses of life that while (with a bit of luck and a following wind) it is possible to make a steady and even comfortable living from music journalism over a number of decades, the majority of the talented and charismatic musicians the writer first got into the business in the hope of bandying words with will probably have spent a large part of that time surviving on or around the breadline. But the appropriate response to this blatant inequity in fiscal rewards and overall job security is to feel humble, grateful and slightly ashamed, not to externalise your guilt by stamping on the hands of those who helped you up the ladder towards becoming the new Mark Lawson.

This month's other biggest talking point is supplied by a journalist whose institutional status is even more well established. Fred Dellar has been learnedly dispensing information about Eel Pie Island and the first rock festival since just after the last ice age (and long may he continue to do so). But his column in this month's *Mojo* demonstrates the dilemma facing the twenty-first-century music press as starkly as the ominous clunk of a falling stalactite signals rapidly rising sea-levels.

Under the heading 'Download Blues', Dellar suggests that the advent of the illegal internet-enabled musical acquisition 'brought a whole new meaning to the word freeloading'. Of course, the *old* meaning of the word 'freeloading' was as closely bound up with the profession of rock journalism as 'gazump' is with estate-agency. And Dellar's anguished restatement of the music industry's now largely abandoned zero-tolerance policy on downloads ('Much as it pains me to admit it, The Man was right…') would carry more conviction if it came from someone who had received slightly fewer free albums over the last eon.

But this isn't just a matter of people who live in glass houses being better advised not to throw stones. Clearly visible within the ruined greenhouse of Dellar's intellectual position is a thriving tomato-plant of enlightenment. For if his argument looks like a last-ditch attempt to defend the rock journalist's ancestral rights not only to hear new music before everyone else but also to do so without paying against the democratising impact of the internet (which it does), might this not imply that the free download has made music journalists of us all?

On a practical level the consequences of this seismic shift can already be discerned in the music press's increasingly desperate struggle to defend its dwindling sphere of influence against the barbarian hordes of the blogosphere. And it is in this context that the traditional print media's ambivalent attitude towards the internet can most easily be understood. Elsewhere in the same edition

of *Mojo* as Fred Dellar's Canute-like stand against the encroaching digital tide, a leaked version of 'Rat Patrol From Fort Bragg' – Mick Jones's fabled original mix of *Combat Rock* – is conspiratorially described as being 'just an internet search away'. Yet the apparent contradiction between these two opposing approaches to what are still sometimes quaintly termed 'new media' can be quickly reconciled with the help of a further application of that trusty old proverb about inhabitants of vitreous dwellings.

The music magazine which reminds its readers too often that a broadband connection is the only key they need to unlock the bounteous treasure-house of twenty-first century pop is playing fast and loose with its own future, as the rock press's survival in physical form is contingent upon the enduring allure of the artefact. Anyone who doubts this need only consider how closely the most fondly remembered eras of Britain's best known pop and rock publications were associated with particular physical formats. For the *NME* of the late seventies it was the vinyl single and album, for *Smash Hits* in its early '80s pomp, the cassette single and 12-inch took centre stage, for *Q* the CD established a new benchmark of character-free audio reproduction, while *Mojo* rejoiced in the advent of the lavishly annotated boxed set.

It's a measure of the extent to which the live show has superseded the recorded album as the music industry's primary income generator that the closest the 2008 vintage *NME* comes to a totemic object is probably a Reading or Leeds Festival wrist-band. And the breathless 'You were there, and we were too' tone of that paper's coverage of such events reflects the rapidly narrowing divide between punter and critic – an aesthetic

'self-styled media elite.'

restructuring whose consequences have yet to be fully understood.

In theory, such a *bouleversement* of rigid intellectual hierarchies can only be a positive development. And yet, if the privileges which were once the exclusive domain of a self-styled media elite are now open to all, surely this renders the listening population at large susceptible to those very moral failings – cynicism, ennui, an ill-founded sense of infinite entitlement – which were once the rock hack's particular button-badges of shame? At the risk of proposing music journalists as people who might have some form of guidance to offer, the ranks of this oft-despised profession contain many a washed-up hater-of-all-that-they-once-loved who could sorrowfully affirm that if you are not obliged to consider the possibility that anything might have a price, it is all too easy to forget that it actually has a value.

November 2008

—

You know that feeling of mingled joy and frustration when the set of keys you've just spent ages looking for turns out to have been lurking in the pocket of your chinchilla overcoat all along? Such was the mix of emotions prompted by a belated run-in with the November issue of *The Wire* (still available at many discerning retailers, especially Ray's Jazz in Foyles).

For all those wondering how the music magazine can continue to justify its existence as an old-school analogue-style artefact when the cultural landscape it endeavours to map is increasingly navigated using digital co-ordinates, *The Wire*'s 'Unofficial Channels: A Tour of Music's Unauthorised Domains' was simultaneously reassuring and revelatory.

Not only was this the most considered, eloquent and downright useful collection of music journalism I've read this year – either online or on the printed page – it also came in a beautifully designed cover.

From Simon Reynolds's even-handed assessment of the 'sharity' whole-album-blog bonanza, to Derek Walmsley's heartfelt appreciation of the home-made Grime DVD, each of this series of short pieces shone a light through a different window of the imposing mansion of digital abundance. And by incorporating fond snapshots of earlier generations' landmarks of access-all-areas audio overkill (from Biba Kopf's improbable yen for Grateful Dead bootlegs, to Byron Coley's more predictable teenage entanglement with John Peel whole-show cassettes), an already vivid picture was given a valuable extra historical dimension.

In avoiding the bogus year zero hoopla which so often surrounds such investigations, this issue of *The Wire* not only established a powerful sense of continuity between pre- and post-internet listening patterns, it also created the perfect showcase for the virtues of the printed word. (If there is a website out there consistently offering critical analysis of this quality, I would dearly love to know its address.)

The Wire's best attribute has generally been an unusual willingness to ask difficult questions of its readers (daring to raise the controversial but fascinating possibility that consumers might have responsibilities as well as rights would certainly come under this heading). Its worst (as seen to truly gruesome effect in the October issue's Neil Young 'primer') is an adolescent desire to appear iconoclastic even when it doesn't actually have anything at all radical to say.

Happily, this month's issue finds the magazine again operating much nearer the top end of its game than the bottom, courtesy of vivid and informative pieces on Radio Ballads and West African Psychedelia (the latter featuring superb photos of Prince Nico in platform boots, the ever elegant Orchestre Poly-Rythmo De Cotonou and Sir Victor Uwaifo's funky dwarf associate King Pago), as well as a priceless digital tip-off (that tip-off being: go to www.grimetapes.com if you want to find out what Dizzee Rascal sounded like on Deja Vu FM in 2000).

The music title with real problems this month is *Q*. Having endeavoured with some success to reposition itself as the new *Word*, the second instalment in the magazine's new era finds it losing the courage of its convictions faster than a 'Brown Bounce'-befuddled Conservative front bench. While AC/DC's Angus Young was an excellent choice of stand-alone cover attraction, Razorlight's Johnny Borrell simply does not have the star wattage to illuminate an entire front page. In fact, he may be the most eloquent living argument for the magazine's old policy of packing its frontage with as many familiar faces as possible in the hope that there'd be someone there readers might be interested in.

It is a telling judgement on the horrendously low quality of this edition that the ten-page Razorlight interview is not the worst thing about it. Everywhere you look, regular features are engaged in a headlong descent down the evolutionary scale. The reactivated 'Who the Hell . . .' interview slot slumps from Will Self to Toby Young, the 'Round with . . .' lapses from Sugababes to Kelly Jones of the Stereophonics. Coming up next month . . . Richard Littlejohn enjoys a good old piss-up with the Pigeon Detectives.

Publish each edition as if were your last – that seems to be the mantra in ever straightening economic circumstances. And for those who worry that the magazine *Disappear Here* – Peaches Geldof's brave literary blueprint for 'the eradication of the ego', as featured in the grimly hilarious MTV reality show of the same title (think of it as *Some Kind of Monster* to *Nathan Barley's Spinal Tap*) – may never actually make it onto the news-stands, this month's edition of *Artrocker* supplies some consolation.

If even the sage interventions of former *NME wunderkind* James Brown as a kind of Noriyuki 'Pat' Morita to Peaches's Karate Kid cannot save La Geldof's venture from the scrapheap, admirers of the superbly po-faced band Ulterior (seen being interviewed on a recent episode) can breathe a sigh of relief, sure in the knowledge that a magazine already exists which is willing to take Ulterior as seriously as they take themselves. *Artrocker* is that magazine.

'Kids today don't have posters on their walls,' proclaims Ulterior guitarist 'Simmons' in the course of a memorable interview by the excellently named Lee Puddefoot. 'Why not? Why's that changed? That's what got us into music, that obsessive commitment.'

We should all find our own means of honouring that obsessive commitment which once led kids to have posters on their walls. My way is to strive to overcome the recently acquired mental block which is currently preventing me from opening each new edition of *Uncut* magazine. (You would think such a synaptic reflex would be an obstacle to writing a heartfelt appreciation of all that is best in Britain's music press, but up to now it actually seems to have made life easier.)

I wonder what's on the cover . . . 'Paul

Weller – A Year with the Guv'nor'? No, sorry . . . just . . . can't do it. Oh well, maybe next month.

December 2008

—

Before we can get down to the real business of this month – which is to use the swishing fly-whisk of truth to dispel the toxic cloud of hyperbole which currently engulfs the two most overrated albums of the year – a little bit of background is called for. An aesthetic virus has afflicted the language of music journalism over the past twelve months which is only explicable within a much broader historical context. And as a declaration of faith in our ability to get through this explanation together, I hereby solemnly undertake that the words 'language', 'context' and 'historical' will play no further part in it.

One of the key underlying themes of Simon Reynolds's landmark 2005 volume *Rip It Up & Start Again* (and indeed, some might argue, of Reynolds's whole career) is a sense of nostalgia for a time – specifically the late '70s and early '80s – when a vanguard of British music journalists (Paul Morley and Jon Savage being the most notable survivors of this elite cadre) not only tracked and analysed the changes taking place in a rapidly evolving post-punk scene, but actually seemed to shape and direct them. But once you begin to look carefully for examples of musical genres which seem expressly tailored to reflect the preferences of the critics whose job it is to evaluate them, it's surprising how many of these symbiotic relationships survive.

Regular readers of the *Sunday Times* have long ago learnt to group together a certain kind of Dutch improvised jazz with the complete works of Giant Sand in the catch-all category 'Stewart Lee Music'. Long-term *Daily Telegraph* subscribers now recognise a certain strand of inexplicably undervalued Irish pub rock as 'Neil McCormick Jazz'. The *Independent on Sunday*'s Simon Price will always be associated with Ro-Mo – the movement he helped to start. And fans of Peter Robinson's estimable *PopJustice* website have been heard to Twitter of a 'Pop Justice Sound' – generally the preserve either of a certain kind of sardonic Scandinavian, or of veteran minor-league Xenomania staffers making a brave but ultimately doomed bid for their own share of the spotlight.

Of all these bespoke musical movements, there is one which transcends the kind of individual association outlined above to make a far broader connection. And it was this shadowy aesthetic upsurge – initially known as 'Pitchfork Rock', but now more catchily termed 'Pitchfolk' – which in 2008 reached what even people who own books by Malcolm Gladwell will hopefully one day tire of calling a tipping point.

The first sign that a distinct kind of music might be emerging whose virtues and vices reflected the mentality of the American indie website *Pitchfork*, came in early 2005, when the previously unknown Arcade Fire's debut UK show at King's College London sold out before it had even been properly announced. Future generations of cultural archaeologists may also cite as significant the revelation that the best-selling title in US publisher Continuum's 33⅓ imprint (a series of in-depth pocket-size studies of cult albums) has not been the one pertaining to *Electric Lady-land* or *Unknown Pleasures* or even *OK Computer*, but rather the story of *In the Aero-plane Over the Sea* by Neutral Milk Hotel.

Jeff Mangum's spiritually inclined Athens, Georgia, ensemble (gracefully acknowledged by Arcade Fire as a formative influence) established the same kind of subliminal template for the music that followed them as Louisville's Slint had earlier done for legions of post-rock inheritors. And as the subsequent stampede of internet talking horses (Clap Your Hands Say Yeah!, Broken Social Scene and Cold War Kids to name but three) tried and failed to follow the same path Arcade Fire had taken from the foothills of indie obscurity onto the high plains of U2-style bombast, the key attributes of Pitchfork Rock became increasingly distinct.

A wilful disconnectedness from the grubby business of everyday social and economic interaction; an occasional tendency to preciousness and/or religiosity; a vague aspiration to counter-cultural collectivity, often paradoxically expressed through unfettered solipsism – these were just some of the many shared propensities that seemed to bind together the earlier progenitors of Pitchfork Rock and the contributors to the website that wrote about them. But rather than condemning them to a self-sustaining virtual backwater, the coming generation of Pitchfolkers were about to find that their inward-looking dreams of digital arcadia chimed precisely with the desires of a broader reviewing public.

Anyone who doubts the almost totalitarian hold Pitchfolk paradigms Bon Iver and Fleet Foxes have exercised over the mainstream critical imagination in 2008 should probably turn to the introduction to *Uncut* magazine's review of the year. 'Ideally,' writes John Mulvey, 'we would have compiled this comprehensive survey of 2008 in a state of splendid isolation. In a shed in the wilderness, where the sub-editors would head out each morning to slaughter animals for the *Uncut* cooking pot. We would revel in the head-clearing silence, commune with nature, and eventually decide which albums, films, DVDs and books had made the biggest impact on us over the last 12 months.'

Albums, films, DVDs and books? Not exactly *Grizzly Addams* is it? Oh well, I guess you can take the man out of *Uncut*, but you can't take *Uncut* out of the man. And far from being an isolated lapse into bucolic hyperbole, Mulvey's consumerist *Iron John* fantasy perfectly encapsulates the manner in which the euphoric reception accorded to Bon Iver's *For Emma, Forever Ago* (or, to give the album its original title, *Boo-Hoo, My Girlfriend Left Me*) has been conditioned by the supposedly dramatic circumstances of the album's making.

'The story of Justin "Bon Iver" Vernon's debut was seductive,' admits the year-end issue of *The Word*, 'the three snowy months spent alone in a hunting cabin in a remote corner of Wisconsin, the deer hunting, the song-writing, the broken heart. That *For Emma* should also prove an album of extraordinary beauty . . . made it almost an embarrassment of riches.'

Oh, I see. So if only it had been an album of pleasant but fundamentally unremarkable Bonnie 'Prince' Billy knock-offs, multi-tracked into pseudo-experimental infinity by a man who seemed to think borrowing a wintry greeting from cutesy Alaskan TV drama *Northern Exposure* made him the new Jack London, then this whole hokey pseudo-survivalist farrago would have been rendered substantially *less* embarrassing?

Well, that's a relief. Because just for a moment there I was starting to worry that the jarringly uniform tone in which seemingly universal admiration for this bewilderingly one-dimensional record has been expressed might mark the final triumph of lifestyle over art. But then I listened again to Will Oldham's *Palace Brothers* (also known as *Days In The Wake*) – an album which bears the same relation to Bon Iver's debut as Little Richard's originals bore to the cover versions of Pat Boone – and suddenly the whole thing started to make sense.

In the early '90s, when Oldham and fellow travellers like Kurt 'Lambchop' Wagner and Bill 'Smog' Callahan defined the archetype of the super-literate post-hardcore singer-songwriter, they were flying in the face of a clearly established sonic order. In the dog days of grunge, it took real artistic courage to swap 'faster, louder' for 'slower, quieter'. But over the ensuing decade and a half of half-assed alt. country scenesterism, the clichéd iconography of the back-porch troubadour has coalesced into an orthodoxy every bit as stale and indigestible as any music the Stone Temple Pilots ever put their name to. (Hence the strenuous attempts that Oldham in particular has made to dis-associate himself from it, whether by appearing in R. Kelly's online soap opera *Trapped In The Closet*, or being rude to the man from the Red House Painters.)

What separates the songs of Bon Iver from those of his more illustrious forebears is that there isn't any tension in them. The music and the lyrics are both leading you in the same direction, which is towards an un-abashed celebration of the emotional priorities of a particular individual, who is not a meticulously constructed artistic persona, but a guy just like you and me, who split up with his girlfriend and then dramatised his ensuing state of isolation by going to stay in his dad's hunting cabin in Wisconsin. It's what disgraced Country Life [butter] poster-boy John Lydon would once have called 'a cheap holiday in someone else's misery'.

It's the absence of contemporary cultural reference points in the music of plaid-clad Seattle quintet Fleet Foxes which seems to have reduced reviewers to a state of elemental hysteria. 'As ancient as the seasons, as fresh as morning dew . . . a reminder of what humanity is capable of,' writes the year's final *Mojo* of the eponymous debut by this harmless bunch of less than pitch-perfect Crosby, Stills and Nash revivalists. 'Sounding both as ancient as the mountains from which their music seemed to flow and as fresh as a flower,' agrees *Q*, while *The Word* found Radio 2's Stuart Maconie acclaiming 'their radiant, pure and transcendent allure'.

It is worth remembering that had the website Metacritic.com been operational in the era when the story of 'The Emperor's New Clothes' was set, the combined weight of UK/US critical opinion would undoubtedly have awarded the head of state's fashion-forward anti-garb a mark in excess of 90 out of 100 (Bon Iver's *For Emma, Forever Ago* scored 88, *Fleet Foxes* 87). And while my confidence that friends and colleagues at the *OMM* would have the courage and good taste to buck this pernicious trend proved sadly misplaced (OK, Fleet Foxes stalled at no. 23 in our top 50 albums of the year, but Bon Iver was no. 1 with a bullet), it's heartening to note that there is one major British music title which has remained ambivalent about this suffocating blanket of cosy late-onset Americana.

So hats off – rather surprisingly – to the *NME*, whose 13 December issue (the one with the top 50 albums of the year in it) at least had the decency to give house-room to a few dissenting voices, and thereby made a bold and entirely unexpected reconnection with the buccaneering iconoclastic spirit which once fired the imagination of the young Simon Reynolds. Check out James McMahon's lyrically impassioned advocacy of (of all the ridiculous albums) Oasis's *Dig Out Your Soul* if you doubt me.

Author's note

Some correspondents have viewed Maggoty Lamb's use of an alias as the last word in moral cowardice. So why the assumed name? 'First,' Maggoty writes, 'because this blog is the work of a professional music journalist who wishes to remain active in that field. Second because for me – as for Bruce Wayne – anonymity is a pre-condition of true even-handedness. And thirdly because the origin of the whole endeavour was the sight of a young sheep, which had sadly drowned in a South Coast drainage ditch. This poignant vista quickly took on a macabre aspect, when the ovine cadaver turned out to be positively heaving with new life. And just as it was becoming apparent what an excellent metaphor this was for the state of the twenty-first-century music industry, the spirit of that maggoty lamb entered my soul, exactly as those Native Americans' did to Jim Morrison after that car crash on the highway!'

ROB YOUNG
Hearken to the Witches Rune

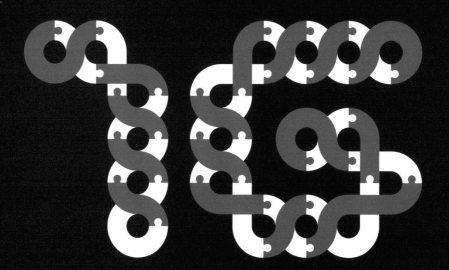

Anyone of a certain age, exposed to BBC children's television during the '70s will recall Toni Arthur: the enthusiastic, polo-necked co-presenter of toddler show *Play School* and its all-singing, all-dancing big brother *Playaway*, plus the folksy round-Britain travelogue series *Take A Ticket To*. But would parents have been so keen on exposing their little ones to the acoustic guitar-wielding wrangler of Big Ted, Humpty and their stuffed chums, had they known that Toni had recently attended naked pagan ceremonies conducted by Britain's self-styled 'King of the Witches'?

Dave Arthur first met Toni in the 12 Stringer, an after-hours espresso bar he was running in central London as a refuelling stop for the red-eyed refugees from Soho's early '60s nocturnal club scene such as Davy Graham and Wizz Jones. When Toni wandered in one night, she was enrolled in a nursing course at London's University College, but had been an exhibition scholar at the Royal Academy since the age of 9. 'He played American folk songs,' she recalls, 'Carter Family stuff mainly, with "Will The Circle Be Unbroken" being top favourite. Intrigued by this totally unheard music, I sang with him. I remember him asking why

I didn't sing the tune. I said I preferred making the harmonies, and that was it. Love!' They married shortly afterwards and moved to Oxford, where they both found work in the university bookshop. While Toni peddled science and medicine textbooks, Dave beavered away in the basement arts department, building up a formidable stock of printed folk song and folklore writing. Around this time a friend gave them a pile of tapes of English old-time music, and the couple were transfixed by the voices of Harry Cox and the Copper Family.

'At that time,' says Toni, 'English un-accompanied folk music was entering the clubs. I loved it and we started singing Copper Family songs and some of the more obvious material. Then we decided to un-cover the less well-known songs. The Euing Collection and the Child Ballads and the wonderful *Pills To Purge Melancholy* were all in publication and, as I could read music – not generally admitted to in the folk move-ment of the time – our research was made easy. The music thrilled me, as it broke so many of the rules I had to adhere to in the classical world. And the modal structures were divine. I thought they had all died out with the ancient Greeks. David researched the words and I did the music. A good marriage of ideas.'

After a few years they moved back to London, where Dave had found a job at the Performing Rights Society (PRS), which gave him access to the card index of songs and their copyrights – a gigantic, unofficial web of music history. 'I used to go through them in my spare time,' he remembers, 'pick out odd songs and track them back, and see where they'd come from, all these folk, traditional things. I ended up doing some cross-referencing on "The Derby Ram" song, and the jazz version, the New Orleans jazz thing, the English version, the American version, there's so many hundreds of recorded versions, and all of them, down there with copyright under various people – some say traditional and under public domain, some of them have got claimed copyright on them.'

Arthur contacted A. L. Lloyd with a view to making a radio documentary about the way the song had been bounced between cultures and countries through history. The idea came to nothing, but Arthur found he and Lloyd were near neighbours in south-east London, and Lloyd wound up as artistic director of the duo's 1969 album of folk songs, *The Lark In The Morning*, on Topic. 'He was besotted with the range of my voice,' remembers Toni, 'nearly three octaves, saying it was more like Bulgarian or Hungarian singers.' Staying in Lewisham at the time, they ended up in a babysitting circle with Shirley Collins, who lived across the heath, and Pete Maynard and Marian Gray of Martin Carthy's former folk/skiffle group The Thamesiders. Around the same time they made friends with Mr Fox's Bob and Carole Pegg on their visits to London

clubs, and with another resident of that area of south-east London, fiddler Dave Swarbrick.

So by the time Toni Arthur began her television career in September 1971, she and her husband Dave were established figures on the traditional folk circuit, with a handful of Bill Leader-produced albums under their belts. Like the Peggs, and later Tim Hart and Maddy Prior, they were a couple drawn together in a romantic and professional quest through their country's folk heritage. Also like the Peggs, they were determined not to sever the music from the people and places it emanated from. 'We were interested in the fact that folk music, the popular culture, involves song, dance, storytelling, a whole range of things,' Dave Arthur tells me. 'Everything impinges on everything else in traditional culture. Dancers tell stories, singers dance, it's all mixed in.' While the Peggs were conducting their researches in the deep dales up north in the early '60s, the Arthurs were devouring the whole gamut of English traditional culture, fraternising with the Hammersmith Morris and learning clog dance steps from champion Johnson Elwood. 'I had to feel this music,' insists Toni, 'feel it and understand it with its total intensity. I could see how the "airy-fairy" Irish traditional dance went exactly with the skipping, sliding, slurring sound of traditional Irish folk song. But I couldn't feel English music with my body. I needed to feel the rhythms through my feet. I tried morris dancing and country dancing but that did little. Then I met Johnson Elwood in County Durham and learned the north-east style of clog dancing from him. The clogs are flat and not curved up at the toe. The style, with its double shuffle, was unique to the form. Supposedly, Jimmy Elwood, Johnson's father, had taught Dan Leno, who had taught Fred Astaire, and thus tapdancing began. And boy, did I understand the music more through this clonking, jumping, heart-pounding dance.'

'It seemed logical that if you could dance, you felt innately the rhythms, particularly the English rhythms, then it must affect your singing and the songs,' adds Dave Arthur. 'If you play a melodeon, you must imbibe some-how this English rhythm thing that I was looking for. So we were morris dancing, clog dancing, playing instrumental music, singing ballads and songs, researching, going off to manuscript collections and working on material, original stuff that nobody else was working on. And there was nobody else doing it then, we were really the only people mixing these things up at folk clubs. I would do a morris jig in the first half, Toni would do a clog dance on the table in a pub, and we'd play a couple of instrumental tunes, we'd sing songs. We'd talk about magic, as we'd got into witchcraft and studying it, to find out how witchcraft was reflected in traditional song – if the magical ballads were anything to do with what was perceived then as the Wicca, the witch covens that were going round in England, and whether they were actually related or whether it was a separate thing. And so we started going to meetings of witches and going through their ritual books and things, and we were invited as guests to all sorts of coven meetings, and then we were stuck in "Tam Lin" and all these magical ballads and somehow trying to relate them to what was going on in the occult world and find out what the connections were.'

In terms of their status in popular under-standing, British witchcraft and folk music are strikingly similar. Both are believed, even by many of the people who practise them, to afford a link to the distant medieval past or even earlier, unaware that many of their identifying features are actually relatively modern inventions. A vastly simplified outline of modern witchcraft would go like this: the art had kept a low profile since what adepts call the 'Burning Times', in other words, the aggressive witch hunts of the English Civil War and its aftermath. The revived Druids of the late eighteenth and nineteenth centuries preserved certain aspects of hermetic lore in a relatively benign form. The highly influential late Victorian Hermetic Order of the Golden Dawn, which included authors such as Bram Stoker, W. B. Yeats, Arthur Machen, Algernon Blackwood, E. Nesbit and Aleister Crowley among its membership, set off a chain of organisations around the country which combined practising Thelemic magic and personal development with Masonic-style hierarchies, most prominently Crowley's OTO (*Ordo Templi Orientis*).

Gerald Gardner, acknowledged as the founder of modern Wicca, was an OTO initiate. A civil servant who had spent much of his working life based in Malaya and had a keen interest in magical artefacts, Gardner retired to a dozy village near the New Forest and was inducted into a local witch coven around the beginning of the '40s. The details of who exactly provoked who to do what over the ensuing fifteen years are sketchy and much disputed, but by 1954 Gardner had become the most prominent leader among Britain's nationwide witch covens, and had written a book, *Witchcraft Today*, that described the modern Wicca movement as a resurgence of ancient pre-Christian

CROSSING BORDER

THE HAGUE / THE NETHERLANDS
NOVEMBER 19, 20, 21
ANTWERP / BELGIUM
NOVEMBER 22

Where literature and music clash and collaborate

In November 2009 we proudly present the 17th edition of Crossing Border.
The foremost international literature and music festival of its kind in Europe.

Save the date

FOR MORE INFORMATION CHECK
WWW.CROSSINGBORDER.NL

religion, a direct continuation of European pagan cults. Would-be initiates to what became known as 'Gardnerian Wicca' were required to make their own handwritten copy of the *Book Of Shadows*, a workbook of spells, incantations and ritual instructions, which had to be borrowed from another coven member.

In the early 1960s, Alex Sanders, a young member of his local Manchester Gardnerian coven, became his group's High Priest, and through a charm offensive towards the media (tipping off tabloid reporters and TV stations about forthcoming 'secret' coven meetings, taking care to alert them to the likely presence of telegenic nude virgins), contributed to a huge surge in coven membership across the UK. For this reason, his followers nominated him King of the Witches, which was also the title of a biography of Sanders which added to the movement's notoriety on its publication in 1969.

By that time, Sanders and his wife Maxine were living in London's Notting Hill. One day he took a call from a researcher wanting permission to borrow Sanders's own *Book Of Shadows* as part of a study of English folk-song origins. It was Dave Arthur. 'Alex Sanders, the King of the Witches, gave me his copy,' remembers Arthur, 'and I sat there for bloody weeks, copying by hand. And then I started going through it, and there's all these bits and snippets of rhymes and things, and one of them appears in the horn dance: "Take thou no scorn to wear the horn/It was a crest ere thou wast born/Thy father's father wore it/And thy father bore it". And, of course, that came from Shakespeare, from *As You Like It*, someone had found that and said, "Oh, that sounds authentic," so they dropped that into it.

Then I was reading things like Charles Leland's book *Aradia*, the gospel of the Italian witch cults that Leland collected during the nineteenth century. And I found all these rituals in there that were identical, they had just been lifted piecemeal and dropped into the *Book Of Shadows* as authentic English rituals, and I also found a couple of things I had found in Crowley manuscripts and W. B. Yeats.

'People at that time, in the '60s and '70s, were very much influenced by Margaret Murray and her *God of the Witches* (1933) – that was the bible of folksy people who were into the occult. She was saying that modern witchcraft was a direct descendant of a pre-historic cult in England, undercover all these years, and they'd taken to the hills and all these little people who were living in holes in the ground had taken their witch beliefs with them.'

The cobbled-together nature of the *Book Of Shadows* sharpened Dave Arthur's scepticism about the origins of many of the folk songs in the English tradition. 'So then we were looking at things like "Tam Lin" and these various ballads – "Thomas Rhymer", "Alison Gross", "John Barleycorn" – which at that point everyone was thinking was some kind of ritual song, the spirit in the barley and all of that, and of course, it was just a drinking song in print in the 1700s. The conclusion I came to was that it was a completely made-up thing, by Gerald Gardner, primarily in the 50s when the witchcraft laws were repealed. He put all this stuff together and made a religion from it.'

Legend Of The Witches, a documentary made by Malcolm Leigh in 1970, shows the Sanders coven as Dave and Toni Arthur would have found it, on their frequent visits to the basement flat in Notting Hill Gate. Intriguingly, the coven can be seen to have adopted some of the technology of modern psychedelia, using stroboscopic lights and flickering Op Art circles reminiscent of the hypnotic 'dreamachines' invented by William Burroughs and Bryon Gysin. Sharp cuts between interior and exterior shots draw a clear connection between the ancient use of fire as a ritual focus, and these artificially induced flicker effects. In one ceremony, shot in what looks suspiciously like a cheap television studio, and soundtracked with fashionably muzzy sitar and tabla music, an initiate is brought, unclothed, towards a stroboscope. 'His senses are constantly switched from one extreme to the other,' narrates the voiceover, 'so that he may come to the [scrying] mirror with all normal preconceptions swept from his mind.'

'In this particular group,' recalls Toni, 'Alex had a lot of mentally disturbed people. Especially those who heard voices and saw things. In the normal world they would have been considered ripe for ECT or very strong medication. However, he told them they were privileged to have contact with the other world. That they must learn to know when the "visitors" should invade their lives and to learn to live quietly with them. And it seemed to work remarkably well – at least they were happy, did no one any harm, and were able to live in society and without drugs.'

Alex Sanders even released an album under his name, *A Witch Is Born* (on A&M Records, home to Strawbs, among others), a recording of Sanders and Maxine leading a girl called Janet Owen through three successive degrees of initiation into their coven. Sanders's sense of theatre was com-

pounded by his dramatic appearance on the sleeve, grimacing like a balding Vincent Price next to a floating ankh. In 1970 he acted as 'consultant' to Leicester-based progressive rock group Black Widow, dabblers in occult trappings whose stage act including the simulated sacrifice of a naked woman. Their somewhat overwrought track 'Come To The Sabbat', from *Sacrifice* (1970), purportedly bears traces of Sanders's hand.

'We went down for rituals occasionally when he invited us,' continues Dave Arthur. 'There was a particular one where a German TV company went down to film. And he asked us as a favour to sing "John Barleycorn" and he would do a John Barleycorn ritual. We must have worn cloaks – we weren't naked, all the others were. I don't think we were. We sang "John Barleycorn", and Alex had just invented this bizarre ritual, where he got this girl from the coven and threw flour over her, and then they tipped beer over her, and then it got so out of hand it was ridiculous. And the Germans who were filming it thought it was unbelievable, it was wonderful. He just went through the song as we sang it and made it up: the cutting down of the corn, the springing up, the threshing, and at the end of it this big libation with the beer and flour thrown everywhere.'

Toni adds: 'The idea of wise women sitting in the corner of a house and singing songs of the supernatural appealed to us. We'd read about Alex and Maxine and visited them in order to find out if they had any knowledge of old songs and balladry. Of course, Alex, the great showman that he was, told us we had to attend his coven meetings to truly "understand". With fear and trepidation we did this. Yes, we stripped naked and danced round in a circle. But this was surprisingly unsexy. We went about four or five times – and every time the magic seemed less and less plausible. I had a problem with religion of any kind. Wicca seemed perfectly harmless. It's not to be confused with Black Magic. It's not the purposeful reversing of Catholic ceremonies in order to gain power over others. It's just a sweet nature-revering religion. As one of the main premises is "anything you do you'll get back threefold", it's hardly given to evil work.

'What finished any involvement for me was when we took our dog Bess with us one time we were visiting. Alex leaned mysteriously over and felt her stomach and said, "Yes, the pups will come in about seven weeks." Magic indeed – she'd just been sterilised!'

Hearken To The Witches Rune, which Dave and Toni recorded for Bill Leader's Trailer label in 1970, is one of English folk's great lost recordings, if only because it's been out of print since its first pressing. On their 1967 album, *Morning Stands On Tiptoe*, Toni stands bathed in a dewy golden dawn in front of the White Horse at Uffington in Oxfordshire. On *Witches Rune* they are abroad in the thick of night, squinting out of the midnight shadows, as if about to disrobe for a Gnostic mass. The pair have mixed feelings about the record now: the memories of Leader's cramped and ramshackle apartment, and the lack of concentration thanks to passing traffic hum, have coloured the experience ('I do sometimes regret the close mic work necessary in his studio to cut out street car noises – you could hear every intake of breath as if we were asthmatics,' explains Toni). But this collection of the magical ballads they were steeped in at the time – 'Alison Gross', 'The Standing Stones', 'The Cruel Mother', 'The Fairy Child', et al – has the raw immediacy of what they might have been like if incorporated in magic rituals. Fans have long been baffled by the verse printed on the sleeve, under the title 'Hearken To The Witches Rune', even though there's no song of that name among the tracks. In fact, Dave Arthur reveals, it's Sanders's own adaptation of the 'Witch's Chant', written by Gerald Gardner's High Priestess, Doreen Valiente, which has been adopted as a kind of supernatural 'come-all-ye' by successive Wiccans: 'Darksome night and shining moon/East South West then North/Hearken to the witch's rune/Here I come to call thee forth'.

If Wicca is a patchwork invention, shaped by the likes of Alex Sanders to fit the permissive mores of his time, then Dave and Toni Arthur's conclusions should equally be applied to our understanding of folk music – that its authenticity cannot be trusted. But should that completely invalidate it as a modern religion, or discount the music? There is no fixed origin, no one-and-only author, only a transmitting process from mouth to mouth, age to age. The version of 'The Cruel Mother' on *Witches Rune* is substantially different, textually, from the one in, for instance, Geoffrey Grigson's *Penguin Book of Ballads*. But the story is essentially the same: a young woman gives birth in secret, stabs the baby (or twins in some versions) with a penknife, and buries it by moonlight. Later, the dead child appears to the mother in the porch of a church, cursing her and reminding her that eternal damnation awaits. It is a song that has been collected in many parts of the country over the decades; some versions feature the refrain lines, 'All alone and a-lonely', others have 'Fine flowers in the valley'. Academics will wrangle forever over the urtext, but in reality there is no 'correctness'. The cruel mother will continue to be haunted by the guilt-inducing spectre of her child, because the song itself is undead, a ghost that refuses to be forgotten, whether sung by a Highland crofter, an acoustic duo in a folk club, an electric rock band at an outdoor festival, or in a home studio with an electronic ambient backing track. For Toni Arthur, the present perception of folk music is 'a total illusion, but a nice one. Most of us that bothered to research knew that this was not a continuation of anything. But it was a re-invention of something that we thought had been before. It was a look at values that we seemed to be losing.' 'The old ways are changing, ye canna deny', as the song went. The day of the noble savage never was, but we wished it was. I think we were a group of people who knew life was going to change, and that someday somebody would say, 'There's no such thing as society.' And that, instead of living life and sharing it with others, we'd have to be politically correct in all things until honesty and courtesy finally disappeared up the arsehole of the government.

Girls Just Wanna Have Fun?

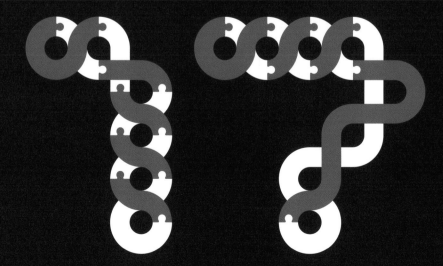

Who was the first teenage girl recorded to camera, caught screaming out for her musical idols? Probably no person alive knows her name, but more than fifty years on from Jerry Lee Lewis and bobby socks, a young woman in the throes of hysteria is still the signal image of the teenage girl's relationship with popular music. Her hands are clenched into fists near her chin, and her shoulders are raised. Occasionally she gives a convulsive shiver. Her face is wrinkled into an expression of ecstasy verging on pain, her eyes closed, her mouth open and wet. Perhaps she is crying as well as screaming. In this state she is helplessly transported, but the transport is threatening. When will the fit be over? Who will shut her up? It is not that she has words – she is beyond and before those. Wordless, intensely emotional and undeniably sexual – this is the state in which teenage girls are understood to connect with music, and with those performing it. It is all in their bodies: they do not intellectualise; their opinions are instinctive rather than considered. Without rational judgement or the ability to articulate it, a teenage girl will always be a fan, never a critic.

From time to time the absence of female music critics is noted, alongside the absence of female producers, female DJs, female radio hosts, female roadies, female photographers, female managers, female label heads and female artists who are not automatically tossed into a box marked 'female performer', as if there was an open paddock where male artists grazed, free-range, and a cramped stall reserved for the women and queers. We need not rehearse the arguments about sexism in the music industry over again. It is so obvious that only those trying to wilfully ignore it could deny the material facts, and so entrenched that it almost always goes unremarked upon, acceded to and accommodated by nearly everybody, regardless of gender, including myself. Many of us traversing one or another circle of this generally repugnant business simply grumble and muddle by and otherwise live with it. Out-and-out battles must be chosen strategically or you risk exhaustion, disheartenment and defeat, so what I intend to do here is focus on a single trope – the figure of the teenage girl – and examine how it functions within music criticism, particularly – and curiously – in the writing of those critics who would probably think of themselves as being quite explicitly on the teenage girl's side. How does the rhetorical enlistment of the teenage girl by most music critics – and most of these male – reinforce the gendered division between the fan and the critic?

Upon first glance – and perhaps upon second and subsequent glances, too – what follows might seem like an internecine squabble between critics, of limited interest to a general reader. Now that a great deal of music criticism happens informally, on blogs which fall outside the gambit of either print or web-based publications, an equally informal and nearly instantaneous apparatus of dialogue has sprung up around it, in comments boxes and on message boards. If you disagree with a critic's opinion, you don't have to write a pithy letter to the *NME* and cross your fingers that it gets printed. You respond on your own blog, and other people respond to you, and so a critical debate arises which can be as over-heated and pernickety as it can be invigorating, thoughtful and wonderfully intelligent. Tiny and quite possibly inconsequential semantic distinctions or gradations of taste assume all the tactical importance of captured territory on the Western Front, at least until the next distraction arrives. This cycle of clamour, over-inflation and subsequent obsolescence in music criticism matches the adrenalised pace of online music consumption, where stars are born and then die by their daily hit-rate. And yet, the fact that popular music is – has always been – intimately connected to the destructive cycles of capitalism, that its libidinal drive can only be created by the insatiable desire for novelty that capitalism demands, does not make popular music, at the last, a trivial or flimsy art form. On the contrary. Enmeshed within commerce to a degree that no other art form is, popular music is invaluable – forgive the mercenary pun – for what it can reveal about how and why capitalism functions, and for those of us whose hatred of capital is matched only by our love for music, the dialectic between the two is as much a fascination – an obsession – as a torment.

Obsession makes the fan (and find me a music critic alive who hasn't used their formative obsessions as an impetus to write), and young women, it is supposed, are particularly vulnerable to obsession. I would argue that this vulnerability is, to a very large degree, a consequence of a girl's socialisation within capitalism as she trains for her most important role, the ideal shopper. The indiscriminate, emotive impulses of fan obsession are not an inherent ontological fact; teenage girls make good fans because it is presumed that they are, and will continue to be, good consumers: their cravings and purchases irrational, and extremely profitable to others. But it is crucial to understand – especially for those who have never been a teenage girl – how this learned behaviour is, to a greater or lesser degree, both conscious and consciously willed. Teenage girls are never less than extremely aware of their own behaviour, because they have been taught from the youngest age that constant awareness is the best guard against social disapproval for any action deemed indecorous, unattractive or otherwise lacking in feminine qualities. To be female is to be subject to a double surveillance – one's own and that of others – and the watching never ceases. It is difficult to describe the mixture of pleasurable, knowing surrender and also disquiet which goes into becoming a fan; into conforming to a behaviour which is both expected but still, somehow, inexplicable and even frightening to those who do not participate in it. (Female consumption is understood in terms of female desire, which is seen to be insatiable. Where will it end?) If the fandom of a teenage girl can have a disturbingly intensive quality, and I am not denying that this is true, I think it is because, rather than in spite of, a girl's awareness that her relationship to the commodity on offer – the music or the performer – is both all that is expected of her and significantly less than she is capable of being. Into her fandom is channelled the frustration of thwarted opportunities to be something other than a consumer – to be, ultimately, a creator. Alienated labour and alienated creativity are the twin devils of life under capitalism, and the compensations of fandom are earned via the former in order to stop up the hole left by the latter. You consume music in order to make up for a bigger want, yet the music itself can speak to that wanting perfectly, painfully, completely.

Within the field of music criticism, however, the teenage girl has always figured as an innocent: an unknowing, non-judgemental listener, whose taste is highly malleable. Her untaught opinions provide a music critic with the ultimate barometer – the ultimate other with which to measure the critic's own sensibilities against. The fandom of the teenage girl is a mark upon the music either wholly positive or entirely negative, depending on the critic's own orientation; that a teenage girl – or rather, a large number of teenage girls – inclines towards one performer or style of music is a sure sign either of that music's worth or of its worthlessness. Either way, it is the critic's role to articulate a lasting judgement, which the teenage girl, caught up in the maelstrom of her temporary affections, is incapable of forming.

I am less interested here in reformulating a defence of the music that teenage girls are most generally presumed to like – mainstream chart pop – than in looking at how a particular critical position, which champions this music, uses the teenage girl in the service of its rhetorical strategies. The critical position is known, broadly, as popism, and though on the surface (and popism is big on surface) it appears to be the least snobbish, most adolescent-friendly of all critical strains, a closer reading of the popist argument does not bear this out.

The two leading popist critics are both American, and both men – Sasha Frere-Jones, a staff writer for *The New Yorker*, and Frank Kogan, whose 2006 book *Real Punks Don't Wear Black* devotes as much energy to Mariah Carey as it does to the Contortions. The evolution – or rather devolution – of the popist approach need not concern anyone without a quasi-professional interest in spending their daylight hours trawling blog archives. The history is there to find, should you wish to find it. It began – and well before either Frere-Jones or Kogan achieved their current level of clout – as a necessary attempt to punch some holes in the received Rock Canon: The Beatles, Rolling Stones, Bob Dylan, Bruce Springsteen, et al. Questioning the notion of authenticity that had wrapped itself around such artists like a pernicious ivy was an effective way of clearing some space for the kind of music and performers most often dismissed in the face of these 'craftsmen' and 'geniuses': disco and dance, rap and R'n'B, chart pop – not, incidentally, all genres with a far higher percentage of female performers than guitar rock has ever been noted for. But an attempt to uncover and to celebrate what is genuinely complicated, intelligent, thrilling and vital about pop music has become, more recently, a hollow victory parade for banality and dumbness. How else to explain Frank Kogan's briefly notorious assertion in 2007 that critical divide over Paris Hilton's debut album was analogous to the rift in American society caused by the Vietnam War? As several other critics and bloggers were quick to point out, America was (and still is) actually embroiled in a war that bears some resemblance to the conflict in Vietnam in terms of its social effects – one does not need to look to celebrities for proof that America is in conflict, both inside and outside of its own borders. It is also worth pointing out that Ms Hilton's musical recording vanished, even from the truncated attention span of pop cultural discourse, with chastening rapidity – the 'debate' about her album was over before it could properly begin, because her music was so boring that it was not worth arguing over. That Kogan could mistake such a trite artefact, not even vulgar enough to rise to the level of kitsch, for something of merit, signals, I think, the wilful abandonment of the critic's first duty: discernment.

Discernment, however, or judgement; deciding between what is good and bad music, is something which the popist critic is very unwilling to do. (To throw such intellectually threadbare and outmoded accusations as 'postmodern relativism' at these critics is, I must stress, to entirely miss the point: anyone itching to unleash their inner Harold Bloom can line up elsewhere.) This statement needs further qualification: critics such as Kogan are unwilling to give the impression of being critical in any context which might underline the difference in position – and in authority – between themselves and their idealised listener, the teenage girl. The teenage girl is discerning – about music like Paris Hilton's – only in so far as her critical acumen is instinctive, rather than consciously developed. For a teenage girl (or in this case, a bunch of imaginary teenage girls, as not many real ones could be found buying the record in question) to 'like' this music is proof enough of the need to defend it against the vengeful critic – also largely imaginary, these days – who would wish Paris Hilton locked in a small room and forced to listen to Bob Dylan albums until she experienced a complete existential crisis over her inadequacy in the face of such profound artistic achievement.

The point can be examined further by looking at another piece that Kogan penned in 2007, entitled 'What's Wrong With Pretty Girls?' Here the same dichotomy – between pop's detractors (a young male Nirvana fan) and pop's defenders (Kogan, on behalf of all the pretty girls, in praise of the Backstreet Boys) is set up, in order to celebrate the instinctive judgement of one while subjecting the other to close examination. Kogan concludes – and rightly, though his argument is hardly groundbreaking – that a knee-jerk dismissal of polished chart pop, in favour of rock, relies on a series of dubious assumptions about the merit of those who write their own songs versus those who only perform them, pain and anguish versus sunshine and bliss, etc.,

etc. As has been de rigueur since their revelatory MTV Unplugged set in 1993, Kogan observes that Nirvana wrote pop songs too, just like the Beatles, and that to judge one pop song as better than another because of its mode of production is rather misguided.

But Kogan has some misguided, dubious assumptions of his own, namely about the girls – the 'screaming sexual girls', the 'mainstream girls' and the 'pretty girls' – who constitute his projected Backstreet Boys fan base. There is his assumption that 'pretty girls' is an interchangeable category with 'mainstream girls' in the first place, as if these pretty girls participate in mainstream taste by default of their looks. For Kogan, beauty does indeed appear as a virtue: 'Is beauty bad for us? Does it oppress us?' he asks. Frankly, Kogan, yes and yes. Eager as he is to tease out the social constructions that lie behind musical choice, when it comes to physical appearance Kogan overlooks the fact that beauty itself is not an inherent or a universal value. As measured against the bodies of girls and women with excruciating narrowness, the abstract norm of beauty does real and enormous damage. Kogan can sense the resentment that is directed at teenage girls, by those who snigger at their taste, without understanding or addressing the fact that this resentment is a social effect of the ruthless competition among teenage girls – and between girls and boys – that is taught, from as early an age as possible, as the one route to success. Positioning himself as the voice of girls who are too busy screaming, dancing and being beautiful to speak for themselves – 'feelings aren't necessarily right' he claims, in answer to the disgruntlement of Nirvana and their fans, though the 'feelings' of pretty girls are just fine as they are, lying below the level of conscious thought – Kogan erroneously identifies this group as a class, and he their fearless champion.

If class is a factor in shaping the kind of fan that you become – and undoubtedly it is – then it requires a more nuanced analysis than Kogan is capable of providing. 'Mainstream' is not a class, though conflating mainstream taste with being working class is a common enough critical gesture, undertaken with varying degrees of cynicism dependent on the critic's own stake in maintaining class distinctions. The fact that popular, modern art forms can also be aesthetically and politically radical, and that the first innovators and audiences for these forms are nearly always working class, is either forgotten or wilfully overlooked by most contemporary critics. Such revisionism is not entirely the fault of critics, but a symptom of a wider disavowal of the idea that art in our time can take us somewhere genuinely new – can create a newness in our understanding of the world that is not just a new format, a new marketing angle, or a new way of recycling past ideas. Any avant-garde – and we live with an atrophied understanding of what this could be – is assumed to be bourgeois; in terms of contemporary music, it is understood that only those with a certain amount of economic security will bother to tinker at the edges of aesthetic acceptability, while those who need to 'make it' – prosper or starve – will necessarily align themselves with the fortune-making potential of chart pop. And so it is for audiences, eccentric or experimental interests being clear signs of affluence, while popular pursuits identify you as one of the people. Popular is synonymous with populist, and artists and performers are praised for their ability to 'speak to everybody', which in practice means producing art that does nothing to challenge the values most useful to the functioning of capitalism.

Hence the nightmare vision – at least I see it as one – that concludes Sasha Frere-Jones's hugely influential 2003 opinion piece for Slate, 'When Critics Meet Pop: Why are some writers so afraid of Justin Timberlake?' It's the piece that shaped the popist approach for this millennium: choose a pop star, invoke an audience of girl fans, show how both star and fans have been snobbishly dismissed by other critics, invoke arguments over authenticity in music, be sure to use the Beatles as an example, and champion the girls as final arbiters of value, to whit: 'And all of u...are dwarfed by the sea of meaning that these fans create when they dance with Justin in front of their own mirrors.' Meanwhile, all I can see is a solipsistic trap, a locked groove for these girls, stuck eternally in front of the mirror with nothing to refer to but themselves and a pop song. Pop songs can take you far, to be sure, but they need to function as more than simply reflections of what we already know. Frere-Jones's sea of meaning is, I would argue, a dead sea.

In order to get out from in front of the mirror, and consumer capitalism's endless treadmill of self-absorption disguised as self-knowledge, what does a song or an artist need to be? I want to borrow here a term – portal – that has been used over the past year by a small handful of British critics, in order to designate music that is capable of carrying a listener out of their received understanding of the world, and equally, out of their own expectations of what they might be capable of becoming. The mirror versus the portal, though like all oppositions, it's not really as simple as that.

It's no accident that British critics – going back to the '80s pioneers of the popist approach, Paul Morley and Ian Penman – have focused on the potential for popular music to be a space in which class expectations and designations are scrambled, or maybe even escaped. British sensitivity to class is precisely honed, and British pop music has a strong tradition of working class autodidacts, proletarian intellectuals and visionaries. I could even mention the Beatles, if you like. Such artists were particularly apparent during the post-punk years, when bands such as Joy Division and the Fall used the conditions of their learning – teenage years spent scouring second-hand bookshops – as an aggressive tactic in trying to claw their way out of straitened economic circumstances. Most importantly, this learning was handed on to fans via references to books, films and other cultural artefacts that were scattered through the songs. These references have survived, like shards recovered from an archaeological dig, to inform those who weren't originally present. I can't tell you how much time I spent during my own adolescence hunting, fruitlessly, for a copy of J. G. Ballard's *Atrocity Exhibition* because it shared a title with the opening track on Joy Division's second and final album, *Closer*, and because I wanted to understand more about the terrible psychosis of the song – its vista of desolate urban spaces and writhing bodies – and because I figured that the two things, song and book, were clues to each other. And so they were: aesthetic clues, moral clues, if I can dare to use that word in discussing popular culture; ways of seeing how a particular vision of the world was stitched together from numerous sources.

It is worth noting, I think, that for all the resurgent influence of Joy Division on a new generation of bands, few contemporary artists have picked up on this part of their legacy. Particularly in America, the Joy Division most often invoked – by artists and critics – is used as a shorthand for the alien-(ated) disco most transparently expressed in 'Transmission', their greatest single: 'Dance, dance, dance, dance, dance to the radio.' The robotic, paranoid sheen of the song's dystopian vision has been transformed into a robotic, paranoid celebration of alienated pleasures: where Ian Curtis flails desperately in a locked groove, his inheritors place us into a narrow circuit between dancing self and song precisely because they have nothing else beyond the song to refer to. A dancing self is by no means a necessarily alienated self – let me not be misunderstood – but to be stuck in front of the radio, or in front of the mirror, forever atomised – that is alienation, whatever the beat.

A catch with the autodidact model is that nearly all of the bands are male, and their fans are presumed to be predominantly male, too. It's one way in which assumptions about fandom are very precisely gendered: female fans channel their obsessions into reading about artists, while male fans read around them, navigating their way through an increasingly complicated chain of references, and arming themselves with the kind of obscurantist knowledge that it takes to become an expert, or possibly a critic. At least, that is the geekcore version of the autodidact impulse, which largely ignores the way in which pop music can provide a very potent, potentially liberating form of self-education – an alternative education to an official curriculum that was inadequate, misleading, and taught you nothing about how the world really functioned. The impulse was certainly there in Riot grrrl, one of the few female examples that lends itself to the argument, but true to the differences in class analysis between American and British culture, Riot grrrl was more con-cerned with viewing women and girls as a class within their own right. This under-standing, combined with an emphasis on consciousness-raising, aligned Riot grrrl quite closely with second-wave US feminism of the '60s and '70s, in which gender, rather than class, was seen as the primary category of oppression.

It is a viewpoint that takes us back to Frank Kogan and the pretty girls (now there's a great band name if I ever heard one: Frank Kogan And The Pretty Girls) chafing under the yoke of Nirvana fans and of critics over-invested in rockist notions of authenticity. Of course, Nirvana had numerous ties of their own to the Riot grrrl scene of the Pacific Northwest, but what Kurt Cobain and Kogan's girls share most in common is not their love of pop melodies, nor their good looks, but their inartic-ulateness. Neither Cobain's inchoate rage nor the teenage girl's sexual ecstasy provides a way out of the confines of the self. The former has no channel for its anger but self-destruction, while the latter circumvents any opportunity for precisely the kind of anger – a *ressentiment* at one's economic superiors – that could lead to social change. It should not be forgotten that the original, ancient role of the critic – and of critique – was a judiciary one, *krisis*: to examine evidence and make judgements based on the evidence, with the aim of repairing a social order that had been damaged. It is an urgent task for the contemporary critic to reinhabit this notion of judgement, and to not be afraid of calling the cultural artefacts produced by a cruel and damaging economic system dissatisfying, inadequate, or just plain bad. It is a particularly difficult task for the feminist critic, when feminism today is so often understood in terms of a liberalism that synchronises altogether too well with capitalist values. To be a feminist is to be required to affirm every woman's 'choice', conveniently ignoring the fact that our 'choices' are largely determined for us by social and economic circumstances, and by the behaviour that we learn is most desirable. I can enjoy the sound of Beyonce's most recent chart hit, 'Single Ladies (Put A Ring On It)', and the fact that its wobbling, minimal synth melody evokes a panoply of digital devices and distractions; on a musical level the song truthfully reflects a sense of being alive in the world today. But I cannot in good faith endorse the sentiment, or celebrate a world in which this sentiment is understood to express a popular belief. Why can't we have popular songs that are as politically daring as they are musically exciting? It must be possible.

SIMON REYNOLDS

Sonic Fiction
. . . or, If This Is the Future,
How Come the Music Sounds So Lame?

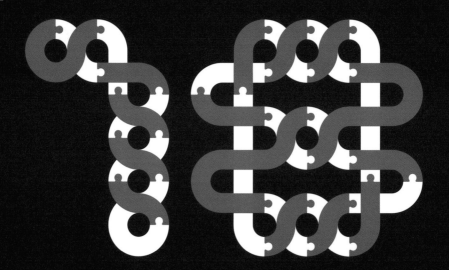

I can remember my memory clearly – the original memory, the false one. My favourite scene in *Star Wars* is the shady bar, known to buffs as Cantina, in the 'pirate city' of Mos Eisley. Entering this den of intergalactic lowlife, Luke Skywalker and Obi-Wan Kenobi meet and hire Han Solo and Chewbacca to fly them off the planet Tatooine. I saw the movie as a 13-year-old when it first came out in 1977 and was captivated by the bar band of dome-headed, insect-eyed aliens who played freaky-sounding music on futuristic-looking instruments.

Catching the movie again on television as a grown-up some years ago (but prior to its reconfiguration as *Star Wars Episode IV: A New Hope*) I was gobsmacked to realise that the music I'd remembered as so out-there was in fact positively musty with old-timey quaintness. No longer an impressionable teen but an adult with learned ears, I instantly recognised the alien music as pre-World War II jazz – *Star Wars* composer John Williams doubtless aiming to play upon our received associations of the Prohibition-era speakeasy as depicted in countless Hollywood gangster movies. As for the 'weird' instruments, they turned out on close inspection to be just superficially snazzed-up and plasticised versions of the saxophone, trumpet and clarinet.

Conceiving the piece, which he titled 'Mad About Me', Williams imagined 'several creatures in a future century finding some 30s Benny Goodman swing band music . . . and how they might attempt to interpret it'. Watching the scene yet again for this article, I noticed that the music isn't a completely retro reproduction antique. There's a steel drum, of all things, bubbling in there as rhythm-pulse, and the bass line appears to be played on a synthesiser. But the essence of the tune is totally of a piece with the music you'd hear in a Woody Allen movie or indeed the gangster-spoofing nostalgia musical *Bugsy Malone*, released a year before *Star Wars* in 1976. It sounds archetypal to the point of seeming déjà entendu, plagiarised from something famous you can't quite place. Williams's lame attempt at futurising it imparts a fusion-tinged gloss which has the unfortunate effect of double-dating the music to the '70s as well as the '30s. It sounds like something Weather Report might have done at their absolute creative nadir . . . or worse, like Manhattan Transfer.

This jarring experience – the fondly-remembered freakadelic music revealed as not-the-least-bit-alien – did plant a seed in my mind, however: a mounting curiosity about science fiction's spotty record when it came to imagining the music of the future. There's two areas, adjacent but separate, up for investigation here: soundtrack composers and their valiant (if arguably always pre-doomed) attempts to come up with 'tomorrow's music today', and SF novels and short stories where music features either prominently or passingly. As a former science fiction fanatic who abruptly jilted the genre for punk and the rock press at the age of sixteen, I felt ideally placed to spot the overlap between my two youthful obsessions, SF and music. When I came to think about it, however, out of the hundreds and hundreds of novels and story collections I'd read in my early teens, borrowed out of Berkhamsted Public Library or bought with odd job money, I could hardly recall any that had dealt with music – impressively or dismally. Cyberpunk, a genre I'd checked out when my interest in SF made a slight return in the '90s, certainly felt rock 'n' roll in vibe and often manifested a self-consciously flashy hipness when it came to pop culture references. But it was also hard to recollect many instances of cyberpunk stories where music (either as a sonic experience or in terms of its social function) was imaginatively projected into the future.

As it turns out, there is a submerged but reasonably substantial lineage of SF writing that deals with music. That, however, is something I'll explore in the second instalment of this piece; here, I'm going to focus on science fiction movies and their soundtracks. (There's at least one other area of intersection between SF and music – the former's massive influence on pop music of every kind, but especially heavy metal, post-punk, industrial, and techno-rave. But that's an immense topic and one that I'm placing beyond my present remit with a sigh of relief.)

To the movies, then. To expect contemporary composers to somehow reach beyond the horizon of present sonic possibility and bring back music that really is 'of' the future is a tall order. Still, there are soundtrack composers who have attempted precisely that, and they're the heroes of this essay. For the most part, though, SF movies have been scored pretty much as the action and suspense movies they generally are beneath the futuristic or extraterrestrial trappings. John Williams is the archetype and apogee here, his scores sticking with the symphony orchestra's sound-palette and using the vocabulary – all tempestuous majesty and swashbuckling derring-do – of the late Romantic composers of the second half of the nineteenth century and first few decades of the twentieth (Mahler, Strauss, Holst, Elgar, Dvorak, et al.). In particular, Williams revived a device used in Wagnerian opera, the leitmotif, a recurrent phrase associated with particular characters, moods, or 'moral forces'. Williams's neo-Romanticism is perfectly apt for the job in hand, given that genre connoisseurs don't even regard *Star Wars* as true science fiction but as 'space opera' or sword-and-sorcery epic, closer to J. R. R. Tolkien's *Lord of the Rings* than Philip K. Dick's *Valis*. Despite the Death Stars and space fighters, it's an essentially medieval reality – all princesses and pirates, knaves and loyal servants (the droids). Its core revolves around the Manichean struggle between the Force and the Darkside, as represented by the pure-hearted Jedi knights and the minions of the Evil Empire; there's even swashbuckling hand-to-hand combat in the form of the light-sabre jousts. The retro-ness of the Cantina scene music is of a piece with the throwback aspect of the entire movie, something blatantly signalled by the opening legend 'a long time ago in a distant planet' but also apparent in echoes of the pulpy heroics of *Buck Rogers* and *Flash Gordon*. (George Lucas had in fact earlier attempted to buy the remake rights to *Flash Gordon* but they were out of his price range.)

Close Encounters of the Third Kind is actually considered one of John Williams's more modernistic scores, darker, venturing here and there to the brink of atonality. But there's a famous and much-loved scene in the movie, in which music plays a direct role in the story rather than just accompanying the action, that's inadvertently comic if you know even a smidgeon about the history of twentieth-century music: the duet between the human reception committee at Devil's Tower mountain in Wyoming and the alien mother ship hovering a few hundred feet above the landing strip. The chief technician mutters, 'If everything is ready here on the dark side of the moon, play the five tones', and the young keyboard player strikes up that famous euphonious motif, selected by Spielberg out of some 350 candidates prepared by Williams. The aliens respond with a basso-profundo ostinato, opaque and sub-melodic, forbidding and yet familiar (since its timbre is essentially that of the tuba). After a minute or so of tentative interplay, during which the aliens hit a bottom note so deep it shatters the glass in an observation tower, the 'jam' suddenly takes off and the technical crew struggle to keep up:

Chief Technician: Give her six quavers, then pause.
Expert no. 1: She sent us four quavers, a group of five quavers, a group of four semi-quavers . . .
Keyboard Operator: What are we saying to each other?
Chief Technician: It seems they're trying to teach us a basic tonal vocabulary.
Expert no. 2: It's the first day of school, fellas.
Expert no. 1: Take everything from the lady. Follow her pattern note for note.

The ensuing piece – titled 'Wild Signals' by Williams – is frantic and dense, the inter-twining patterns of Mankind's arpeggios and Alienkind's counterpoint only brushing elliptically against anything you'd call a melody. Yet even someone like myself, a layperson when it comes to the evolution of classical music during the twentieth century, can tell that this 'basic tonal vocabulary' is no further advanced than, at most, the '20s. It's amazing enough that the alien civilisation, who are capable of traversing the light-year distances between galaxies and sundry technological marvels beyond human fathoming (like keeping air pilots they kidnapped in the '40s from aging), just so happen to use the exact same octaves and intervals favoured by the Western classical tradition. But why has their development halted somewhere in the vicinity of Stravinsky and Shostakovich (composers that Williams was partial to as a youth – funny that!), instead of vaulting through the twelve-tone scale and serialism on to the 'source

shudder

judder

Simon Reynolds